In the Beginning

In the Beginning

The Navajo Genesis

Jerrold E. Levy

UNIVERSITY OF CALIFORNIA PRESS

Berkeley / Los Angeles / London

University of California Press
Berkeley and Los Angeles, California

University of California Press, Ltd.
London, England

©1998 by
The Regents of the University of California

Library of Congress Cataloging-in-Publication Data
Levy, Jerrold E., 1930–
     In the beginning : the Navajo genesis / Jerrold E. Levy.
        p.   cm.
     Includes bibliographic references and index
     ISBN 0-520-21128-6 (cloth : alk. paper).—ISBN
0-520-21277-0 (pbk. : alk. paper)
     1. Navajo mythology.   2. Navajo Indians—Religion.   I. Title.
     E99.N3L62   1998
     299'72—dc 21   97-21487

Printed in the United States of America

9   8   7   6   5   4   3   2   1

Contents

Tables

Acknowledgments

I would like to thank my friends and colleagues Joseph Jorgensen, Stephen Kunitz, and Jim Greenberg as well as the two readers for the University of California Press for the time they took to read an early version of the manuscript and for offering many helpful criticisms and suggestions.

PART 1

Background

1

Introduction

In every age and place, people have sought to understand the world about them and their place in it. They have asked how and by whose agency the universe came into being, whether it is finite with a definite beginning and end, and whether it has a purpose. People in all societies have been concerned with the problem of order and chaos: that is, whether events are inevitable and predictable or are subject to interference that renders them unpredictable. And they have wanted to know whether events may be controlled by humans. They have sought to understand the meaning of life and death, and have searched for ways to deal with suffering and the forces that threaten both individual and social life. Taken together, these questions are the concerns of what, in the West, is called religion—"a set of symbolic forms and acts which relate man to the ultimate condition of his existence" (Bellah 1964, 358).

This is a book about the religion of the Navajo people of western North America, despite the fact that neither they nor many other peoples make a clear distinction between the religious and the secular, the sacred and the profane. By comparing Navajo answers to these questions with those offered by Christianity, Judaism, and modern science, I hope to show that Navajo religion is as sophisticated as the "great" religions of the Western world.

Until well into the twentieth century, anthropologists sought to discover the origins of religion by assuming that the nonliterate societies of the world represented the culture of early humanity. Influenced by the Darwinian theory of evolution, they were convinced that human culture had evolved in a similar manner proceeding from the simple to the complex. Despite Franz Boas's rejection of the comparative method, which placed technologically simple, albeit contemporary societies at the beginning of a series of stages that culminated in the most "evolved" societies of the civilized Western world, anthropologists found it difficult to abandon the evolutionists' mindset. Certainly the so-called primitive societies of today each have a history and have changed over the millennia since *Homo sapiens* emerged (or evolved). And certainly many of these societies are complex rather than simple. But, because the history of technology has progressed from the simple to the complex, anthropologists clung to the idea that culture, along with humankind's knowledge and beliefs, must also have evolved and progressed from the naive to the sophisticated.

Although the search for the origins of religion has been abandoned by today's anthropologists, as have evolutionary schemes for the development of social organization, there has been no new anthropological approach to the study of religion. There have, of course, been theories—psychological and social—concerned with the nature of religion, but a comprehensive model that replaces that of the evolutionists escapes us. In a recent critique of anthropological approaches to religion, Morton Klass observes that "for some time many have seen the anthropological study of religion as essentially dead in the water," and that there have been no theoretical advances since midcentury (Klass 1995, 2). But why should this be so? I think that in large part the difficulty lies, first, in the fact that the cross-cultural study of religion involves understanding the mental life of people of radically different societies and, second, in the nature of the data available to us.

To illustrate the first problem, consider Paul Radin, who argued that philosophical speculation was and is performed by intellectuals in primitive societies (Radin 1927). Despite rejecting the evolutionists' assumption that as human society evolved so had the human mind, only ten years after the publication of *Primitive Man as Philosopher*, he writes:

[Early man's] mentality was still overwhelmingly dominated by definitely animal characteristics although the life-values themselves—the desire for success, for happiness, and for long life—were naturally already present. . . . No economic security could have existed, and we cannot go far wrong in assuming that, where economic security does not exist, emotional insecurity and its correlates, the sense of powerlessness and the feeling of insignificance, are bound to develop. . . .

It is but natural for the psyche, under such circumstances, to take refuge in compensation phantasies . . . the main goal and objective of all his strivings was the canalization of his fears and feelings and the validation of his compensation dreams. (Radin 1937, 6–9)

With no evidence to support his assumption that early humans lived in an area of scarce resources, this student of Franz Boas was nevertheless still in thrall to an evolutionary perspective and equated their mental capacities with their technology. What are the animal characteristics of early *Homo sapiens*'s mentality and how do they differ from the animal characteristics of contemporary humans? Radin thought that the early mind was different in degree, but not in kind, from the modern mind and that the early human's responses to life's main challenges were profound, sophisticated, and comprehensible. He was, moreover, skeptical of notions of progress in moral awareness. With this point of view, I am in complete agreement. But if this is so, then in what degree was the early mind different? And what were these "definitely animal characteristics?" Do animals desire success, happiness, and long life? Or did Radin believe that even after the emergence of *Homo sapiens,* biological evolution continued to occur as culture gradually evolved?

Let us look at this problem from another perspective. Virtually all who have seen them stand in awe before the ancient cave paintings in southern and central Europe: "We look at the best and most powerful examples of this art, and we just know that we have fixed a Michelangelo in our gaze" (Gould 1996).[1] Radiocarbon dating places the origin of these paintings from between 32,410 years ago at Chauvet Cave to 11,600 years ago at Le Portel. They were executed by members of our own species, *Homo sapiens* commonly called Cro-Magnon, who occupied Europe and who were overlapped in time by the earlier Neanderthals, who did not produce representational art. Neanderthal and Cro-Magnon were two separate species, and not end points of a smooth evolutionary continuum. Neanderthal died out; Cro-Magnon continues as modern humanity.

With only internal evidence, early scholars sought to date the cave paintings by classifying them in stages proceeding from the simple to the more complex, despite the fact that Darwinian evolution is not a theory of progress. According to Stephen Jay Gould, "The equation of evolution with progress represents our strongest cultural prejudice against a proper understanding of this biological revolution in the history of human thought" (71). Perhaps there was a general mental advance for a

---

1. The discussion of this topic is taken from Stephen Jay Gould's article in *Natural History* (1996).

time immediately after the appearance of *Homo sapiens*, but the twenty-thousand-year period during which the cave paintings were made does not reach very far into humanity's past. By best estimates, modern humans evolved in Africa some two hundred thousand years ago: The creators of the first known cave paintings were much closer in time to us in the twentieth century than to the original *Homo sapiens*.

Most species do not alter much during their geological lifetimes, and widespread species such as human beings are particularly stable. Consequently, there is no reason to assume that Cro-Magnon was less developed than ourselves or evolved biologically over a period of twenty thousand years, and even less reason to believe that the so-called primitive societies of today, which have as long a history as urban societies, are any less sophisticated despite their less complex technologies.

We must, therefore, study all the religions of the world in the same manner as we do the "great" religions: without assuming that, because they are not "great," they are "lesser." Unfortunately, this is easier said than done, which brings us to the second reason there have been no advances in the field in half a century: we are hampered by the data available for the task. What we know of religion and philosophy among preliterate people is essentially timeless; it has no historical depth, having been learned almost without exception during the past two hundred years. Whereas the written texts of Christianity are plentiful and may be dated, which allows us to reconstruct the development of Christian ideas, the synchronic materials we have for preliterate people do not readily allow for similar approaches to their religions.

An interview with a single religious expert, no matter how knowledgeable, would not be acceptable as an accurate, general description of Christianity, nor indeed of any other aspect of modern urban society. We know that the views of a Protestant clergyman will not adequately describe Catholic or Greek Orthodox Christianity, much less Judaism or Islam. Yet anthropologists and others have not hesitated to generalize from transcripts of conversations with a preliterate individual in order to represent the religion of an entire society. Similarly, even when several versions of a myth have been gathered by a number of scholars, variations are attributed to the vagaries of individual tellers. A general version is derived by including only the elements found in all or most of the variants, and the resulting text is examined as a phenomenon independent of the society that created it.

Anthropologists have made some very important simplifying assumptions about the nature of preurban societies and, on the basis of these assumptions, generalized from the individual to the society as well as from one society to preliterate societies as a class. Robert Redfield summarizes the characteristics of these societies: they are distinctive, as evidenced by the group-consciousness of the people in the community; they are small, so that either the community itself or a part of it may be studied by making direct personal acquaintance with one section of it; they are homogeneous; and "activities and states of mind are much alike for all persons in corresponding sex and age positions; and the career of one generation repeats that of the preceding. So understood, homogeneous is equivalent to 'slow-changing'" (Redfield 1955, 4). In sum, the views of a single individual may be taken to represent the culture as a whole. Moreover, because the culture is slow-changing, it represents the distant past as well as the present and thus is presented to the reader as tightly integrated, lacking in internal contradictions or conflicts, and representative of early society in general.

To learn what pre-civilized men were like, . . . we may look to what has been written in great detail about many hundreds of present day tribes and bands and villages, little communities of the never civilized. I do not assume that these latter people have experienced no changes in the several thousands of years since the first cities were built. The particular thoughts and beliefs of the present-day preliterates have probably changed a good deal during many hundreds of generations. The customs of these people are not "earlier" than is our own civilization, for they have had as long a history as have we. But what I do assert is that the surviving primitive peoples have remained substantially unaffected by civilization. Insofar as the conditions of primitive life remain . . . so, too, the kinds of thoughts and beliefs, however changed in specific content, remain of a kind characteristic of primitive society. That there is such a kind is evidenced to us from the fact that we can generalize as to this manner of thought and belief from the surviving primitive peoples in the face of the very great variety of content and belief which these exhibit. (Redfield 1953, 2–3)

In sum, by *assuming* that these preliterate societies are homogeneous and slow-changing, that the conditions of life have not changed, we may generalize from the present to the past, *and* the evidence that this is possible is the "fact" that we can and do find certain features of pre-civilized life held in common by the hundreds of societies studied. But if thoughts, beliefs, and customs have changed over time, what has remained unchanged? Certainly, technology has changed from spears to atlatls to bows and arrows, and hunting and foraging have been superseded in many parts of the world by the invention and spread of agriculture and pastoralism. Redfield does not answer this question, but he details what, in his opinion, makes preurban society qualitatively different from civilized society.

In *The Primitive World and Its Transformations,* Redfield describes the differences between the two types of society (1953, 7–25). Preurban societies had a strong sense of group solidarity, and the groupings of their members were based on status and role rather than on practical usefulness. The incentives to work and exchange labor were not economic but based on tradition and derived from a sense of obligation "coming out of one's position in a system of status relationships" (1953, 11). In contrast, the urban society rests on mutual usefulness with an economy determined by the market.

Redfield discusses what Robert Nisbet has called the five unit ideas of sociology: community, authority, status, the sacred, and alienation. Linked to their conceptual opposites—society, power, class, the secular, and progress—these ideas were the major concerns of European sociology in its great formative period, 1830–1900, when the foundations of contemporary sociological thought were being laid by such men as Tocqueville, Marx, Weber, and Durkheim (Nisbet 1966, 4–6). "Considered as linked antitheses, they form the very warp of the sociological tradition. Quite apart from the their conceptual significance in sociology, they may be regarded as epitomizations of the conflict between tradition and modernism, between the old order, made moribund by the industrial and democratic revolutions, and the new order, its outlines still unclear and as often the cause of anxiety and hope" (Nisbet 1966, 7).

Moreover, these ideas were deeply rooted in the persisting moral conflicts of the nineteenth century; none came into being as a consequence of problem-solving research strategies. Today, we are "in a late phase of the classical age of sociology. Strip from present-day sociology the perspectives and frameworks provided by men like Weber and Durkheim, and little would be left but lifeless heaps of data and stray hypotheses" (Nisbet 1966, 5). This, in my opinion, goes a long way to explain why anthropological approaches to religion have not progressed since the ideas of cultural evolution were discredited during the latter half of this century.

In the opinion of these early sociologists, the transition from the *Gemeinschaft* to the *Gesellschaft,* from the traditional community to modern society with its large-scale, impersonal, contractual ties, involved the loss of a prior state during which mankind was intimately connected to the natural environment. The world that had been lost was represented by European culture prior to the industrial revolution and the rise of the great cities. Later anthropologists, following social philosophers like Rousseau, have believed that this was the state of precivilized people in general. The idea is deeply embedded in the social sciences and has reached into popular culture: primitive people lived in harmony with the natural world in a "Golden Age," whereas civilized urbanites have become rootless and alienated in the artificial world of the city.

But whereas all of the early sociologists with the exception of Karl Marx were mistrustful of the idea of progress, at least as envisioned by the thinkers of the Enlightenment who saw it as a freeing of the individual from the bonds of tradition and the development of individual analytic reason and rationality, later liberal anthropologists and philosophers such as Adam Smith or Alexander Robertson embraced not only the notion of progress but also that of evolution. Redfield, for example, was explicit in his support for the idea of progress:

The standards as to the good have changed with history. The moral canon tends to mature. . . . On the whole the human race has come to develop a more decent and humane measure of goodness—there has been a transformation of ethical judgement which makes us look at noncivilized peoples, not as equals, but as people on a different level of human experience. . . . I find it impossible to regret that the human race has tended to grow up. (1953, 163)

This "evolution" involved both cultural and physiological development: "We may suppose that fifty thousand years ago mankind had developed a variety of moral orders, each expressed in some local tradition comparable to what we find among aborigines today. Their development required both an organic evolution of human bodily and cerebral nature and also the accumulation of experience by tradition" (Redfield 1953, 17). Nevertheless, according to Redfield, the people who made the cave paintings, although fully human and possessing the same degree of moral sensibility, were not capable of the same degree of theoretical sophistication as we (1953, 18).

The idea of progress supports the notion that human society has changed qualitatively since the development of civilization. It is also an idea that antedates Charles Darwin's theory of evolution and is deeply embedded in the culture of the Christian West. It was St. Augustine who fused the early church's idea of a unified humanity with the conception of a single, unified, linear flow of time (Nisbet 1980, 59–68). As Christianity was universal and available to all humans regardless of race or culture, so the notion of progress applied to the development of humanity as a species rather than the development of a single society that might eventually decline. And humankind, possessing the capacity to progress over a long period of time, was gradually educated and improved. Time itself—real, linear, and finite—was a creation of God along which humanity progressed through successive emergent stages toward fulfillment of all that was good in its being.

Unilinear cultural evolution is nothing but a recasting of these ideas in a secular mode: it rephrases an old Christian idea in the language of biological evolution. Even the stages of culture through which humanity was thought to have progressed—savagery, barbarism, and civilization—are reminiscent of Augustine's epochs of advancement during which humanity progressed from *infantia,* a preoccupation with the satisfaction of basic material needs, through *pueritia,* the birth and proliferation of languages and cultures, and on through the various periods of increasing maturity.[2] Needless to say, unilinear evolutionists were not millennialists, as were early and even later Christians. Nevertheless, they perceived the stage of "civilization" as one which embodied a more mature humanity, if not the final stage of perfection and enlightenment.

Those raised in the Christian West need not have been Christian to imbibe this vision of time and development. Those who were to become anthropologists breathed it in with the very air during their years in universities. It was, therefore, within this tradition that even contemporary scholars who have eschewed the theory of unilinear evolution if not the idea of progress faced the materials that pertained to non-Western religions. Much of North American ethnographic material was gathered in an attempt to record as much as possible before what still remained of the precontact cultures of the continent was lost forever. One consequence of this "salvage ethnology" was the recording of hundreds of myths but remarkably few philosophical discussions between anthropologists (or other observers) and their informants that might help interpret myths that are remarkably difficult for westerners to understand. Though the myths are narratives, they do not often follow Western narrative traditions. What they purport to explain most often seems trivial, and the images they project seem, to a westerner, hardly rational. Take the opening statement of a Paviotso version of a myth about the theft of pine nuts by Coyote and Wolf: "Coyote smelled pine nuts in the east,

---

2. By midcentury, the terms described stages in the development of subsistence technologies: foraging, horticulture, agriculture, and on through the industrial revolution.

and blood gushed from his nose" (Bierhorst 1985, 124). What methods of analysis should be used to interpret such a statement? And, as myths were gathered from any individual willing to tell them, there was often no attempt made to ascertain the position of the narrator in his or her society, with the result that, for any given myth, we do not know whether it was told by a knowledgeable person or even if it was in a form designed to be told only to children.

In some societies the grand myths of creation appear to have a structure; in others they appear fragmentary and disconnected. Events do not follow one after the other with any logic recognized by current observers and rarely is there a conclusion that makes sense. Yet anthropologists, linguists, theologians, and many others have recognized that without an understanding of myth, there can be no understanding of the religions of nonliterate societies.

Informed by the theoretical models of their times, anthropologists have attempted unitary explanations designed to embrace all types of myth. These have invariably failed, from the early evolutionist to contemporary structuralist, symbolic, and psychological explanations, if only because there are so many different types of myth. Myths do not have a single form or function, nor do they act according to one simple set of rules. Adding to the confusion, there is no one definition of myth. Myths differ enormously in their morphology and their social function. Some are closely related to rituals, but many are not. There may, however, be a

primary mode of mythical imagination or expression which is then applied in different ways and to different ends. . . . There is no invariable connection between myths and gods or rituals. Myths may possess significance through their structure, which may unconsciously represent structural elements in the society from which they originate or typical behavioristic attitudes of the myth makers themselves. They may also reflect specific human preoccupations, including those caused by contradictions between instincts, wishes, and the intransigent realities of nature and society. (Kirk 1970, 252)

It is not my intention here to critique the various approaches to the study of myth. Each has had a degree of success analyzing those myths that serve a particular function. For example, Bronislaw Malinowski's analysis of Trobriand myths accounting for the origin of an entire clan system demonstrates that these accounts are charters that reaffirm institutions (Malinowski 1954, 111–126). They support the status quo and can be accepted because the genealogy of the institution may be stated and their origins placed in the mythical time when "everything was placed in order and achieved once and for all its proper nature" (Kirk 1970, 257).

But what about myths that do not serve this function? Malinowski's theory does not apply to myths that appear to have little or nothing to do with social institutions. Take the myth of the *vagina dentata*. It is widespread but has nothing to do with either biological or social reality. Psychiatrists have noted that many patients fantasize that the female vagina has teeth, and these patients are said to suffer from castration anxiety and fear of women (Abraham 1949, 463). That the phenomenon is common among neurotic and psychotic males leads to the inference that myths of *vagina dentata* indicate the presence of widely held anxieties in societies that tell these myths. Some have posited a connection between *vagina dentata* myths and vaginismus, an involuntary spasm of the vaginal muscles that protects a woman from the pain she fears. "Since the vagina is a receptive organ, vaginismus can be considered as an expression of powerful incorporative tendencies; it seems to be the realization of the idea of 'vagina dentata,' the hurtful female genital" (Benedek 1959, 735). Myths "about cases of *penis captivus* (a prolonged form of vaginismus which immobilizes the inserted penis in the female) . . . have an almost global circulation. . . . In reality no case has ever been observed or treated or reported. . . . The story shows only the ubiquitous character of the latent castration fear in men" (Gutheil 1959, 720).

Here, interpreters of myth face their greatest challenge; how to verify the interpretation. Malinowski, working in a relatively undisturbed society, could observe the uses to which the myth was put and, in the event of conflict, might even have been able to observe it functioning as a charter that supported the status quo. But how shall we do this for the innumerable societies that have been transformed forever by exposure to the modern world? We cannot administer psychological tests to people long dead to see whether they were plagued by castration anxieties. And where something like this has been done—administering such tests to Eskimo shamans, for example—we have found them to be eminently normal and not the neurotics proposed by theories purporting to explain the nature of the shamanic trance (Murphy 1964). Moreover, regardless of how these myths originated, their meaning for a given society is problematic depending upon whether the myth has been retained over time or has been borrowed. Undaunted by such difficulties, scholars have created theoretical concepts, such as the basic or modal personality, which are then used to analyze myths as if they were the collective dreams of an entire people.

The problem facing the mythologist is the same as that confronting interpreters of the early cave paintings: the myths come to us without context, and we are forced to rely on internal evidence alone. The approach of most anthropologists has been to treat myths of preliterate peoples as representing an ahistorical and unchanging culture, one that has existed—at least until the recent past—as homogeneous and without internal conflict. Different versions of a myth are ascribed to differences among individual tellers, some more creative than others, and some perhaps more knowledgeable. The result is a Platonic version of the myth created by the anthropologist that erases all internal inconsistencies and includes only those elements that appear in all or most of the variants. This version may reveal something about the myth, but it reveals nothing about the mythmakers.

Rarely have anthropologists used biblical scholars' methods of analyzing the Bible, or, lacking written historical contexts, fitted a myth or legend into a known period of history. Without a written text, it is impossible to see stylistic changes in the use of language over time. And without an historical framework to provide context, it is virtually impossible to identify persisting traditions that represent differing points of view within the nonhomogeneous and changing preliterate society. Yet this is precisely what I attempt in this book, because at no time during its known history was Navajo society either homogeneous or unchanging.

A large corpus of Navajo myths has been recorded in great detail during the past century. Usually, the status of the narrator is known—whether a layman or a religious practitioner—as well as the particular ceremonies the narrator knew and performed. This knowledge allows us to determine whether the variations in the telling of the myth of creation are patterned and correspond to specific ceremonies, or whether they are random results of the individual's narrative skill or level of knowledge. These myths were most often recorded by scholars such as Washington Matthews, Father Berard Haile, Leland Wyman, Clyde Kluckhohn, and Gladys Reichard, or knowledgeable amateurs such as Mary Wheelwright, all of whom spent many years working with the Navajos. In addition, Haile, Reichard, Kluckhohn, and Wyman had some command of spoken Navajo.

We know the general outlines of Navajo history: that they originated in what is now western Canada and, over several centuries, moved southward until, circa A.D. 1500, they settled in the Southwest and made contact with the Pueblos. We have many of the myths told by their linguistic congeners in the north and by the peoples of the Plateau, Basin, and Plains with whom they came into contact on their journey south. We also have many Pueblo myths and can, in consequence, see which myths were borrowed from neighbors, which were retained over the centuries, and which were created *de novo*. Most important, we know something of the great transformations that occurred in their society. From a hunting and gathering society with a religion much like those of other hunter societies of western North America, they became agriculturalists after their contacts with the Pueblos. But no sooner had this transformation taken place, than they began another shift to pastoralism that lasted from the late eighteenth century until well into the reservation period in the late nineteenth century. Then, with the dislocations taking place in the twentieth century, they began another transformation as they became integrated into a wage-work economy. All of these major changes in subsistence led to changes in social organization and religion. And change generates conflicts within the body politic itself, which in turn lead to changes in myth. Let us turn briefly to consider how this may be seen in societies with written texts.

Scholars have identified four major "documents" that make up the first five books of the Bible. The earliest are called J and E, the one reflecting the traditions of the southern kingdom of Judah, the other those of the northern kingdom of Israel. There is also a later "priestly" document, P, that builds upon J and E, as well as an almost complete retelling of the story of Moses contained in the book of Deuteronomy, called D.[3] These sources are identified by differing styles of writing as well as terminology. More important for our purposes, they represent different political and religious points of view that fit known historical events.

There are two very different myths of creation. The first is the P version (Gen. 1:1–2:3), in which humankind is created after all other living things, and male and female are created together. The earlier J version follows (Gen. 2:4b–25) but insists that the human male was created first, followed by the creation of the flora and fauna of the world, which were placed in the Garden of Eden. Only after this was the human female created from the male's rib. The former myth is concerned with establishing the law of the Sabbath, the seventh day, as well as with the orderly

3. The reader is referred to Richard Friedman's *Who Wrote the Bible?* (1987) for an accessible discussion of the subject.

sequence of creation of order out of chaos. The latter accounts for original sin, which is blamed on the female, and for the subordinate status of women in general. The internal contradiction of the total account is not objected to by religious Christians and Jews.

There are also two accounts of the flood myth that differ in terminology, actual details, and conceptions of God.[4] J pictures an anthropomorphic deity who regrets things that he has done, is "grieved to his heart," and can "smell" Noah's sacrifice. P regards God more abstractly as a transcendent controller of the universe.

Political motivations also provide different accounts of events and major actors. The E document, reflecting the views of the northern kingdom of Israel, is pro-Moses but anti-Aaron, the high priest, and thus expresses the resentment of Levitical priests who were expelled from Jerusalem during the reign of Solomon when the high priesthood was put in the charge of the descendants of Aaron. E attacks Aaron and praises Moses. In the E story of the golden calf, it is Aaron who commits the heresy (Exod. 32:1–33:11). After Aaron and his sister Miriam excoriate Moses for having a foreign wife, E describes how they are personally reprimanded by God (Num. 12). Years later, after the fall of the northern kingdom and the arrival in the south of northern refugees, the author of P is faced with a problem. By this time both J and E are sacred texts, so that neither can be totally censored. Moreover, northerners raised in the E tradition are now a part of the southern kingdom. How may the account be fashioned so that both traditions are accommodated without having Aaron and the priests of Jerusalem appear as villains? In effect, P writes a second Torah that parallels the accounts of E and J. Now Moses and Aaron together are attacked by their cousin, Korah, and a group of Levites. Korah does not challenge Moses's leadership but Aaron's exclusive hold on the priesthood (Num. 16). Here, Moses defends Aaron, and God destroys Korah.

We are led to ask whether similar political and religious conflicts may be detected in orally transmitted traditions. Once sacred texts have been committed to writing, later writers find themselves constrained, forced to work around the preexisting traditions or create new ones. Either way, internal contradictions become obvious. One may denigrate Moses, but he cannot be removed from the text entirely. The emphasis may be tilted

---

4. "P has one pair of each kind of animal. J has seven pairs of clean animals and one pair of unclean animals. . . . P pictures the flood as lasting a year. J says it was forty days and forty nights. P has Noah send out a raven. J says a dove" (Friedman 1987,59).

somewhat so that Aaron's rather than Moses's staff turns into a snake.[5] But oral traditions are free to reshape their myths as they choose. At any given time, they may be thought of as an integrated whole.

However, when political divisions have been documented in an oral society and myths have been gathered during the period of conflict, similar manipulation of the creation myths have been documented. In 1904, after many years of intravillage conflict, the Hopi village of Orayvi split in two as one faction left the village and started a new one a few miles away. Both before and after the split, several observers recorded creation myths as told by the leaders of the two factions. Some of these narratives were recorded within five or six years of each other. Two were narrated by the same individual before and soon after a change in the leadership of the faction to which he belonged. The two accounts differ greatly, featuring different creators, and reflect the political changes. Members of a rebellious political faction told the Hopi myth of creation in which Spider Woman, a beneficent deity and guardian of the hero Twins, led the people out of the underworlds. This faction was led by the Spider clan, and the prominence of Spider Woman in the narrative was taken as proof that their cause was blessed. In contrast, the faction loyal to the village chief told of a creation led by the female deity, Huru'ingwuuti, who created humanity. The emergence from the underworld was not mentioned because Spider Woman and the Twins could not be omitted from that narrative. Spider Woman could, however, be identified as the creator of imperfect and evil humans who brought dissension into the world (Levy 1992, 123–154). The question is whether similar phenomena can be identified in Navajo myths for which we have no well-documented internal historical conflicts.

This problem is addressed in part 2 of this book: I analyze the myths and identify two opposing traditions. Despite the large number of myths that have been gathered and translated—some fifty myths by 1957—most account for the origin of specific healing ceremonies rather than the creation of the cosmos and the present world. Part 2 compares only translations of complete creation myths as narrated by practitioners of various ceremonies as well as by a knowledgeable layman. Ceremonial myths are only referred to when they amplify or elucidate the manner in which practitioners of a particular ceremony narrate the myth of creation. Each of the chapters in part 3 deals with a single question posed and answered by most religions and compares how the answers provided

5. In Exodus, J is 4:1–5 and 7:14–18. P is 7:10–13.

by Navajos compare with those offered by Judaism, Christianity, modern science, and sociology.

The primary purpose of part 2 is to demonstrate that two philosophically opposed points of view are expressed in the creation myth and in the later origin myths of the various Navajo healing ceremonies. As noted by other scholars—notably Karl Luckert (1975) and Bert Kaplan and Dale Johnson (1964)—motifs that the Navajos carried with them from the north can still be found in the myths. Luckert believes that these early myths are survivals of the Navajos' distant hunting past and can be viewed much as archaeologists reconstruct the past by examining strata deposited over time. He does not claim that they express points of view that have persisted beyond the period during which the Navajos subsisted primarily on hunting. Kaplan and Johnson take the position that the tradition of the hunters was gradually replaced by that borrowed from the agricultural Pueblos and that the earlier tradition focuses on personal and magical "power," whereas the latter tradition functions primarily to maintain social control and harmony. Unlike Luckert, they go on to claim that, as the agricultural tradition came to dominate, not only was conflict generated but the hunter tradition found expression in contemporary cases of social pathology and psychiatric disorder such as interpersonal violence, alcoholism, and hysteria.

Kaplan and Johnson believe that the personality produced by hunting and gathering societies is still to be found in contemporary Navajo society—that this personality has somehow survived, despite two centuries of major changes in the subsistence economy. They believe that, because prevailing social values emphasize the community as opposed to the individual, contemporary hunter personalities can only be deviants. To me, their position is untenable: It is inconceivable that "hunter" personalities could be created by a society that today is thoroughly integrated into the wage-work economy and dependent on federal and state welfare.

The position taken here is that changing economic and social conditions engendered diverging interpretations of events that sought their justification in and expressed themselves by utilizing preexisting myths as well as by creating new ones. In order to clarify the transitions undergone by Navajo society, chapter 2 reviews what we know of Navajo history from the time they left the western subarctic, through their migration to the Southwest, their contact with the agricultural Pueblos, the adoption of pastoralism, and the reservation experience of pastoralism and its displacement by wage-work.

The intent of chapters 3 and 4 is to demonstrate that the differences that distinguish several versions of the creation myth are patterned rather than random. The account of the creation provided by a man who was knowledgeable but not a ceremonialist is followed by a comparison of other narrations given by several ceremonialists.

Two traditions may be discerned depending on the ceremony or ceremonies performed by the narrator. The general structure of the myth follows that of the agricultural Pueblos. It is a myth of emergence from the underworlds and an account of the creation of the present world, of humankind, and the origin of the Navajo clans. The myths told by men who performed the most Pueblo-like ceremonies emphasize agricultural symbolism, a major female creator deity, and an orderly world as opposed to an unpredictable one. In this tradition, which I have called the Blessingway tradition, disorder and unpredictability, represented by the trickster deity Coyote, are demonized. Dualism has developed and is also kept separate in the ceremonial sphere: There are ceremonies according to the Blessing and Holy ways as well as ceremonies according to the Evilway side. Evilway practitioners include more references to Coyote, the prime trickster figure of the Great Basin and Plains, and to shamanic possession than do Blessingway and Nightway singers. There are, however, men who perform such ceremonies as Waterway, Hailway, Frenzy Witchcraftway, and Mothway. These narrators preserve Coyote's importance as a creator but give even more prominence to a deity named Begochidi. I have called this more monistic emphasis on unpredictability as inseparable from creativity the Coyote-Begochidi tradition.

The number of ceremonies referred to in the preceding paragraph may confuse the reader who is not already familiar with the literature. A detailed discussion of these ceremonies is provided in chapter 6. Here it is sufficient to point out that, after the adoption of agriculture and exposure to Pueblo influences, the ceremonial system was transformed radically and the number as well as the form of healing ceremonies proliferated.

The Blessingway is considered by nearly all ceremonialists to be the "skeleton" that gives form to the whole system. Many think it the most important of the ceremonies. It is performed for blessing as a prophylactic and prevention of untoward events. Opposed to the Blessingway but its indispensable antithesis are the Evilways, which function to exorcise evil expressed as sickness and witchcraft.

The ceremonies of the Coyote-Begochidi tradition do not easily fit into this scheme. They exorcise as do the various Evilways, but rather than demonizing Coyote, they utilize his creative power to heal. Two of these ceremonies—Frenzy Witchcraftway and Mothway—have been especially difficult for both Navajos and anthropologists to classify. Of special concern is Coyoteway, which does not fit comfortably in any classification. It appears to be a ceremony in transition that began to die out before it had reached a final position in the system. These problematic ceremonies of the Coyote-Begochidi tradition express a continuing concern with unpredictability and chance.

Chapters 5 and 6 attempt to show how the Coyote-Begochidi tradition developed and to relate it to changes in Navajo life that are discussed in chapter 2. In chapter 5, I examine an ancient and widespread myth, the Hiding and Release of Game, as it is told among the tribes along the route of the Athabascan migrations from Alaska and Canada to the Southwest. As the route is followed, the principle hero of the myth changes from a northern Athabascan, vaguely human trickster-creator to Coyote in the Basin, Plateau, and Plains. Some Apaches retain Coyote as the hero, but the Western Apaches, Jicarilla, and Navajos—those Apacheans with the most agriculture—replace Coyote with one of the Hero Twins of the Pueblo Southwest. I discuss how the two traditions have utilized and changed myths from the Athabascan north and note that some of these myths coexist in different forms depending upon which ceremony utilizes them. I then examine motifs that feature Coyote and Begochidi, to show how shamanistic notions of soul possession are retained as well as to demonstrate that Begochidi was borrowed from Zuni and Keresan Pueblos in order to clothe a trickster-creator in more acceptable Pueblo clothing as the Puebloized Blessingway tradition gained acceptance.

In chapter 6, I use the myth motifs of the Navajo healing ceremonies to classify the various ceremonies according to whether they include shamanic themes of soul loss, possession, and trickster figures. The two traditions are located in the various sings. The Coyote-Begochidi tradition does not represent a survival from the distant hunting and gathering past so much as an adaptation that took place to cope with important new problems that became acute during the transition to pastoralism as well as the later period of conquest and life on the reservation.

In part 3, the focus changes from myth analysis to the comparison of Navajo answers to the perennial questions of the creation of the cosmos and why the world is the way it is. The purpose of these chapters is to demonstrate that Navajo religion is as sophisticated as Judaism and Christianity.

Chapter 7 examines the Navajo creation of the cosmos and life and finds the account closer to contemporary scientific cosmology than to Christian belief. The position of humankind in the creation, the nature of life and death, and the relationship of the body to the soul are also discussed.

The reader may question why I have included a discussion of contemporary scientific cosmology that is, after all, of a different order than religious speculation. My intent is threefold. First, I want to show that scientific knowledge cannot be taken as a standard of truth against which religious truths may be measured and found either wanting or satisfactory: Scientific theory changes even more rapidly than religious philosophy. Second, I wish to show that modern science, as exemplified by the recent development of chaos theory, is as sensitive to the sociocultural environment as is religion. And third, I hope to demonstrate that scientific theories cannot answer the eternal questions dealt with by religion. Whether one accepts that there is a single universe or many universes, and whether the universe is constantly expanding finally to experience entropy death or will ultimately collapse into a black hole, one is still faced with the question of whether there was a beginning and will be an end to the process. Perhaps more important, one cannot decide whether the order of the universe—that is, the laws of physics and life—are the result of a divine plan, or a happy accident, the consequence of the nature of matter itself.

By these statements I do not intend to imply that a religious truth is as valid as an empirically derived scientific one and that both may be accepted simultaneously. Rather, my intent is to show that when we consider issues of concern to religion, we often find ourselves at the limit of current scientific knowledge and cannot rely on current scientific speculation and theorizing to answer our questions.

Chapter 8 takes up the relationship between notions of order and chaos and good and evil. It is here that the two Navajo traditions diverge the most. The Pueblo-like Blessingway tradition tends to be dualistic, opposing good and order to evil and chaos. In this, it is more similar to Christianity than to modern secular thought. The Coyote-Begochidi tradition is more monistic and similar to contemporary science and psychology. Unpredictability is not totally random, and humankind is neither completely good nor entirely evil. Moreover, evil is not as inclusive as it is for Christians and Jews because untoward events of the natural world—famines, plagues, and other disasters—are part of the unpredictable natural world and not of themselves evil. Evil is confined to malevolent human acts.

Chapter 9 examines how Navajo myths define the nature of the masculine and feminine as well as the hermaphrodite, a symbol that unites the two. Unlike Judaism and Christianity, which clearly place the female in an inferior position, Navajo myth is ambivalent: Some events place women on a par with men, whereas others see the male superior to the female. Similarly, the role of the hermaphrodite as mediator of the polarities is not clearly stated; the hermaphrodite's position is as ambiguous as that of the sexes.

Because some degree of sexual conflict is found in societies worldwide, the chapter presents evidence that this conflict is more acute and persistent in Navajo society than is generally the case elsewhere. The myths reflect this antagonism between the sexes as well as the ambivalence felt toward the institutionalized transvestism of true hermaphrodites and physiologically normal males.[6] On the subject of sexual conflict, Navajo religious concepts do not provide clear answers, and the conflicts themselves are most likely the result of the major and fairly rapid transitions undergone by Navajo society over the past five hundred or so years.

The final chapter considers the nature of religion and myth and the reasons why most westerners view the so-called primitive religions as less coherent and perfect than the world's "great" religions. The major cause of this view, beyond the tendency to see one's own religion as more advanced and therefore superior, is the nature of myth itself. Small, preliterate societies must preserve their traditions in a form that can be memorized and understood by a wide range of listeners, not just the most philosophical ceremonialists. This constraint, in conjunction with the relative paucity of myth material gathered from each society, has made it difficult to read the language of myth as an intellectual treatise exposing the philosophy of a given society. Used to reading books specifically designed to explicate religious and philosophical issues, westerners are baffled by narratives with plots seemingly devoid of logic that rely on cryptic symbols for much of their meaning. The result of this bafflement has been the tendency of most westerners to believe that the religions of preliterate societies are incomplete and disorganized and to discount the intellectual content of myths and provide

---

6. Most anthropological literature refers to the person who assumes the role of transvestite as a *berdache* because this was the term used by early French explorers who observed the practice among tribes of the Southeast. The French assumed these individuals were homosexuals; *berdache* means a male prostitute. Because the role does not necessarily involve homosexuality, it is preferable to use *institutionalized transvestism* in its stead.

instead psychological interpretations or speculations concerning the evolution of religion.

To the extent that Navajo myth and religion represent North American religions in general, I conclude that the religions of precontact North America are no less comprehensive or sophisticated than those of the civilized Western world, and that our lack of understanding results from the paucity of data rather than any deficiency of the primitive intellect. The story, of course, is not yet finished. I do not detail developments during the last half century. Yet suggestive questions come immediately to mind. First and foremost, what changes in Navajo religious life may be observed today and can they be related to the changing social and economic conditions of the reservation? Will Navajo religion disappear entirely, supplanted by Christianity and other religious phenomena currently observed in the United States? Will myths recede in importance as they have in modern societies in general? None of these questions can be answered here, but trends may be suggested and the need for continued interest and research emphasized.

2

Historical Background

The outline of Navajo prehistory, from the time they left their homeland in the western subarctic until their arrival in the Southwest and subsequent contact with the Pueblos, has involved major changes in subsistence economy and social organization as well as changes of customs and beliefs consequent upon these transitions. After some time in the Southwest as neighbors of the Pueblos, the Navajos' economy shifted from one based primarily on hunting to one that relied on agriculture supplemented by hunting. Later, after a period of intense contact with the Pueblos and the introduction of sheep and cattle from the Spaniards, pastoralism became the dominant subsistence pursuit. In fact, pastoralism persisted long after the conquest of the Navajos by Americans and the establishment of a reservation in 1868. The most recent transition was the decline of pastoralism and the increased reliance on wage labor and unearned income provided by the federal government. Associated with these changes was the shift from bilateral to matrilineal descent, the development of matrilineal clans, and a shift away from shamanistic religion with its focus on survival of the individual to a priestly religion with a focus on community well-being. However, the rise of pastoralism and limited agricultural resources made the development of sedentary communities impossible, with the result that Navajo ceremonialism retained its focus on individual healing. And as the society changed, so did myths and beliefs, until the corpus of recorded myth available for study today became both extensive and complex. Because the analysis and interpretation of the myths presented in this book is based on the associations of various myths with specific economic and social transitions, it is helpful to detail what we know as well as what we don't know of the Navajo past so that the reader may better follow the subsequent examination of the myths.

Despite general agreement on the major transitions, anthropological opinion remains divided on virtually all of the details: one, whether matrilineal descent was developed after the arrival of Athabascan speakers in the Southwest or was already in existence in the subarctic; two, whether the migration southward was along the western edge of the Plains, through the intermontane valleys of the Rocky Mountains, or across the Plateau and the Great Basin; and three, whether, by the time the Spaniards noted their presence in the Southwest, the Navajos had been in the area for a long time or had arrived only a short time before the Spanish *entradas*.

Table 1 *Major Historical Periods*

Period	Society and economy	Religion
ca. 1000 Migration from Subarctic	Bilateral descent and bands	Shamanism
By 1500 Arrival in Southwest	Bilateral descent and bands	Shamanism
By 1600 Practicing agriculture	Matrilineal descent and clans Agriculture and hunting	?
1690–1770 Host Pueblo refugees	Pueblito settlements and new marriage prohibitions	Shift from shamans to priests
1770–1830 Dispersal of population	Shift to pastoralism Transhumance and independent families	Proliferation of ceremonials
1864—1868 Conquest	Incarceration at Fort Sumner	
1868—present Reservation period	Expansion of population and of reservation area	Christianity
1930s—1940s Stock reduction	Shift to wage-work economy	Peyote religion
1945—present	Wage-work settlements	Growth of Peyotism and Christianity, decline in number of ceremonialists

Navajo is one of a number of Athabascan languages spoken by groups in the western subarctic, northern California, the Plains, and the Southwest. It is one of the southern Athabascan languages referred to as Apachean, and has over 92 percent of its basic vocabulary in common with the Apache languages, which suggests that the southern Athabascan tribes separated from each other only after they arrived in the Southwest. This, along with the fact that Apachean speakers occupy a large area of the Southwest, indicates that they separated from each other and became recognizably distinct societies no more than five hundred to seven hundred years ago, sometime between A.D. 1300 and 1500 (Jorgensen 1980, 71–73). This method of dating, known as glottochronology or lexico-statistics, can hardly be called exact but may be accepted as a rough method of estimating the time taken for one language to separate from another. Some archaeologists, however, place the arrival of the Apacheans on the South Plains as late as 1525 (D. Gunnerson 1956; Gunnerson and Gunnerson 1971).

Navajo has a much smaller proportion of its basic vocabulary in common with the northern Athabascan languages, and it is estimated that it may have taken between two hundred and five hundred years for the Apacheans to complete their migration from the subarctic to the Southwest. This was almost certainly time enough for generations of Apachean speakers to learn and borrow from the tribes with which they came into contact on their journey. Navajo appears to have the greatest lexical commonalties with Chipewyan (76 percent), Carrier (73 percent), Kutchin and Hare (71 percent), and Han and Beaver (70 percent). These tribes are on the periphery of Athabascan territory—Kutchin, Han, Hare, and Chipewyan along the north from the central to eastern limit, Beaver and Carrier on the southern border.[1] It would seem reasonable to expect that the myths of the southern Athabascans would be more similar to the myths of these groups than to those of the western Athabascans, whose myths were more influenced by the Northwest Coast tribes.

That the westernmost Athabascans of the subarctic were in contact with and much influenced by the tribes of the Northwest Coast has led most anthropologists to believe that the Athabascans of the eastern half of the area represented the original form of northern Athabascan social organization. Thus George Murdock (1955) and Harry Hoijer (1956)

1. That the movement was from north to south has been established by the fact that Navajo retains words referring to things such as boats, which are found only in the north (Morice 1907; Sapir 1936).

believed that the early Athabascans had bilateral descent and Hawaiian terms for cousins, whereas Alfred Kroeber (1925) believed they were bilateral but with Iroquois terminology.[2] Isadore Dyen and David Aberle (1974) have disputed the conventional view and maintained that early Athabascans had matrilineal descent and Iroquois terminology and that the eastern tribes changed later to a bilateral system.

I believe that the Navajos and Western Apaches developed matrilineal descent and unilineal descent groups, referred to here as *clans* rather than *sibs,* after their entry into the Southwest. Dyen and Aberle argue that the northern Athabascans with bilateral descent lost matrilineal descent after moving further inland toward the east. In a similar manner, all the Apacheans except the Navajos and Western Apaches must have lost matrilineal descent sometime after they began their migration south. But if the groups who became the southern Athabascans were already living on the edges of the northern Athabascan homeland, and if it took between two hundred and five hundred years to reach the Southwest, how would it have been possible for the Western Apaches and Navajos to be the only ones to retain unilineal descent, especially given the fact that the Apacheans were essentially one group until after their arrival on the South Plains? It seems more likely that, even if they had once been matrilineal, they would have had to redevelop matrilineal descent after settling in the Southwest. This is not the place to go into detail; suffice it to say that although the issue is not and probably never will be settled, the preponderance of the evidence supports the conventional view.

Anthropologists have also been divided over the route the Navajos took on their journey south. Linguistic as well as early historical evidence suggests that most, if not all, Apacheans moved south along the western flanks of the Plains and did not begin to separate one from another until after having been on the South Plains for some time. The argument that the Navajos traversed the eastern reaches of the Plateau and Great Basin and entered the Southwest via the intermontane valleys was proposed primarily because the old Navajo area of settlement in the San Juan River drainage in what is now northwest New Mexico lies directly south of a large, easily traversed intermontane valley in southern Colorado.

By 1630, the Spaniards recognized the Navajos as a people distinct from other Apacheans by virtue of their greater reliance on farming and

---

2. The term *Hawaiian* is used when all children of both parents' siblings are referred to by the same terms as siblings. When, however, the children of father's brother and mother's brother are ferred to by a separate term that distinguishes them from siblings and the children of mother's sister and father's brother (all referred to by the same term), the terminology is called "Iroquois."

more sedentary lifestyle. I am inclined, because of myths from both the Plains and the Basin that have been adopted by the Navajos, to agree with David Brugge that Apacheans utilized both the Plains and Basin (Brugge 1983, 489). Survival on the Plains prior to the arrival of the horse sometime after 1650 was difficult, and retreating to the mountains during the harsh winters after hunting buffalo on the Plains during the spring and summer would have been preferable to remaining on the Plains throughout the year. On the Plains they would have come into contact with eastern Shoshones and Comanches who had left the Basin for the Plains somewhat earlier, as well as with the Crow, Blackfoot, Kiowa, Wichita, and Caddo. An initial introduction to farming may have come from the Caddos and Wichitas or from riverine tribes on the headwaters of the Missouri. And from these tribes the Apacheans would have learned how to make pottery (quite distinct from Puebloan pottery) as well as how to farm the flood plain.

Once in the Southwest proper, Navajos had frequent contact with the Pueblos, from whom they would have learned irrigation techniques. Intensive interaction with the Pueblos began in 1690, when the Spaniards reconquered New Mexico after the Pueblo revolt of 1680, and lasted until about 1770. Prior to this time, the Navajos probably developed matrilineal descent as well as named clans. The Western Apaches also practiced more agriculture than did other Apache groups and appear to have developed along lines similar to those followed by the Navajos. Neither the Navajos nor the Western Apaches were entirely sedentary, as were the Pueblos. Although they established settlements near their farms, they left for a part of each year to hunt and gather wild plants. In early Navajo country, farming resources did not permit a major reliance on agriculture.

It is likely that the clan system developed independently and was not borrowed from the Pueblos. Pueblo clans are named after animals and natural phenomena such as bear, bluebird, water, or corn. In contrast, the names of Navajo and Western Apache clans appear to be derived from earlier band names that refer to location or the characteristics of the people: "By the Water's Edge," "House Standing Up," or "Many Goats." Early Navajo local groups are thought to have been very much like those of the early Western Apaches: relatively small congeries of localized matrilineages, each controlling farm land and practicing patrilateral classificatory cross-cousin marriage—that is, marriage into father's clan (Aberle 1980; 1981).

The transition from a hunting and gathering economy to a reliance on both hunting and agriculture was gradual, and the changes in social organization most likely did not require any major changes in the religion. But after 1690, when they were joined by Tewa, Jemez, Keresan, and Zuni refugees, the Navajos underwent a period of intense interaction with the Pueblos that radically changed the Navajos social and religious life. During the eighty years in which many Navajos lived with Pueblos in sedentary settlements called *pueblitos,* the Navajos adopted marriage regulations designed to ensure intermarriage among the various ethnic groups. It was also during this time that shamanism was abandoned and "priests" who learned their skills rather than receiving them in visions became the religious specialists. There was also a wholesale adoption of Pueblo myths and agricultural symbolism and the introduction of community-oriented ceremonies.

I believe that both of these transitions—the social and the religious— were difficult and engendered conflict that may still be discerned in the myths. Shamans probably resisted the devaluing of the vision experience and the individual power attached to it. And some Navajos as well as Pueblos must have resisted the pressure to ally themselves in marriage to people who were culturally different and who were, in effect, strangers. It also appears likely that many men resented the enhanced status of women as intermarriage with the strongly matrilineal Pueblos proceeded. How these changes and the conflicts they engendered are reflected in the myths is discussed in greater detail in the appropriate chapters. Here it is useful only to review what is known of marriage regulations among the Apacheans and Pueblos and to identify the contrasts between shamans and priests and between religions focused on individual well-being and those focused community well-being.

Changes in marriage regulations and preferences during the period of intense contact with the Pueblos are important for the interpretation of the Navajo myth of Mothway, which deals with the consequences of incest. After settling in the Southwest but before 1690, the Navajos developed clans, and as the population grew, small local communities settled near farming resources. Aberle (1980) believes that marriage into father's phratry was preferred by the Navajo at that time for the same reasons it was favored by the Western Apaches.[3]

Like the Western Apaches, Navajos probably lived in small settlements (local groups) near farm sites for most of the year. The local group was

---

3. The term *phratry* refers to a group of clans thought by the society to be related to each other in some manner so that, despite being distinct unilineal descent groups, marriage among their members is usually prohibited.

the largest unit with a definite leader and important functions (Bellah 1952, 82–107). Usually two or three named clans were represented in each local group, which contained anywhere from two to ten matrifocal extended families, some containing ten to thirty households (Goodwin 1969, 146–147). In each group, one clan predominated, and the group was known by that clan name whether or not it contained others of equal size. Farm lands of a group were spoken of as belonging to its dominant clan, although use rights were not confined to members of that clan. The head of the local group was also spoken of as the chief of its predominant clan.

When the population of a local group exceeded the carrying capacity of its farmland, several extended families left to start a new settlement. As groups hived off and multiplied, leapfrogging over neighboring settled areas, named clans scattered all over the Western Apache area. Although members of a given clan were often widely distributed, there seem to have been places where each clan was the strongest.

Clan linkages occurred in a variety of ways. Among the White Mountain Apaches, four or five related clans were grouped into exogamous phratries. In other areas, the linkages were more like chains. Clan A, for example, might be related to clans B and C, but B and C might not be related to each other. Marriage to someone of one's own or a related clan was prohibited, but marriage into father's clan was preferred, as was the marriage of two people whose fathers were of the same clan (shared father's clan). There was a preference for patrilateral cross-cousin marriage, which, as clans developed, was represented by marriage to someone of the clan of a cross cousin rather than to a genealogically close first or second cousin.

There would have been a tendency to local group endogamy as the reliance on agriculture and group size increased. Successive marriage alliances among two or, at most three clans sharing localized farm sites decreased internal competition for land. At the same time, however, cultural homogeneity would be found over fairly large areas because of population expansion and the hiving off of local groups. Relatedness among people of the same clans and phratries would provide the basis for intersettlement cooperation.

During the early eighteenth century, when the Navajos incorporated refugees from several Pueblo groups, more marriage prohibitions would have served to integrate a growing number of exogamous clans and phratries as well as local settlements. Prohibitions against marrying classes of kin increasingly more distant from oneself force the individual and the descent group into alliances with a decreasing proportion of available mates. According to Kathleen Gough, if such prohibitions were not in place, there would be a tendency to marry back into father's group and so "form small knots of closely in-marrying groups within the larger political unit, thus leaving the larger unit without a firm basis for structuring its relations as a whole" (1961, 615). It was during this period that the Navajos came to prohibit marriage into father's clan and phratry, as well as marriage between individuals whose fathers were of the same clan.

The prohibition against marriage into father's clan and phratry is found among all the matrilineal Pueblos, and it is likely that a simple borrowing accounts for its adoption by the Navajos (Aberle 1980, 130–132). However, the Navajos and Hopis also extended prohibitions to marriage between individuals whose fathers were of the same clan and phratry and to grandparents' clans and phratries. Although Aberle believes the prohibition of marriage between individuals whose fathers were of the same clan and/or phratry is a uniquely Navajo invention, Mischa Titiev notes its presence among the Hopi prior to the twentieth century.[4] Among the Pueblos, only the Hopi have a restriction against marriage into mother's father's clan and phratry, although it is not adhered to presently, and the Navajos also adopted this restriction.[5]

In my opinion, the proliferation of local settlements, especially the *pueblitos,* during the eighteenth century was sufficient reason for the Navajos to develop these prohibitions. All the Pueblos practiced village endogamy, and the village was the largest political unit. In contrast, the Navajos were faced with the task of absorbing the Pueblo refugees at the same time they needed to preserve their separate identity by maintaining contacts with other Navajo settlements.

Turning now to the effect this period of interaction had on Navajo religion, it appears that reliance on shamanism was replaced by a preference for ceremonialists who learned their skills rather than receiving supernatural power from one or more spirit helpers during a vision experience. Subsequent to the spread of horticulture in the Southwest, shamanism and the vision quest were overlaid by the development of annual fertility and rainmaking ceremonials among those tribes most dependent on farming. Most Pueblos organized shamanistic curers into so-

4. An instance of marriage between two individuals whose fathers were of the same clan is found in Mischa Titiev's household census of Old Oraibi, with the informant's comment that, although prohibited in the past, it was no longer (Titiev n.d.).

5. For a more detailed discussion of Navajo marriage prescriptions, see Jerrold Levy, Eric Henderson, and Tracy Andrews (1989).

dalities and vested some curing functions in the hands of the priests of the rainmaking sodalities. The most serious diseases were thought to be of supernatural origin—in particular, the result of witchcraft. The belief that disease was caused by intrusion of a foreign object was ubiquitous. The cure by "sucking" or extracting was the most prevalent shamanistic activity. Equally important was the belief that disease was caused by soul loss. In such cases, it was necessary that the shaman identify, defeat in combat, and kill the witch and then restore the stolen soul to the patient. The vision quest was generally absent from Pueblo practice: Pueblo shamans were recruited by the curing sodalities, and a vision was not a prerequisite for selection, although visions were induced through the ingestion of psychoactive plants during the initiation rituals.[6]

The Hopis differed from this pattern in several important respects. Hopi healers did not utilize the trance state, did not have spirit quests or confirmations in sodality initiations or group rites, and did not believe in illness caused by soul loss. In addition, according to Ruth Underhill (1948, 37), the Hopis did not have curing sodalities, and they believed that breach of taboo was a major cause of disease, perhaps even more important than witchcraft. Over time, the Navajos were influenced more by the Hopis than by other Pueblos. They did not develop curing sodalities, and their ceremonialists did not attain their status after a vision experience. They abandoned the belief that illness was caused by soul loss and adopted the belief that taboo was the cause—without, however, emphasizing the responsibility of the individual for his actions, as did the Hopi. In the myths, disease is most often caused by possession and soul loss, but actual cases are always attributed to inadvertent breach of taboo (Levy, Neutra, and Parker 1987, 19–38).

I suspect that the Hopi influence came both before and after 1770, and that Navajo interaction with Hopis was more sustained than it was with the other Pueblos. During the drought years from around 1690 to about 1770, many Hopi families left their villages because of famine and took refuge among the Navajos, particularly in Canyon de Chelly. And as the Navajo population pushed westward, increasing numbers of Navajos came into contact with the Hopis of First Mesa, and a long period of intermarriage took place.

After 1770, drought, intensified Ute raiding, and a resumption of warfare with the Spaniards led Navajos to migrate to the south and west of their center of settlement in the upper San Juan River drainage. The

6. For a detailed discussion of Pueblo shamanism, see Levy (1994).

relatively large *pueblito* settlements were abandoned, and the population became more dispersed. Farming presumably declined somewhat in importance at this time, and Pueblo elements of social organization became more diluted. By the early 1800s, stock raising had become as important as agriculture; during the early years of the reservation period, stock raising became the dominant subsistence pursuit.

These developments precluded the formation of a community-oriented ceremonial cycle based on the agricultural year or the creation of curing societies. Instead, Navajo religion remained oriented around ceremonies aimed at curing the individual. The only ceremony that retained a strong agricultural focus in its myth of origin and some clan ownership and community orientation was the Blessingway, which became the preeminent ceremony. The trance state was utilized only by "diagnosticians," who occupied a less prestigious status than did the ceremonialists. But the stimulus to develop a complex ceremonial system remained, so that, instead of reverting to a fairly simple series of healing rituals like those commonly found among hunting and gathering societies, the Navajos developed one of the most elaborate and complex ceremonial systems of North America.

The shift to pastoralism also generated conflict between men and women as well as introducing intrafamilial conflicts. As hunter-gatherers with bilateral descent, Navajo men were the principal providers, and although the women were not oppressed, men made all the economic decisions. With the development of matrilineal descent and female ownership of the key agricultural resource, women's status and influence was enhanced considerably, particularly given Navajo-Pueblo intermarriage.

The Navajos are unique among North American Indian societies in having been pastoralists. Pastoralism is a male-managed subsistence pursuit associated with patrilocal or virilocal residence the world over (Textor 1967). Moreover, according to Robert Lowie, the status of women in these societies is almost "almost uniformly one of decided and absolute inferiority" (1961, 193). The Navajos' shift to pastoralism coincided with an increase in raiding and warfare that also served to elevate the managerial roles of men in a society that was already matrilineal and in which women enjoyed considerable control over the use and distribution of resources.

Men contended with women for their prerogatives, but the men's position was made difficult by the fact that, after marriage, they took up residence with their wives' families. The young married male was in many respects a servant in his wife's camp and took orders from his father-in-law. In chapter 9, I present the mythological relationships between men and women as well as ethnographic evidence to support the interpretation that conflict between the sexes was more intense among the Navajos than it was among the Pueblos and many other tribes.

The opposition between the supporters of shamanism and the supporters of the more community-oriented agricultural religion created two opposed traditions. The latter, which I refer to as the Blessingway tradition, put Changing Woman and agricultural symbols in direct conflict with Coyote, the trickster-creator of the hunting past. This resulted in a demonization of the trickster figure and all it represented. In effect, a strong dualistic tendency developed. The ordered regularity of the agricultural cycle became opposed to the unpredictability represented by the trickster Coyote. In bowing to Pueblo influence, however, a trickster figure was borrowed from Zuni and given pride of place in the myths of the shamanistically inclined. Coyote was not entirely abandoned but was retained in the shadow of Begochidi, the new creator-trickster, and as the opponent of order in the Blessingway tradition.

Over time this shamanistic resistance would have been overcome, were it not for the adoption of pastoralism and the dispersal of the population. New uncertainties were introduced along with new anxieties as the Navajos faced renewed warfare with Utes, Spaniards, and later with Mexicans, until their final defeat at the hands of the Americans in 1864. The years following the establishment of the reservation were punctuated by a series of cold winters and years of drought that decimated herds and forced many Navajos to settle new areas further to the west that were only later added to the reservation. Subsistence anxiety as well as the experience of conquest and domination all served to keep the perception of an unpredictable universe alive. By the early years of the twentieth century, the pastoral life that has come to be thought of as "traditional" Navajo culture was a success, and the reservation had become home.

Yet the very success of this federally sponsored pastoralism carried the seeds of its own destruction. The population expanded until, despite constant additions to the reservation, the land could no longer support the herds and flocks. The end came during the 1930s and 1940s, when a stock reduction policy was inaugurated that, in effect, destroyed the pastoral economy without replacing it with adequate wage-work opportunities. The persistence of an uncertain and unpredictable economy reinforced the point of view that sought accommodation with chaos and unpredictability, and thus this less well-known philosophy has survived in a somewhat covert manner.

The study of Navajo religion since the stock reduction years has yet to be undertaken. The influence of Christian missionaries, which had been minimal prior to World War II, grew after Protestants saw the value of ordaining Navajo ministers. The peyote religion, known formally as the Native American Church, also became popular among those who had suffered the most loss during the stock reduction years and continued to gain converts after that time (Aberle 1966). Today there are few younger Navajos who claim to adhere exclusively to the traditional religion.[7]

In 1990, 76 percent of men over age sixty had some affiliation with traditional religion. Only 39 percent were exclusively traditional, because many were also either Christian or members of the Native American Church. In 1990, 15 percent of men aged between twenty-one and sixty-five years of age claimed exclusive adherence to traditional religion, although 39 percent claimed some affiliation. The various Christian denominations had the largest number of adherents: some 42 percent, with 29 percent exclusively Christian. The difference in the proportion of men claiming no religious preference in the two cohorts was significant, from 4 to 22 percent. Moreover, only 65 percent of those claiming some religious affiliation were active participants.

As the wage economy expanded after 1930, the number of younger Navajos who could afford to spend years as apprentices to practicing ceremonialists declined radically; it has become difficult for the remaining traditionalists to have the requisite ceremonies performed (Henderson 1982). By 1980, there were only twenty-four ceremonialists alive on the Kaibeto Plateau, and of these, only eighteen were still practicing. Between 1905 and 1980, the ratio of ceremonialists to the population declined from 1:30 to 1:175 and the repertoire of ceremonies available was severely restricted.

Paralleling the decline of traditional Navajo religion has been the increased use of English in the home and the rapid gains made in educational attainment. In 1990, 60 percent of the men and 66 percent of the women we interviewed had graduated from high school, a level of edu-

---

7. The figures presented are derived from a sample of 530 men between the ages of twenty-one and sixty-five selected as a control group for men in alcohol treatment programs. They were randomly selected but matched to the men in treatment by age and community of residence in two large areas of the reservation. Information was also gathered on their fathers. The research was conducted under the direction of Stephen Kunitz and myself between 1991 and 1996. Wood (1982) has reported 12 percent of family heads in the Navajo-Hopi Joint Use Area claiming exclusive adherence to traditional religion, compared to 25 percent exclusively Christian.

cational attainment comparable to the national average of 63 percent in 1980 (Hacker 1983, 250).[8] Of those men between the ages of twenty-one and thirty, 47 percent spoke only Navajo at home compared to 87 percent of men over forty. Moreover, whereas 4 percent of the older men spoke only English in the home, 20 percent of the younger men did so.

What effects these developments have had on Navajo religious thought is as yet unknown and is not, therefore, a part of this book. It remains to be seen whether myth will continue to be the vehicle by which religious tradition is maintained or will itself decline as it has in the nation at large, or whether the new sense of Navajo nationalism will renew and create distinctive Navajo religious forms. The story presented here must, of necessity, end with the years during and immediately following stock reduction.

8. In the same study, there were fewer women in treatment, so that the control group numbered only 230.

PART 2

The Myths

3

The Underworlds

Like the creation myths of many of the New World's agricultural societies, the Navajo creation myth describes an emergence of all life from within the earth.[1] In common with the myths of the Pueblos of the Southwest as well as those of the Aztecs, the Navajo creation myth observes a number of formalities: the cardinal directions have colors and characteristics; four, or multiples thereof, are ever present—there may be four underworlds and deities often appear in four manifestations; and deities are often presented as male and female pairs.[2]

These formalistic aspects may vary among narrators but are found even when a single individual has recorded the myth on two different occasions. For example, First Man and First Woman accompanied by a variety of deities proceed through the underworlds together until they reach the present surface world. This first group of beings is variously given as four, eight, or twelve. In most versions, the entire group of beings is introduced by narrators in the first underworld, but sometimes one or more of the beings do not appear until the third or even the fourth underworld.

Emergence myths are found among most of the agricultural tribes of North America. They are based on an analogy to the cycle of germination and growth followed by maturation, death, and rebirth. Thus, life

1. On myths of emergence among the agricultural societies of the New World, see John Bierhorst (1985; 1988; 1990).
2. Unlike the Aztecs' creation myth, the Mayan creation myth is not one of emergence. However, it contains directional symbolism, paired deities, and a succession of world destructions and new creations.

is conceived in the womb of the earth and, as with seeds, all that appears in the present world was contained in embryonic form in the lower worlds. The Zunis describe how life in the "lowermost womb or cave world" became overfilled with being. "Everywhere were unfinished creatures, crawling like reptiles one over another in filth and black darkness, crowding thickly together and treading each other, one spitting on another or doing some other indecency" (Cushing 1896, 381). The motivation for leaving one world for another may be social disorder or evil that existed from the very beginning.

The Navajo emergence emphasizes that the essence of everything in the present world already existed in the underworlds, although the earlier forms are not described as graphically as in the Zuni myth. For example, in the Navajo third underworld, the six sacred mountains are created, although not in the form they will take in the present world, and First Man brings soil from each mountain with him to the present world.

The principle of procreation is present immediately: The essence of femininity and masculinity appear as clouds, mists, or winds. From these clouds, First Man and First Woman are created; the male principle is associated with light and life, the female with blackness and death. Blackness is death, but it is also the darkness of the womb and birth, and immediately, these oppositions seek to come together. Uniquely Navajo is the great emphasis placed upon the tension between male and female that culminates with the separation of the sexes in the third underworld. Coyote is included in the First Man group in almost all versions, although his importance varies with the narrator. All versions maintain that insects were present in the first underworld and that they were evil and represented witchcraft.

The version of the myth presented in this chapter is that told in 1928 to Aileen O'Bryan (1956) by Sandoval. Sam Ahkeah, Sandoval's nephew and chairman of the Tribal Council, served as interpreter. According to Goddard (1933), who recorded a version of the myth from Sandoval in 1923 and 1924, Sandoval was not a ceremonialist but was very learned. O'Bryan's recording is referred to as Sandoval I, Goddard's as Sandoval II. Because Sandoval was not a ceremonialist, his version is not weighted toward the point of view of any particular ceremony and may serve as a narrative against which the other versions may be compared.

Gishin Biye', an Evilway singer, dictated an emergence myth to Alexander M. Stephen (1930) in 1885 and again to Father Berard Haile (1981) in 1908. These versions are referred to as Gishin Biye' I and II. A version compiled from Haile's notes was published by Mary Wheelwright (1949). Although Haile was still relatively inexperienced in 1908, the fact that he was a sympathetic man of the cloth encouraged Gishin Biye' to include far more ceremonial detail than he gave to Stephen several years earlier. Many of the differences between Gishin Biye's version and those provided by others may be accounted for by the emphasis he placed on the origins of the Evilway.

In 1950, Stanley Fishler (1953) recorded an emergence myth told by Frank Goldtooth from Tuba City in the western portion of the reservation. Goldtooth was a Nightway and Frenzy Witchcraftway singer who also knew the Mothway, although he claimed never to have performed it. Goldtooth told Fishler that he was taught two "ways of learning" and that the two ways are the same except that in the one, Begochidi does everything, whereas in the other, White Bead Woman (Changing Woman), First Man, and Talking God are the important gods (Fishler 1953, 2–3). When he was a tribal councilman, Goldtooth had been severely criticized for his support of the government stock-reduction programs, and the fact that he knew Frenzy Witchcraftway and the Mothway led many of his opponents to believe he was a witch. In consequence, he became guarded about his ceremonial knowledge, and this, I believe, is the reason that he gave Fishler little information about Begochidi, a deity who has puzzled anthropologists for many years. I worked with Goldtooth during the 1960s when I was studying seizure disorders, and he provided much information about Mothway and Frenzy Witchcraftway but not about Begochidi. It is possible that he might have been more forthcoming had I been more aware of Begochidi's importance and asked him direct questions.

Mary Wheelwright (1942) also recorded an emergence myth in which Begochidi figured prominently. The myth was told in 1928 by Hosteen Klah, who, referred to as Lefthanded by Wyman (1970, 39), was a Hailway and Nightway singer, a transvestite, and the grandson of Narbona, a famous Navajo leader.[3]

Washington Matthews (1897) recorded several versions of the emergence myth during the later years of the nineteenth century. Much of his material was obtained from Torlino, a Blessingway singer, as well as from two Nightway singers, Hatathli Nez and Smiling Chanter. It is not clear, however, whether Torlino's version comprises the greatest portion of the

3. According to Gladys Reichard, when Klah was still a baby, he was emasculated in an attack by the Utes on the return from Fort Sumner (1963, 141). See also W. W. Hill (1935), who gives an account of Klah as well as of a woman transvestite who claimed to be a true hermaphrodite.

story with additions and elaborations provided by the two Nightway singers or the other way around (Matthews 1897, 50–51; Zolbrod 1984, 7, 343 n. 6). In any event, this is a version from the point of view of the Blessingway and the Nightway. I will refer to this recording as Torlino's. In 1984, Paul Zolbrod published this version in a sensitive and literate style with the addition of episodes he believes that Matthews omitted.

Here, then, is the myth told by Sandoval to Aileen O'Bryan.

THE FIRST WORLD

The First World, *Ni'hodiłhił,* was black as black wool. It had four corners, and over these appeared four clouds. These four clouds contained within themselves the elements of the First World. They were in color, black, white, blue, and yellow.

The Black Cloud represented the Female Being or Substance. For as a child sleeps when being nursed, so life slept in the darkness of the female being. The White Cloud represented the Male Being or Substance. He was the Dawn, The Light-Which-Awakens, of the First World.

In the East, at the place where the Black Cloud and the White Cloud met, First Man, *Áłtse hastiin,* was formed; and with him was formed the white corn, perfect in shape, with kernels covering the whole ear. . . .

The First World was small in size, a floating island in the mist or water. On it there grew one tree, a pine tree, which was later brought to the present world for firewood.

Man was not, however, in his present form. The conception was of a male and a female being who were to become man and woman. The creatures of the First World are thought of as the Mist People; they had no definite form, but were to change to men, beasts, and reptiles of this world.[4]

Now on the western side of the First World, in a place that was later to become the Land of Sunset, there appeared the Blue Cloud,

---

4. The appearance of the supernaturals is described in a variety of ways by different tellers to accomplish the task of describing "conceptions" or "essences" of beings who lacked definite form until after their emergence into the present world. Most tellers of myths among the Navajo as well as other tribes opt for a method of description to which the average listener can relate: the supernaturals could change their form from human to animal at will. Sandoval, however, appears to suggest that, without definite form, they cannot be described adequately.

and opposite it there appeared the Yellow Cloud. Where they came together First Woman was formed, and with her the yellow corn. This ear of corn was also perfect. With First Woman there came the white shell and the turquoise and the yucca.

First Man stood on the eastern side of the First World. He represented the Dawn and was the Life Giver. First Woman stood opposite in the West. She represented Darkness and Death.

First Man burned a crystal for a fire. The crystal belonged to the male and was the symbol of the mind and of clear seeing. When First Man burned it, it was the mind's awakening. First Woman burned her turquoise for a fire. They saw each other's lights in the distance. When the Black Cloud and the White Cloud rose higher in the sky First Man set out to find the turquoise light. He went twice without success, and again a third time; then he broke a forked branch from his tree, and, looking through the fork, he marked the place where the light burned. And the fourth time he walked to it and found smoke coming from a home.

"Here is the home I could not find," First Man said.

First Woman answered: "Oh, it is you. I saw you walking around and wondered why you did not come."

Again the same thing happened when the Blue Cloud and the Yellow Cloud rose higher in the sky. First woman saw a light and she went out to find it. Three times she was unsuccessful, but the fourth time she saw the smoke and she found the home of First Man.

"I wondered what this thing could be," she said.

"I saw you walking and wondered why you did not come to me," First Man answered.

First Woman saw that First Man had a crystal for a fire, and she saw that it was stronger than her turquoise fire. And as she was thinking, First Man spoke to her. "Why do you not come with your fire and we will live together." The woman agreed to this. So instead of the man going to the woman as is the custom now, the woman went to the man."

About this time there came another person, the Great-Coyote-Who-Was-Formed-in-the-Water, and he was in the form of a male being. He told the two that he had been hatched from an egg. He knew all that was under the water and all that was in the skies. First Man placed this person ahead of himself in all things.[5] The three began to

---

5. Here is the clearest indication of a tradition that gives Coyote priority over First Man and First Woman. Few tellers of the myth follow this tradition.

plan what was to come to pass; and while they were thus occupied, another being came to them. He also had the form of a man, but he wore a hairy coat, lined with white fur, that fell to his knees and was belted at the waist. His name was 'Átsé hashké, First Angry, or Coyote. He said to the three: "You believe that you were the first persons. You are mistaken. I was living when you were formed."

Then four beings came together. They were yellow in color and were called the Wasp People. They knew the secret of shooting evil and could harm others. They were very powerful.

This made eight people.

Four more beings came. They were small in size and wore red shirts and had little black eyes. They were the spider ants. They knew how to sting and were a great people.

After these came a whole crowd of beings. Dark colored they were, with thick lips and dark protruding eyes. They were the black ants. They also knew the secret of shooting evil and were powerful; but they killed each other steadily.

By this time there were many people. Then came a multitude of little creatures. They were peaceful and harmless, but the odor from them was unpleasant. They were called "that which emits an odor."

And after the wasps and the different ant people there came the beetles, dragonflies, bat people, Spider Man and Woman, and the Salt Man and Woman, and others that rightfully had no definite form but were among those who peopled the First World. And this world being small in size, became crowded, and the people quarreled and fought among themselves, and in all ways made living unhappy.

THE SECOND WORLD

Because of the strife in the First World, First Man, First Woman, the Great-Coyote-Who-Was-Formed-in-the-Water, and the Coyote called First Angry, followed by all the others, climbed up from the World of Darkness and Dampness to the Second or Blue World.

They found a number of people already living there: blue birds, blue hawks, blue jays, blue herons, and all the blue-feathered beings. The powerful swallow people lived there also, and these people made the Second World unpleasant for those who had come from the First World. There was fighting and killing.

The First Four found an opening in the World of Blue Haze; and they climbed through this and led the people up into the Third or Yellow World.

THE THIRD WORLD

The bluebird was the first to reach the Third or Yellow World. After him came the First Four and all the others.

A great river crossed this land from north to south. It was the Female River. There was another river crossing it from east to west, it was the Male River. The Male River flowed through the Female River and on; and the name of this place is *Tóbił dahask'id,* Where the Streams Come Together.

There were six mountains in the Third World. In the East was *Sisnaajiní,* the Standing Black Sash.[6] Its ceremonial name is the Dawn or White Shell Mountain. In the South stood *Tsoodził,* the Great Mountain, also called Mountain Tongue.[7] Its ceremonial name is the Blue Bead or Turquoise Mountain. In the West stood *Dook'o'słííd,* and the meaning of this name is forgotten.[8] Its ceremonial name is the Abalone Shell Mountain. In the North *Dib'nitsaa,* Many Sheep Mountain.[9] Its ceremonial name is Obsidian Mountain. Then there was *Dził ná'oodiłii,* the Upper Mountain.[10] It was very sacred; and its name means also the Center Place, and the people moved around it. Its ceremonial name is Precious Stone or Banded Rock Mountain. There was still another mountain called *Ch'óol'į́į́,* or Giant Spruce Mountain, and it was also a sacred mountain.[11]

There was no sun in this land, only the two rivers and the six mountains. And these rivers and mountains were not in their present form, but rather the substance of mountains and rivers as were First Man, First Woman, and the others.

---

6. *Sisnaajiní* refers to Mt. Baldy near Alamosa, Colorado. Others say it is Pelado Peak or Sierra Blanca Peak.

7. *Tsoodził* refers to Mt. Taylor, near Grants, New Mexico.

8. *Dook'o'słííd* refers to San Francisco Peak, at Flagstaff, Arizona.

9. *Dib'nitsaa* refers to San Juan Mountains in Colorado.

10. *Dził ná'oodiłii* refers to El Huerfano Peak, New Mexico. Sam Akeah says it is the Mother Mountain near Taos.

11. The mountain called *Ch'óol'į́į́* is also given as El Huerfano or El Huerfanito Peak, New Mexico.

Now beyond Sisnaajiní, in the east, there lived the Turquoise Her-maphrodite, *'Asht'í nádleeh.*[12] He was also known as the Turquoise Boy, *Dootł'izhii náyoo' ałi ashkii* .[13] And near this person grew the male reed. Beyond, still farther in the east, there lived a people called the *Hadahoniye' dine'é,* the Mirage or Agate People. Still farther in the east there lived twelve beings called the *Gháá'ask'idii.*[14] And be-yond the home of these beings there lived four others—the Holy Man, the Holy Woman, the Holy Boy, and the Holy Girl.

In the West there lived the White Shell Hermaphrodite or Girl, and with her was the big female reed which grew at the water's edge. It had no tassel. Beyond her in the West there lived another stone peo-ple called the Ground Heat People. Still farther on there lived another twelve beings, but these were all females.[15] And again, in the Far West, there lived four Holy Ones.

Within this land there lived the *Kiis'áani* (House Dwelling People), the ancients of the Pueblo People. On the six mountains there lived the Cave Dwellers or Great Swallow People. They lived in rough houses of mud and sticks and entered them through holes in the roof. On the mountains lived also the light and dark squirrels, chipmunks, mice, rats, the turkey people, and the lizards and snakes. The beaver people lived along the rivers, and the frogs and turtles and all the un-derwater people in the water. So far all the people were similar. They had no definite form, but they had been given separate names be-cause of different characteristics.[16]

Now the plan was to plant.

First Man called the people together. He brought forth the white corn which had been formed with him. First Woman brought the yellow corn. They laid the perfect ears side by side; then they asked one person from among the many to come and help them. The Turkey stepped forward.

12. The translation of *'asht'í nádleeh* is "wealthy hermaphrodite."

13. The translation of *dootł'izhii náyoo'ałi ashkii* is "boy who is bringing back turquoise."

14. *Gháá'ask'idii* are the hunchback figures connected with seeds, fertility, and phal-lus worship. They are said to have come from the mountain called *Ch'óol'íí* (O'Bryan 1956, 5 n20). These may be the Navajo counterparts to Kokopeli, the Pueblo hump-backed flute player. They have horns on their heads and are in charge of mountain sheep in the Nightway (see Richard 1963, 443–445).

15. The twelve female beings referred to here are the Corn Maidens, deities of fertil-ity (O'Bryan 1956, 6 n22).

16. Again, Sandoval insists that the Holy People have no definite form either animal or human.

They asked him where he had come from, and he said that he had come from the Gray Mountain. He danced back and forth four times, then he shook his feather coat and there dropped from his clothing four kernels of corn, one gray, one blue, one black, and one red. Another person was asked to help in the plan of the planting. The Big Snake came forward. He likewise brought forth four seeds, the pumpkin, the watermelon, the cantaloupe, and the musk melon. His plants all crawl on the ground.

They planted the seeds, and their harvest was great.

After the harvest, the Turquoise Boy from the East came and visited First Woman. When First Man returned to his home, he found his wife with this boy. First Woman told her husband that 'Asht'į nádleeh was of her flesh and not of his flesh. She said that she had used her own fire, the turquoise, and had ground her own yellow corn into meal. This corn she had planted and cared for herself.

Now at that time there were four chiefs: Big Snake, Mountain Lion, Otter, and Bear. And it was the custom when the black cloud rose in the morning for the First Man to come out of his dwelling and speak to the people. After First Man had spoken, the four chiefs told them what they should do that day. They also spoke of the past and of the future. But after First Man found his wife with another, he would not come out to speak to the people. The Black Cloud rose higher, but First Man would not leave his dwelling; neither would he eat nor drink. No one spoke to the people for four days. All during this time First Man remained silent and would not touch food or water. Four times the white cloud rose. Then the four chiefs went to First Man and demanded to know why he would not speak to the people. The chiefs asked this question three times, and a fourth before he would answer them.

He told them to bring him an emetic. This he took and purified himself. First Man then asked them to send the hermaphrodite to him. When he came, First Man asked whether the metate and brush were his. He said that they were. First Man asked him whether he could cook and prepare food like a woman, if he could weave, and brush the hair. And when he had assured First Man that he could do all manner of women's work, First Man said: "Go and prepare food and bring it to me." After he had eaten, First Man told the four chiefs what he had seen and what his wife had said.

At this time the Great-Coyote-Who-Was-Formed-in-the-Water came to First Man and told him to cross the river. They made a big raft and crossed at the place where the Male River flowed through Female

River. And all the male beings left the female beings on the river bank; and as they rowed across the river they looked back and saw that First Woman and all the female beings were laughing. They were also behaving very wickedly.

In the beginning the women did not mind being alone. They cleared and planted a small field. On the other side of the river, First Man and the chiefs hunted and planted their seeds. They had a good harvest. *Nádleeh* ground the corn and cooked the food. Four seasons passed. The men continued to have plenty and were happy; but the women became lazy and only weeds grew on their land. The women wanted fresh meat. Some of them tried to join the men and were drowned in the river.

First Woman made a plan. As the women had no way to satisfy their passions, some fashioned long narrow rocks, some used the feathers of the turkey, and some used strange plants (cactus). First Woman told them to use these things. One woman brought forth a big stone. This stone-child was later the Great Stone that rolled over the earth, killing men. Another woman brought forth the Big Birds; and others gave birth to the giants and monsters who later destroyed many people.

On the opposite side of the river, the same conditions existed. The men, wishing to satisfy their passions, killed the females of mountain sheep, lion, and antelope. Lightning struck these men. When First Man learned of this, he warned his men that they would all be killed. He told them that they were indulging in a dangerous practice.[17] Then the second chief spoke: he said that life was hard and that it was a pity to see women drowned. He asked why they should not bring the women across the river and all live together again.

"Now we can see for ourselves what comes from our wrong-doing," he said. "We will know how to act in the future." The three other chiefs of the animals agreed with him, so First Man told them to go and bring the women.

After the women had been brought over the river, First Man spoke: "We must be purified," he said. "Everyone must bathe. The men must dry themselves with white corn meal, and the women, with yellow."

This they did, living apart for four days. After the fourth day, First Woman came and threw her right arm around her husband. She

17. Note that First Woman encourages the women to do these things, whereas First Man warns the men against unnatural practices.

spoke to the others and said that she could see her mistakes, but with her husband's help she would henceforth lead a good life. Then all the male and female beings came and lived with each other again.

The people moved to different parts of the land. Some time passed; then First Woman became troubled by the monotony of life. She made a plan. She went to *'Átsé hashké,* the Coyote called First Angry, and giving him the rainbow she said: "I have suffered greatly in the past. I have suffered from want of meat and corn and clothing. Many of my maidens have died. I have suffered many things. Take the rainbow and go to the place where the rivers cross. Bring me the two pretty children of *Tééhooɫtsódi,* the Water Buffalo, a boy and a girl.

The Coyote agreed to do this. He walked over the rainbow. He entered the home of the Water Buffalo and stole the two children; and these he hid in his big skin coat with the white fur lining. And when he returned he refused to take off his coat, but pulled it around himself and looked very wise.

After this happened the people saw the white light in the East and in the South and West and North. One of the deer people ran to the East, and returning, said that the white light was a great sheet of water. The sparrow hawk flew to the South, the great hawk to the West, and the kingfisher to the North. They returned and said that a flood was coming. The kingfisher said that the water was greater in the North, and that it was near.

The flood was coming and the earth was sinking. And all this happened because the Coyote had stolen the two children of the Water Buffalo, and only First Woman and the Coyote knew the truth.

When First Man learned of the coming of the water, he sent word to all the people, and he told them to come to the mountain called *Sisnaajiní.* He told them to bring with them all of the seeds used for food. All living beings were to gather on the top of *Sisnaajiní.* First Man traveled to the six sacred mountains, and, gathering earth from them, he put it in his medicine bag.

The water rose steadily. When all the people were halfway up *Sisnaajiní,* First Man discovered he had forgotten his medicine bag. Now this bag contained not only the earth from the six sacred mountains, but his magic, the medicine he used to call the rain down upon the earth and to make things grow. He could not live without his medicine bag, and he wished to jump into the rising water; but the others begged him not to do this. They went to the kingfisher and asked him to dive into the water and recover the bag. This the bird did. When

First Man had his medicine bag again in his possession, he breathed on it four times and thanked his people.

When they had all arrived, it was found that the Turquoise Boy had brought with him the big Male Reed; and the White Shell Girl had brought with her the big Female Reed. Another person brought poison ivy; and another, cotton, which was later used for cloth. This person was the spider. First Man had with him his spruce tree, which he planted on the top of *Sisnaajiní*. He used his fox medicine to make it grow; but the spruce tree began to send out branches and to taper at the top, so First Man planted the big Male Reed. All the people blew on it until it reached the canopy of the sky. They tried to blow inside the reed, but it was solid. They asked the woodpecker to drill out the hard heart. Soon they were able to peek through the opening, but they had to blow and blow before it was large enough to climb through. They climbed up inside the big Male Reed, and after them the water continued to rise.

THE FOURTH WORLD

When the people reached the Fourth World, they saw that it was not a very large place. Some say that it was called the White World; but not all the medicine men agree that this is so.

The last person to crawl through the reed was the turkey from Gray Mountain. His feather coat was flecked with foam, for after him came the water. And with the water came the female Water Buffalo, who pushed her head through the opening in the reed. She had a great quantity of curly hair which floated on the water, and she had two horns, half black and half yellow. From the tips of the horns lightning flashed.

First Man asked the Water Buffalo why she had come and why she had sent the flood. She said nothing. Then the Coyote drew the two babies from his coat and said that it was, perhaps, because of them.

The Turquoise Boy took a basket and filled it with turquoise. On top of the turquoise he placed the blue pollen, *tádidíín doot łizh*, from the blue flowers, and the yellow pollen from the corn; and on top of these he placed the pollen from the water flags, *teełhádidíín*, and again on top of these he placed the crystal, which is river pollen.[18] This basket he gave to the Coyote, who put it between

18. Water flag is European iris, but Sandoval is referring to cattails.

the horns of the water buffalo. The Coyote said that with this sacred offering he would give back the male child. He said that the male child would be known as the Black Cloud or Male Rain, and that he would bring thunder and lightning. The female child he would keep. She would be known as the Blue, Yellow, and White Clouds or Female Rain. She would be the gentle rain that would moisten the earth and help them to live. So he kept the female child, and he placed the male child on the sacred basket between the horns of the Water Buffalo. And the Water Buffalo disappeared, and the waters with her.

After the water sank there appeared another person. They did not know him, and they asked him where he had come from. He told them that he was the badger, *nahashch'id,* and that he had been formed where the Yellow Cloud touched the earth. Afterward this Yellow Cloud turned out to be a sunbeam. (O'Bryan 1956, 1–11)

PRIMARY ACTORS

At the very outset, Sandoval presents the major themes of the creation. The first actors appear to be First Man and First Woman, but soon Coyote claims that he is the first. Coyote appears in two manifestations, as a creator and as the more familiar First Angry. Earlier, Sandoval had told Goddard that there was "Water Coyote" who runs in the water and knows everything about the water and Coyote who wears a coyote skin blanket and knows everything on land.

Gishin Biye' II also mentions two coyotes, First Scolder, or Angry (*Átsé hashké*), and Coyote, but their characteristics are not contrasted. Gishin Biye' I and II introduce Black God, the god of fire, as a major creator along with First Man and First Woman. According to Gishin Biye' I, a variety of beings are created by this trio—Biting Vagina, Water Monster, Salt Woman, and so on—some of whom appear as members of the First Man group in other versions. Although Coyote is not mentioned in Gishin Biye' I, in Gishin Biye' II the people of the First World come to First Man and Coyote to ask what should be done about the crowded conditions, and First Man and Coyote lead the ascent into the next world.

Goldtooth says that in the beginning there were mists that created Supreme Sacred Wind, who in turn created First Man, First Woman, and Coyote (*Átsé hashké*), who was made from an egg and from mists. Although in identifying Supreme Sacred Wind as the initial creator,

Goldtooth may have been taking Christian belief in a supreme deity into account, Supreme Sacred Wind seems to represent a logical search for a unifying life force.[19] In any event, mist or wetness come first, and then comes Wind (*nitch'i*), which in Navajo thought is the life force that enters into all living things. Where Goldtooth differs from the others is in his early introduction of two principle Holy People, Talking God (*Haashch'ééti'í*) and Calling God (*Haashch'éé'ooghaan*).[20] Goldtooth and Klah are the only ones who mention Begochidi in the first underworld. Goldtooth, Klah, and Gishin Biye' I and II also include Black God (*Haashch'ééshzhiní*), the Fire God, otherwise known as Black Body (*Bits'íís lizhin*).

According to Goldtooth, it is Begochidi who created the mountains and the insects, and it is he who "makes the animals disappear and who makes the rules." Klah has Begochidi create the first hermaphrodite (*nádleeh*). He says that Black God destroyed the First World because Begochidi insisted that he was the only one to make the laws, and that Begochidi led the people into the second underworld.

Torlino's account differs from the others by entirely omitting First Man, First Woman, and Coyote. Torlino says that there were Wind People, who were the insects, as well as Water Monster, Frog, Blue Heron, and Thunder. The Wind People committed adultery and so the chiefs (Frog and so on) refused to talk with them. A flood forced them to fly up to the Second World. First Man, First Woman, and Coyote are introduced much later, perhaps in a conscious effort to make them appear less important.

MALE AND FEMALE

Sandoval has the male and female essences created separately in the First World. This creation introduces the detailed descriptions of tensions that characterize the opposition between creativity and death or light and dark. First Man's light is stronger than that of First Woman, and she goes to live with him. Sandoval comments on the fact that formerly women went to live with their husbands' people but that presently postnuptial residence is matrilocal. It is not clear whether this

19. This is also consistent with the role of Wind as described by James McNeley in *Holy Wind in Navajo Philosophy* (1981); McNeley points out that Wind is that which animates all life.

20. *Haaschch'ééh* is a class of supernatural being represented in Navajo ceremonials by masked impersonators.

is to be taken as a simple comment on historical change or whether it is at the heart of tensions between men and women.

Goldtooth presents First Man and Woman as siblings who commit incest and give birth to First Boy and First Girl. He may introduce sibling incest this early in the myth because he knows the Mothway, which treats the seizures caused by this form of incest. Torlino mentions that adultery caused the flood in the First World. Except for these two references to tension between the sexes, Sandoval is the only one who sets the stage for later conflicts between men and women.

GOOD AND EVIL

The beings in the first underworld are called Mist People, and among those identified in the different versions are various insects said to be evil. Sandoval I observes that "some medicine men claim that witchcraft came with First Man and First Woman, others insist that . . . witchcraft originated with the Coyote called First Angry" (O'Bryan 1956, 3). All versions mention that evil insects were present in the First World. Gishin Biye' II says that First Man and his companions—all the beings in the underworld—were evil people who practiced witchcraft. This version associates Black God with witchcraft but does not detail his actions. Gishin Biye' II ascribes the plan to leave the First World to the chiefs, who make the decision in a council. In this respect the story is much like the Hopi myths, which always attribute decisions in the underworlds to the chiefs. The fact that evil is present from the beginning creates a tension between those who wish to polarize good and evil by making Coyote the supreme evildoer and those who seek to preserve a unity of the opposing forces.

THE SECOND WORLD

In some versions, the order of creation of natural beings is presented in the Second World: first insects and swarming things, then birds, and later animals. This order parallels the sequence of creation in the first chapter of Genesis.

Torlino's account is approximately the same as that of Sandoval's except that, instead of the first four leading the people into the next world, it is Wind (*Niłch'i*, a white face peering at them) who shows them the way. As in his account of the First World, this may be an effort to make the First Man group appear less important. It is also similar to Goldtooth's contention, in that both make Wind very important.

Goldtooth does not differentiate among the underworlds after the first creations. Gishin Biye' I identifies the Second World but focuses on the separation of the sexes, which Sandoval places in the Third World. Gishin Biye' II identifies the Second World as red rather than blue and introduces a number of new supernaturals—Sphinx Man and Woman, Wolf, Badger, Kit Fox, Puma, Wildcat, and Mountain Lion—who are like the chiefs in Sandoval's Third World. First Man and Coyote are the leaders and all defer to them. The people practice witchcraft, and First Man makes the Evilway medicines to counter it. First Man withdraws all the evil from the people into himself. By so doing, the First Man group is imbued with witch power.

Klah's account, like that of Sandoval and Torlino, is brief. Begochidi creates twin men and women. Black God does not like these creations and kills them. It rains and everyone is happy, but Black God burns the water and the people leave through reeds to the Third World.

THE THIRD WORLD

In Sandoval I, the sexes separate because the women believe that they do not need men. First Woman uses her own fire, which is said to be weaker than that of First Man. She also plants her own corn. First Man seems to look at his wife's behavior with Turquoise Boy as if it were adultery, but this is not spelled out. Sandoval II, however, says specifically that the cause was adultery.

Gishin Biye' I attributes the separation of the sexes to Wolf's wife, who gambles and neglects her duties and claims that she can get along without her husband. All sexual excesses are described in detail. As in Sandoval I, the women masturbate with various dildos. The results of these unnatural unions are the monsters of the present world, who are slain by Monster Slayer. Coyote, Badger, Yellow Coyote, and Blue Coyote cross over to the women and go into a sexual frenzy, copulating continually and performing cunnilingus.[21] The men copulate with does and

21. The words *mạ'ii dootł'izh* and *mạ'ii łitsoii* have often been translated as "Blue Fox" or "Kit Fox" and "Yellow Fox." In everyday speech, the kit fox is referred to as *mạ'ii dootł'izh*, but *mạ'ii łitsoii* almost invariably refers to a coyote. Given that Coyote is also referred to by the four directional colors in myths, it is likely that two aspects of Coyote are meant here (Haile 1981, 34 n29). The association of Coyote with Badger is based on the frequently made observation that badgers and coyotes often hunt in pairs and, at times, form strong friendships. "Indicative of this type of friendly relationship is the type of effigy occasionally found on pre-Columbian pottery from Mexican and other ruins" (S. Young and Jackson 1978, 94–95).

are struck by lightning. The men also masturbate with the livers of game animals. The women beg to be taken back, but they smell like coyotes and have to be purified. It is the hermaphrodite who makes the final decision to bring the women back. Later, Coyote fails to steal the water baby, so First Man orders Spider Woman to steal it. She hides it, and no one can find it to this day.

Gishin Biye' II places the creation of the first hogan before the separation of the sexes. The hogan is usually said to be created after the emergence into the present world and is a central part of the Blessingway. Salt Man and Woman and Black God are found in this world, and First Man makes elaborate preparations of medicines, placing to the south witchery, bean shooting, evil wishing, and insanity. In a line to the west, he places all sorts of stings and claws. All of these are prepared for the medicine pouches of the Evil Moving Upway (*haneełnéehee*). The hogan was also the first medicine lodge, according to Gishin Biye' II. Two male and two female pouches make up four medicine pouches of *haneełnée-hee*. Each of the nine original beings receive a portion of First Man's medicines and powers. Then a share is given to all the beings mentioned in the lower worlds as being evil.

In Gishin Biye' II, First Man makes genitals, but Coyote identifies their various parts and tells people what they are for. Red-white stone, associated with the evils of the world, is one of the parts used, and Coyote contributes pubic hair. Coyote announces that there is going to be birth. This version says that Coyote was the source of an evil that did not exist before but has Coyote admit that, although he is filled with evil, there is a time to employ evil and another to withhold it (Haile 1981, 19). In other accounts, it is First Man who explains the need for witchcraft and its antidotes.

Gishin Biye' II says that a man who had been missing is found dead in Thunder's house. When Thunder refuses to return him, Black God sets fire to his house until he complies. When Thunder refuses to revive the man, Black God sends his fire again until Thunder acquiesces. From that time on, power songs have all belonged to Black God. When the revived man is brought back to the village, the *haneełnéehee* is performed over him. Various supernaturals are described in detail, as well as the medicine bundle (*jish*) used by the Hero Twins, sandpaintings, and the origins of Owlway, Shootingway, Earthway, and Hailway. Several forms of divining are detailed in this and a subsequent episode: hand trembling by Gila Monster, listening by the Hero Twins, flying out to search by Black God, and stargazing by various birds. The chiefs then make the medicine bundle for the Shootingway and consult Coyote. Coyote sings the four songs, and this is the beginning of the Male Branch of the Shootingway, "which is not widely known."

Gishin Biye' then repeats the story of a missing man, except that now Dark Hail Man has the body. Black God forces the release of the man, and Dark Hail Man gives Black God his songs, which are then given to the *haneełnéehee* and used as fire drill songs. "Therefore if these twelve songs are sung and medicines are administered against witchcraft, the patient becomes well and the witch dies."

After the separation of the sexes and the women are reunited with the men, fed, bathed, and purified, a brother and sister commit incest and plunge into the fire. They were moths, and this is the explanation of seizures, although the Mothway is not specifically mentioned. People begin spitting blood, and the cause is divined. Locoweed, Poison Ivy, Poison Marsh Plant, and Jimson Weed Youths perform a ceremony to heal people sick with "these things."

At this point, another Coyote appears, runs about with no regard for anything sacred, and mocks everyone. He is called *chahałheeł atk'i-naadeeł* (darkness falling down together), and they make arrows to shoot him. The *haneełnéehee* uses these arrows to dispel evil, shooting them over the hogan.

The people hear the crying of a child in the water. Coyote finds the child and hides it in his coat. This starts the flood and, after the people climb into the next world, Monster Slayer and Horned Toad search Coyote and find the child. The child is returned to the water with an offering by First Man, and the waters recede. There is no mention that Coyote is doing the bidding of First Woman, nor is there mention of the Water Monster. To place Monster Slayer, one of the hero twins, in the underworlds is unusual. The twins are the children of Changing Woman, who usually comes into being in the present world. The implication is that, as the people of the lower worlds are evil, so too are the twins. This is a most unusual interpretation. In the version given to Stephen, Gishin Biye' said that it was Spider Woman, not Coyote, who stole the water baby.

In Goldtooth's narration, the identification of the underworlds is confused. He makes a number of general statements about the nature of things. First, he says that "it is Begochidi who makes the animals disappear and who makes the rules." After the separation of the sexes, which is caused by adultery on the part of a chief's wife, First Man makes a law: "The male shall rule and whatever your chiefs say, that must be done." In most respects, the account of the separation is not unusual. Blue and Yellow Fox and Badger cross over to the women and perform a variety of deviant sexual acts. Coyote steals two water babies at the request of First Man as well as First Woman. After the flood, offerings are made to the Water Monster, but the babies are not returned. The female baby is put in charge of all water on the earth. The male baby is put in the sky in charge of all the water there.

In Klah's Third World, it is Begochidi who creates the male and female rivers, First Man and First Woman, and birds and animals. The hermaphrodite takes charge of all created beings and creates the various tribes of people. It is not clear whether these "tribes" are humans or the supernatural ancestors of humans who are created in the present world. In most versions, it is Changing Woman who creates humans, the Earth Surface People, in the present world.

The separation of the sexes is caused by the adultery of First Woman. Blue Fox and Yellow Coyote remain with the women. Both being have flutes, and their flute playing makes the women happy, but Begochidi finds out about this and brings the two men back to the others. All references to sex are omitted in this telling, perhaps because his interlocutor was a woman.

Coyote's theft of the water baby and the coming of the flood are essentially the same as in other versions except that, when the flood comes, it is Begochidi who decides that only the good people will ascend to the fourth world.

In Torlino's Third World, only grasshoppers are found. The adultery of the Grasshopper chief's wife gives cause for the ascent into the Fourth World, where the separation of the sexes takes place.

THE FOURTH WORLD

The Fourth World is the last of the underworlds according to Sandoval I and Torlino, but it is the present world according to Sandoval II, Gishin Biye' I and II, Goldtooth, and Klah. Sandoval and Sam Ahkeah explained to O'Bryan that the four worlds were really twelve worlds, or stages of development, but different medicine men divide them differently according to the ceremony held. For the narrative, they call them the Four Dark Worlds, and the Fifth World is the one we live in. An old medicine man explained that the Sixth World would be that of the spirit and that the one above that would be "cosmic," melting into one (O'Bryan 1956, 11). The version given by

Gishin Biye' to Haile subdivides each world into "speeches." Gold-tooth calls these "laws."

In Torlino's Fourth World, the people find the Pueblos (*Kiis'áani*) who practice agriculture. The land is arid and farming is only possible by irrigation. The Pueblos feed the newcomers, and the Masked Gods, the *Haashch'ééh dine'é*, appear for the first time: "Late in the autumn they heard a distant voice calling to them from far in the east. Four mysterious beings finally appeared" (Matthews 1897, 68). These beings are White Body (*Bits'íís łigaii*), a being like the god of this world whom the Navajos call Talking God (*Haashch'éé'złti'í*); Blue Body (*Bits'íís doołł'izh*), who is like the present Water Sprinkler (*To'nenili*); Yellow Body (*Bits'íís łitsoii*), who is similar to the present Calling God (*Haashch'éé'ooghaan*); and Black Body (*Bits'íís łizhin*), who is the same as the present god of fire, Black God (*Haashch'ééshzhiní*).

The *Haashch'ééh dine'é* are impersonated by masked dancers in the public exhibitions of the great chants, and it is likely that they are the masked katsinas of the Pueblos who appear in Torlino's myth at the same time as the *Kiis'áani,* who also taught agriculture to the people. The impersonators of the *Haashch'ééh dine'é,* like Pueblo katsina impersonators, are not allowed to speak while wearing a mask, and these supernaturals are often referred to as the Failed-to-Speak-People.

All the beings who emerged from the underworlds—as well as Changing Woman and her sons, Monster Slayer and Born for Water, who were created in the present world—are Holy People. Thus, the *Haashch'ééh dine'é* are a subgroup of the Holy People (*Diyin Dine'e*). But, unlike the First Man group and many of the other Holy People who are said to be evil, the *Haashch'ééh dine'é* are good and helpful deities. According to Reichard (1963, 476), "Talking God, one of the great gods, acts as a mentor, often directing mythical characters, warning them, or telling them the answers to test questions which they would not otherwise have known. He is the only god I have found with a sense of compassion." Talking God is also the tutelary of Nightway and is referred to as the maternal grandfather of the gods (*yé'ii bicheii*).

It can be confusing that the *Haashch'ééh dine'é* are referred to by the same term as the monsters who attack people in the present world: Because the monsters are supernatural beings, are they also Holy People? *Diyin,* usually glossed as "holy," is more accurately rendered as "possessing great supernatural power," without indicating whether the power is good or evil. Thus, First Man is one of the *Diyin Dine'e* who uses his supernatural power for both good and evil. But the *Haashch'ééh dine'é,* who are good, are also referred to as *yé'ii,* monsters, who are generally thought of as evil. The root word from which *yé'ii* is derived is *yéé,* which means "fear" or "dread." All supernatural power, whether used for good or evil, is dangerous and may inspire fear. A Navajo may indicate both the nature of the supernatural power—either good or evil— or its strength or degree of dangerousness by using either *diyin* or *yé'ii.* Referring to the Masked Gods as *yé'ii* emphasizes their greater power not that they are evil. In Nightway, the *Haashch'ééh dine'é* are referred to as *Yéé'ii.* In Blessingway, however, there is an indication that not all Holy People are *Yéé'ii*—at a gathering "the numerous Holy People of Blessingway who were not yé'i clothed themselves as the yé'i people do" (Wyman 1970, 312 n219).

After the masked gods appear in Torlino's account, Black Body tells the people that they "want to make more people, but in form like themselves. You have bodies like theirs; but you have the teeth, the feet, and the claws of beasts and insects. The new creatures are to have hands and feet like ours. But you are uncleanly, you smell badly" (Matthews 1897, 69).[22]

The *Haashch'ééh dine'é* then create First Man and First Woman from corn and instruct them to live together as husband and wife. Torlino thus denies First Man and First woman a role as primary creators and makes them subservient to the masked gods. He has this take place in the underworlds, however, because he cannot go completely against tradition. First Man and First Woman then give birth to five pairs of twins. The first pair born are barren hermaphrodites, but the other pairs live together as husband and wife. This is similar to the Zuni account of the siblings searching for the center of the earth who commit incest and give birth first to the hermaphrodite and then to the misshapen beings who become the "Mudhead" clowns, or Koyemsi (Cushing 1896, 399–401). But it runs counter to the view of Klah and Goldtooth, who assign the hermaphrodite Begochidi a role as one of the major creator deities.

Torlino then describes the association of the *Haashch'ééh dine'é* with masks, and of sibling incest with witchcraft (Matthews 1897, 70):

In four days after the last pair of twins was born, the gods came again and took First Man and the First Woman away to the eastern mountain where the gods dwelt, and kept them there for four days. When they returned all their children were taken to the eastern mountain and kept there for four

---

22. Note that similarity to the biblical creation of man in God's image. This indicates that some, if not most, *hataɫi* picture the *Haashch'ééh dine'é* at least in human form.

days. Soon after they all returned from the eastern mountain, it was observed that they occasionally wore masks, such as *Haashch'ééłti'í* and
Haashch'éé'ooghaan wear now, and that when they wore these masks they
prayed for all good things—for abundant rain and abundant crops. It is
thought, too, that during their visit to the eastern mountains they learned
the awful secrets of witchcraft, for the *'ánt'įįhnii* (witches, wizards) always
keep such masks with them and marry those too nearly related to them.

As for the four sets of brothers and sisters who had at first chosen to live
together as husband and wife, when they returned from the eastern mountain they separated. They were now ashamed, it seems, of their incest.

When they return from the eastern mountain, the brothers and sisters
keep their former unlawful marriages secret and intermarry with the Mirage People and the Pueblos, keeping all the mysteries they learned secret also.

After this, the descendants of First Man and First Woman obtain seeds
from the Pueblos and make a great farm. They also attempt to make
hunting decoys but are unsuccessful until the *Haashch'ééh dine'é* show
them how to make deer masks, how to imitate the motions of the deer,
and explain "all the mysteries of the deer hunt" (Matthews 1897, 71).[23]
And, again, this runs counter to the tradition that makes Begochidi the
master of game.

In Torlino's account, it is only after these events—after First Man's
group has been in the Fourth World for eight years—that the sky stoops
down, the earth rises to meet it, and at the point of contact up spring
Coyote and Badger, who are now thought of as children of the sky. This
contrasts sharply with Sandoval's account, which has First Man, First
Woman, and Coyote created in the first underworld.

Torlino also places the separation of the sexes and the flood as the final events of the Fourth World. When the people go to Water Monster's
home to retrieve a mother and daughter who were taken there while trying to swim across the river to rejoin the men, Coyote steals the babies.
Coyote, however, is not ordered to do this by anyone, and it is First Man
who later discovers the theft and throws both babies back to the Water
Monster so that the flood will recede.

Some of the differences in the various versions of the myth may be
the result of the various circumstances under which the myths were told.
The differences between the versions given by Gishin Biye to Stephen

---

23. In the myth of Gameway, hunting ritual and skills are given to humans by a woman
who married a deer.

and Haile may have resulted from the different time allotted for the telling as well as to the fact that Haile was a man of religion who therefore seemed to deserve a more complete narrative. We know that Sandoval devoted a considerable amount of time to his work with O'Bryan, which may account for the length and detail of the narrative. By contrast, regardless of the time it took Goddard to record the earlier version, we know that he was transcribing the original Navajo and then translating it into English, and the burden of this work may account for Goddard's shorter narrative.

Other differences appear less the result of individual circumstance than of differing points of view. Goldtooth and Klah maintain that Begochidi is the prime creator, although they do not neglect Coyote and First Man. Gishin Biye' presents Coyote and First Man as leaders in the underworlds but also depicts Coyote as the originator of all evil. Torlino consistently paints First Man as evil and Coyote as a relatively unimportant deity; both First Man and Coyote appear late in his narrative, and Wind is presented as the principle that leads the way from one world to the other. These patterned differences, which become even more pronounced after the emergence, are dealt with in the next chapter.

4

The Emergence
and the Present World

The various myths that follow the immediate postemergence events do not follow any particular order and are not included by all narrators. In consequence, I have not included the complete text of Sandoval's account but have presented only those episodes that are salient in all versions: the coming of Changing Woman, the birth of the Twins, the slaying of the monsters, the creation of the Navajos, and Changing Woman's departure. The myths of Changing Bear Woman and the Great Gambler, which are included by Sandoval, are dealt with in the next chapter because of their importance for our understanding of Coyote and Begochidi.

THE FIFTH WORLD

First Man was not satisfied with the Fourth World. It was a small, barren land; and the great water had soaked the earth and made the sowing of seeds impossible. He planted the big Female Reed, and it grew up to the vaulted roof of this Fourth World. First Man sent the newcomer, the badger, up inside the reed, but before he reached the upper world, water began to drip, so he returned and said he was frightened.

At this time there came another strange being. First Man asked him where he had been formed, and he told him that he had come from the Earth itself. This was the locust. He said that it was now his turn to do something, and he offered to climb the reed.

The locust made a headband of a little reed, and on his forehead he crossed two arrows. These arrows were dressed with yellow tail feathers. With this sacred headdress and the help of all the Holy Beings, the locust climbed up to the Fifth World. He dug his way through the reed as he digs in the earth now. He then pushed through mud until he came to water. When he emerged he saw a black water bird swimming toward him. He had arrows crossed on the back of his head and big eyes.

The bird said: "What are you doing here? This is not your country." And continuing, he told the locust that unless he could make magic, he would not allow him to remain.

The black water bird drew an arrow from back of his head and, shoving it into his mouth, drew it out his nether extremity. He inserted it underneath his body and drew it out of his mouth.

"That is nothing," said the locust. He took the arrows from his headband and pulled them both ways through his body, between his shell and his heart. The bird believed that the locust possessed great medicine, and he swam away to the East, taking the water with him.

Then came the blue water bird from the South, and the yellow water bird from the West, and the white water bird from the North, and everything happened as before. The locust performed the magic with his arrows; and when the last water bird had gone he found himself sitting on land.[1]

The locust returned to the lower world and told the people that the beings above had strong medicine, and that he had had great difficulty getting the best of them.

Now two dark clouds and two white clouds rose, and this meant that two nights and two days had passed, for there was still no sun. First Man again sent the badger to the upper world, and he returned covered with mud, terrible mud. First Man gathered chips of turquoise, which he offered to the five Chiefs of the Winds who lived in the uppermost world of all. They were pleased with the gift, and they sent down the winds and dried the Fifth World.

First Man and his people saw four dark clouds and four white clouds pass, and then they sent the badger up the reed. This time

---

1. In Hopi myth, when the locust comes into the present world, the people there attack him with lightning or arrows. He survives these attacks and is thought to have great war medicine. Alexander Stephen (1929) gathered one version from First Mesa in 1893. Frank Hamilton Cushing (1923) recorded the other on Third Mesa in 1883.

when the badger returned he said that he had come out on solid earth. So First Man and First Woman led the people to the Fifth World, which some call the many colored earth. They emerged through a lake surrounded by four mountains. The water bubbles in this lake when anyone goes near.[2]

Now after all the people had emerged from the lower worlds, First Man and First Woman dressed the Mountain Lion with yellow, black, white, and grayish corn and placed him on one side. They dressed the Wolf with white tail feathers and placed him on the other side. They divided the people into two groups. The first group was told to choose whichever chief they wished. They made their choice, and, although they thought they had chosen the Mountain Lion, they found that they had taken the Wolf for their chief. The Mountain Lion was the chief for the other side. And these people who had the Mountain Lion for their chief turned out to be the people of the Earth. They were to plant seeds and harvest corn. The followers of the Wolf chief became the animals and birds; they turned into all the creatures that fly and crawl and run and swim.

And after all the beings were divided, and each had his own form, they went their ways.

This is the story of the Four Dark Worlds and the Fifth, the World we live in. Some medicine men tell us that there are two worlds above us, the first is the world of the Spirits of Living Things, the second is the Place of Melting into one. (O'Bryan 1956, 11–12)

After the people reach the present world, First Man builds the first hogan and sweat house.[3] These events figure prominently in the Blessingway myth, which starts at this point. First Man, First Woman, and the "All-Wise-Coyote-Who-Was-Formed-in-the-Water" plan for the future. They decide that there should be day and night but, because First Angry Coyote caused so much unhappiness, he should be excluded.

They then create the Sun, the Moon, and the months of the year. They find Black God at a place where there is fire under the earth and ask him to use his fire to heat the sun. First Man plans to heat the moon with the first crystal that he used for his fire. Turquoise Boy, who had

2. According to Sandoval, the place of emergence is near Pagosa Springs, Colorado. "The white people have put a fence around our sacred lake" (O'Bryan 1956, 12).

3. The material in this and the following two paragraphs summarizes Sandoval's account (O'Bryan 1956, 12–32). Note that Sandoval gives separate roles to the two Coyotes.

been placed in the Sun, and White Shell Girl, who had been placed in the moon, demand a person's life in sacrifice for each time they pass over the earth.[4]

While they are doing these things, First Angry Coyote repeatedly comes to ask what they are up to. After the months have been created, Coyote comes again and notes that they have divided the year equally into summer and winter and plan to count the changes of the moon. "But," he says:

"I will put in some extra days so that the months will not be even. Sometimes frost will come early, and sometimes it will remain late. First plants will sometimes freeze, and so also will animals. Sometimes the full moon will come at the end of the month; and at the end of the year you will have 13 moon periods instead of 12. . . . You have in your minds that it was I who spoiled your way of living down in the underworlds. It was not my plan."

Then he addressed First Woman. "Why did you keep this sacred thing from me? When you asked me to steal the Water Buffalo's babies you said that you had suffered many things because of your husband's plan. Everything was well when I did as you wished. I have kept the female Water Buffalo baby; and by keeping her I am able to call the male rain and the female rain and all the different clouds and vapors. It is well. I followed your desires so that the people might have the seasons and the flowers and all that grows from the earth during different times of year. Your plan was for the benefit of those to come. But I will place the female child back into the River. Whenever you wish rain you will have to go for the Water Buffalo's girl baby; and after you have used her power you will have to return her to the River again." (O'Bryan 1956, 20).[5]

After Coyote had departs, the sky, sun, moon, and the various constellations are created. Although Sandoval omits this episode, most versions have Coyote return after the constellations have been placed and,

4. That Sun demands human life is also found in Pueblo myths, and some have speculated that it is an echo of the human sacrifice practiced by the Aztecs and Mayans. The coming of death before there are mortal humans is an interesting example of the tenuous boundary between mythic periods. Before the creation of humans, there were only the Holy People, who were supernaturals and ought not to have been subjected to mortal ills.

5. One would expect that Coyote born of water would be the one to control the rain, clouds, and mists rather than First Angry. The association of Coyote with fertility is found in the Coyoteway, which is discussed in chapter 6.

as with the months of the year, create disorder by throwing the remaining stars randomly across the sky. "To this very day, those who look at the sky on a dark night can see the unevenly placed stars. And by looking at them they can observe the everlasting disorder created by *Ma'ii* the Coyote in his impatience, it is said" (Zolbrod 1984, 94).

First Man, using the mountain soils he brought with him from the underworlds, creates the sacred mountains. Into each mountain, he places its inner being. "By themselves natural phenomena are lifeless, but an inner human form set within them functions as their life principle. This vitalizes and also personalizes each phenomenon" (Wyman 1970, 24). The personalization of each phenomenon is one of the purposes of the Blessingway, the myth of which begins at the place of emergence.

Life in the present world is good until the people see the first death. Then they remember that the Sun said he would claim lives in payment for his light. They search and, looking down through the place of emergence, find the deceased in the underworld. It had been First Man's and First Woman's plan to have people live forever. They are unhappy with this death and cast a log into a lake, saying that if it floats, people will live forever, but if it sinks, people will die. Just then, Coyote arrives carrying a big stone axe. He throws the axe into the water, saying, "Unless this stone axe returns to the surface there will be death." The stone, of course, sinks, and the log floats. So it is decided that although people will die, sometimes the very ill will recover. This episode combines an old and widely spread account of how Coyote brought death with a Pueblo myth of the first death caused by a witch.[6] After this, old age and illness come into being, although First Man and First Woman had not planned for this.[7]

First Man and First Woman had a plan for how life would be in the present world.

THE PLAN, OR ORDER OF THINGS

There was a plan from the stars down. The woman's strength was not to be as great as the man's strength. They could not attend to the planting and harvesting as the men could, therefore men would be

6. On how Coyote brought death and how death was first caused by a witch, see H. R. Voth (1905, 11–12) and Harold Courlander (1971, 28–29).

7. Death, old age, and poverty are later mentioned as monsters spared by the twins born to Changing Woman.

worth more than women. And the plan was that women would propose marriage to men; but the Coyote came and said: "Brothers, lis-
ten, I have just married a woman." Again he spoiled their plan. Men
propose marriage to women; but because of the older plan there are
still cases where women go after men. Then not long after that, that
which the bird, *chishgahi,* the robin, said came true; but they still
thought it unwise to have babies born in the new way.[8] Just then the
Coyote came and said: "Brothers, I have a little baby."

Then they planned how a husband and a wife should feel toward
each other, and how jealousy should affect both sexes. They got the
yucca and the yucca fruit, and water from the sacred springs, and dew
from all the plants, corn, trees, and flowers. These they gathered, and
they called them *tó 'ałchíní,* sacred waters. They rubbed the yucca and
the sacred waters over the woman's heart and over the man's heart.
This was done so they would love each other; but at the same time
there arose jealousy between the man and the woman, his wife.

After that they planned how each sex would have its feeling of
passion. A medicine was made and it was given to the man and to
the woman. This medicine was for the organs of sex. The organ of the
man would whistle; and then the organ of the woman would whistle.
When they heard this, each organ gave a long, clear whistle. After
that they came together and the sound of the whistle was different.
That is why the voices of the young boy and maiden are different; and
it is why their voices change. (O'Bryan 1956, 32–33)

In Sandoval II, it is First Woman who, wishing to make marriage more
permanent, creates the genitals and sexual desire. Claiming that he will
make them look better, Coyote pulls his whiskers and places the hair on
the boy's penis and the girl's vagina.

According to Gishin Biye' II, First Man makes the genitals in the third
underworld. In the present world, First Man creates the genitals a second time, the penis in the sky, and the vagina on earth (Haile 1981, 132).
Later still, First Man makes the stars and Black God places them in the
sky. Before this task is completed, however, Coyote takes Black God's
bag of stars and scatters them randomly across the sky. "The mixture left
over from Black God's distributions . . . in time became the genitalia of
men. A similar mixture . . . in time became the genitals of women"

8. After old age and illness came into being, the robin caused women to menstruate
(O'Bryan 1956, 32).

(Haile 1981, 129). Even later, after First Man names everything that was placed in the present world, "The genitalia of man and woman united and crossed over to the side of the earth" (Haile 1981, 139).

In Torlino's account of the separation of the sexes, First Woman insists that she can live without men and that the only reason that men hunt and provide meat is because they want to have sex with their wives: "You lazy men would do nothing around here were it not for *jóósh*. In truth, *jóósh*, the vagina, does all the work around here" (Zolbrod 1984, 59; see also Matthews 1887, 218 n32). The rest of the episode is the same as Sandoval's, except for the fact that six clans of the Pueblos accompany the men.

First Man then names all the various animals and sends them to the places where they are to live. Wolf is named *Ma'iitsoh* (Big Coyote or the big wanderer) because he had stolen and thus must "travel far and wide over the face of the earth"(O'Bryan 1956, 34). First Man names another being *Ma'ii* (Coyote), but the original coyote gets angry and says that "he would not have it; and that he would leave; but First Man called him back and told him that he would also be known as *'Atsé hashké*, First Angry. . . . and he went happily away, for he was told that he would know all the happenings on the face of the earth" (O'Bryan 1956, 34). It is strange that Coyote is given a name at this time, considering that the Coyote named First Angry had already been called by this name in the underworlds.

People then lose the ability to transform between human and animal form. They are made to keep their animal forms and live with their own kind in different parts of the earth.

At this point in the narrative, Sandoval inserts a section that refers to Pueblos. It seems that a group of people known as Blue Bird Clan People were led by a very powerful woman. In a footnote, Sandoval says that one of his female ancestors was a Hopi and belonged to Blue Bird Clan.[9] He speaks of how these people, "human beings," went to the mesa country (Mesa Verde) and built their homes in the cliffs (O'Bryan 1956, 35). There were many of them, they practiced agriculture, and they had plenty and could build their houses of stone because they did not have to travel about as hunters did. They built round, underground kivas, where they performed their ceremonies and where some practiced witchcraft.

In time, however, many became witches and traveled about in the forms of the coyote, bird, or wild cat, and planned to kill First Man. In

---

9. Blue Bird clan was a high-ranking clan on the Hopi Second Mesa.

a manner reminiscent of the destruction of the Hopi village of Awatovi, those who were not witches waited until the evil ones were in the kivas, threw chili and other "poisons" into the fires, and sealed the smoke holes so that all inside were destroyed. Those who had not been in the kivas were then killed by First Man, who sent several "plagues" against them; the plagues destroyed all but a few witches.

These house-dwelling agriculturalists wove sandals from yucca fiber covered with pitch, used prayer sticks, and grew and wove cotton. "They lived peacefully and were happy. . . . They raised great quantities of corn. All this made them grow in number; they became a very strong people and their past troubles were forgotten; but this was not to last" (O'Bryan 1956, 38).

Monsters appeared and began to kill people. These monsters were the offspring of the women who had masturbated with various objects during the separation of the sexes in the Third World. Sandoval then relates the story of the Changing Bear Maiden who marries Coyote and learns his witchcraft, and follows this with the story of the Great Gambler. Both of these episodes are important parts of the myths of several ceremonies and are discussed in chapter 6.[10]

The alternating of day and night is explained by a story concerning a Giant (*Yé'ii*), who plays the moccasin game against the animals of the day and those of the night: "It was a rule that all the different persons who grew to be great powers, once they made a mistake, forfeited their lives. So because the Giant made the mistake of letting the owl outwit him the holy people came together and planned how he, and at, the same time, all the monsters who destroyed those living upon the earth must die" (O'Bryan 1956, 70).

Changing Woman and the Creation of the Navajos

The story of Changing Woman is the major focus of the Blessingway and is included by all tellers of the origin myth. As told by Sandoval, First Man finds an infant in a cradle board on the top of

10. The story of Changing Bear Maiden is also included as part of the creation myth by Torlino, Goldtooth, and Gishin Biye' II. The story of the Great Gambler is included by Torlino but not by Gishin Biye', Klah, or Goldtooth.

Ch'óol'įį (Giant Spruce Mountain), one of the three sacred mountains placed in the center after the sacred mountains of the four directions were made. He brings it home to First Woman, and they become its foster parents. Talking God and Calling God appear and tell them that the baby had been their plan. They instruct the parents in the making of the first cradle board and, when the baby utters her first laugh, First Woman gives Coyote gifts. The girl grows rapidly, and after thirteen days she has her first menses. The ritual of a girl's first menstruation is performed over her.

After this, the girl wishes for a mate. Every morning when the sun rises, she lies on her back until noon. As she lies under the ledge, spring water drips over her body. She does this for four days. In another four days, she knows that she is pregnant, and five days later, she bears twin sons (O'Bryan 1956, 75–77).

Torlino, a Blessingway singer, gives a far more elaborate account in which First Man and First Woman play no role (Matthews 1897, 104–105). Instead, an effigy is found by the last four people not to have been killed by the monsters.[11] Holy People, led by Talking God, create two effigies in the form of a woman, one of turquoise, the other of white shell. These effigies also have a white and yellow ear of corn. These are then brought to life as Changing Woman (*Asdzą́ą́nádleehé*), White Shell Woman (*Yoołgai Asdzą́ą́*), White Corn Boy (*Naadą́łgaii ashkii*), and Yellow Corn Girl (*Naadą́łtsoii at'ééd*). Changing Woman mates with the sun, and White Shell Woman mates with water. The son born of Changing Woman is later named Monster Slayer (*Naayéé neizghání*), and the son born of White Shell Woman is named Born for Water (*Tó bájísh chíní*).

In contrast, Gishin Biye' II's account of the origin myth of the Evil Moving Upway gives two versions of the birth of Changing Woman: an Evilway version, followed by the Blessingway version. In the first version, First Man and First Woman do not find the child, and her mating with the Sun and with water are presented as illicit cohabitation (Haile 1981, 150–154). Her offspring are named Monster Slayer and Born for Water, and "these two were to slay the *yé'iitsoh* later on." Haile did not think that this story was part of the Evilway myth proper and did not believe this woman was identical with Changing Woman.

11. If these were the last four people, the others having been killed, they must have been humans, because the next sentence mentions that the Holy People were there.

The second version is clearly concerned with Changing Woman and is said to be the "Blessing Rite version of events" (Haile 1981, 154–161). First Man, First Woman, and Coyote find the baby, name her Changing Woman, and perform the puberty rite over her after she experiences her first menstruation. But, unlike any of the other accounts, she does not give birth to the Twins. She does, however, distance herself from First Man and First Woman, who she knows are not her true parents. When First Woman protests that she raised her and cared for her, Changing Woman replies, "You had nothing to do with me. Others took care of me" (Haile 1981, 160).

This angered them. At once First Woman put blue and yellow jewels into a pot of water and stirred this mess while she was mumbling something, while *Asdzą́ nádleehí* [Changing Woman] was cooking her own meal on the other side of the hogan. "I know who you are," she again addressed them. "Your bellies are filled with evil. You are witches, bean shooters, evil wishers who tell people they will die, just to frighten them. Just go your way and I'll go my own." This speech angered them so much that they did not notice that the food they were eating was hot and steaming. It happened that this food was all sorts of evil, smallpox and chicken pox, whooping cough and similar diseases.[12]

And First Man spoke: "I hope that my thoughts are always fulfilled. May it always be as I think. Let the red and yellow in the east bring on these diseases." And *Asdzą́ nádleehí* replied; "May they all return upon your head. My power will prevent your evil, my streaks shall appear to also prevent your evil influences in due season." They then left in anger and fury and went to *niyá nikéháaghał* where all these evils exist.

She [Changing Woman] then gathered white corn, red, blue, and varicolored corn, put these with seeds and other edibles into a bundle, and left for the west. "My ceremonies will be greater than theirs," she said. "They will help my people more than theirs can injure them." And with these various plants and herbs she took with her Dark Cloud, Dark Mist, Dark Thunder, and so on. Therefore, all good rain (female rain) and good edibles come from the west and from her. (Haile 1981, 160)

Sandoval's account continues with the growth of the Twins, their desire to kill the monsters, and their visit to the home of their Sun father, where they receive the sacred weapons with which they kill the monsters.

12. These are all postcontact diseases. It is unfortunate that we lack the original Navajo and thus cannot tell whether these specific diseases were named by Sandoval or are the translator's interpolations.

Wyman lists eleven monsters killed, six spared, and six obstacles treated as monsters (1970, 57). The monsters most often mentioned by different narrators are Big Ye'i, Horned Monster, Rock Monster Eagle, Kicks-off-Rocks, and the Eye Killers. The spared monsters are Sleep, Hunger, Poverty, Old Age, and Lice. The obstacles most often mentioned are Crushing Rocks and Slashing Reeds. This episode properly belongs to the Enemy Monsterway and not to Blessingway. Nevertheless, it is one of the important myths of the events in the present world prior to the creation of the Navajo and Changing Woman's departure for the west.

The Twins slay Big Ye'i and Gray Big Ye'i, who are killed by Coyote in other myths. They also kill Horned Monster (*Déélgééd*), the Great Elk of early Athabascan myths, and perform other deeds that were once done by the trickster Coyote. This pattern of the Twins performing Coyote's deeds recurs in the accounts of the monsters who are spared.

Monster Slayer kills eleven of the Twelve Antelope, but catches the twelfth, saying: "All the thoughts and spirits of your comrades have departed from you. Those thoughts will never enter you again. People will use your flesh for meat. Your head, also, will be used by the people" (O'Bryan 1956, 93). He then lets the antelope go and sends it to live on the plains. He cuts the heads off the slain antelope so that later people can use the heads as hunting decoys.[13] In this way, another hunting technique is given to humans. Gishin Biye' II also connects hunting ritual with this episode. The antelope say:

"What benefit is it to you to kill us? We may be of some use to the people after all, and we promise to slay no more." "All right, I shall not kill you," [Monster Slayer] said. And because they had been man-eaters their tongues are (now) black. Here the corralling, trapping, and game burning songs start, which at present are no longer in vogue. Hunting only is practiced. (Haile 1981, 201)

With the exception of the Twelfth Antelope who, like his eleven brothers, devoured people, the other monsters who are spared represent unpleasant aspects of the human condition that came into being after Coyote determined that there should be death. Each is spared because, in some way, it benefits humankind (O'Bryan 1956, 99).

Poverty says, "You must not kill me, . . for in six months people will have good clothing, and at the end of that time, called autumn, they will

13. We have already seen that hunting magic and masks were given by the *Haashch'ééh dine'é*. Here they are given by the Twins. In Gameway, they are taught by a woman who married a deer (see chapter 5).

use it for the winter to keep themselves warm." A Blessingway singer puts it this way: "Should you kill me nothing will be threadbare, there will be just one kind of clothing in use all the time. . . . While if I live on it will become threadbare on persons, after which they will clothe themselves in good kind of goods, in various kinds of goods" (Wyman 1970, 573).

The Blessingway singer has Old Age point out that if people didn't age, there would be no death and, in consequence, no birth: the same people would continue to live for all time. And the louse claims that he serves as a pastime when a person becomes lonesome. Sandoval puts it somewhat differently by having the louse claim that picking lice from each other's heads is a sign of friendship and love among humans. And death points out that if nothing died, there would be no room on earth for youth and laughter.

Once the monsters have been eradicated, Changing Woman, the Sun, and the Holy People create the Navajos and the first clans, then leave the present world forever. Sandoval continues:

After the bow and arrows of lightning were returned to the Sun, Talking God and Calling God came to First Man and First Woman and asked them what they thought about all that had happened. "What will take place now will be your plan," they said. "Yes," answered First Man and First Woman, "Now it must be our plan. We will think about it."

The Sun brought a turquoise man fetish and gave it to White Bead Woman. She ground white beads into a powder and made a paste with which she molded a fetish like the one the Sun had given her, but it was a woman. When it was finished they laid the two side by side. Then they took the white corn which was brought up from the Dark World where the First Man was formed and they laid it beside the turquoise man fetish. And the yellow corn from the Dark World, which was formed with First Woman, was laid by the side of the White Bead Woman fetish. (O'Bryan 1956, 102–103)

The two fetishes and the ears of corn move and become human beings.

When they began to move the Coyote came. He jumped on the bodies and put something first up one nostril and then up the other nostril. He said to the first nostril: "You shall be saved by this." To the second nostril he said: "This shall be your shield." The first turned out to be the trickery of men; the second, the lies that they tell. But once in a while they are saved by their own lies. That was what the Coyote had in mind. (O'Bryan 1956, 103)

Human beings are then created by the Sun and White Bead Woman (Changing Woman) from male and female fetishes and white and yellow corn. After this, the Navajo clans are created. Finally, the Holy People leave the present world.

Again the Sun spoke: "First Man and First Woman, the Coyote Who-Was-Formed-in-the-Water, and the Coyote called First Angry, these First Four must go to the East beyond the place of the sunrise. . . . "

After the Four First Beings started for the East, First Woman turned back and said: "When I wish to do so I will send chest colds and disease among the people; when I wish to do so I will send death, and the sign will be the coyote."

So the Four First Ones went East and they took all their powers with them. . . .

Then the time came for the White Bead Woman to depart. Before her stood two persons. . . . There were also 12 male beings, . . . the Four Rain Clouds, and all the flowers, and another 12 persons, female beings, and with them were the Four Vapors. The White Bead Woman spoke to these people. She said that it was her plan to have all tribes, other than her own people, move beyond the sacred mountains. She said that she wanted her children to live on the land within these sacred mountains. Then she rose up in the clouds . . . , and with her went all her power, and there was no more of her power left on the earth. . . .

After that time, the White Bead Woman's home was called the Floating White Bead House, also, the Floating Turquoise house. Around her home is flat country called the White Bead Plain. To the East of her home is the Most High Power, to whom she goes and becomes young again, and by whose power she knows all things.[14] In the four directions from her house, she undergoes a change. She comes out of her house an old woman with a white bead walking stick. She walks towards the East and returns middle aged; and she carries no walking stick. To the South she walks and she returns a young woman. She walks to the West and comes back a maiden.

14. Presumably, "the Most High Power" refers to the Sun, for whom she has prepared her house. As the positions of the Sun determine the seasons, so White Bead Woman changes—aging, dying, and becoming young again.

She goes North and returns a young girl. She is called the White Bead Woman, *Yoołgai Asdzą́ą́*. She has three names, and the second is the Changeable Woman, *Asdzą́ą́ nádleehé*. The third is *Yoołgai at'ééd*, the White Bead girl. She has these three names, that is her power. . . .

Inside the home of the White Bead Woman, on a shelf running east to west on the south side, were four water jars. The first was the Black Water Jar which contained the Black Cloud and the Male Rain. The second was the Blue Water Jar which contained the Blue Cloud and the Male Rain. The third was the Yellow Water Jar which contained the Yellow Cloud and the Male Rain. The fourth was the White Water Jar which contained the White Cloud and the Male Rain. On the north side of the home was a shelf running west to east, and on it were also four jars. The first was a Black Water Jar which contained the Black Vapor and the Female Rain. The second, the Blue Water Jar, contained the Blue Vapor and the Female Rain. The third, the Yellow Water Jar, contained the Yellow Vapor and the Female Rain. And last, the White Water Jar, which contained the White Vapor and the Female Rain. Also, there were jars filled with the seeds of plants and all the beautiful flowers. (O'Bryan 1956, 112–113)

In Torlino's account, the Sun persuades Changing Woman to go with him to the west and make a home for him. Her sister, White Bead Woman, remains behind; she and the Holy People create the Navajos.[15] After the Navajos have increased, White Bead Woman finally leaves them to live at *Dibé nitsaa*, the Place of Mountain Sheep. She takes leave of the young girl she loves:

"I am going to leave you," she said to her. . . . "But I shall not forget your people any more than I shall forget you *sitsói*, my grandchild. I will come often to see them. And I shall watch over them, just as I shall always be watching over you. Their need for me is no longer great. They are growing stronger as a people. They are learning to control the things of this world." So spoke *Yoołgai Asdzą́ą́*, the White Shell Woman. And so saying, she disappeared as if she had vanished into the air.

Then, four nights after her departure, the young girl had a dream. In that dream *Yoołgai Asdzą́ą́*, the White Shell Woman, came to her, stood before her, smiled, and then spoke these words: "*Sitsói* my grandchild," she spoke. "It is as you have supposed. I have indeed gone to *Tséyi'*. From

---

15. Actually, Changing Woman returns with the other gods for the ritual of creation. For a listing of the deities who participated in creating the Navajos, see Matthews (1897, 136–137).

there I will go to *Dibé nitsaa*, the Place of Mountain Sheep, where I will dwell forever in the house of white shell which *Haashch'ééh dine'é*, the Holy People, have prepared for me. . . . Do not think you will never see me again. But do not think either that when you do see me I will appear in the form that has grown familiar to you. Instead look for me in some other form. Look for me when it rains. You will see me in the gentle showers of the female rain. You will see me there when it falls near your dwelling. You will see me in the moisture it brings. Perhaps you will see me in the crops that grow because of that gentle rain." (Zolbrod 1984, 292–293)

Whether presented singly or as a pair, Changing Woman or White Shell Woman is, like the Zuni Corn Maidens, an agricultural deity. Changing with the seasons, she becomes increasingly older until, with the start of a new cycle, she becomes young again. Of all the deities, "Changing Woman alone is consistently well-wishing to the Earth Surface People" (Kluckhohn and Leighton 1974, 183). She is the Navajo version of the Hopi goddess, Huru'ingwuuti (Voth 1905, 1–9).

Huru'ingwuuti in Hopi means "Hard Beings Woman," and she owns all hard substances such as beads, corals, and shells. Like the Navajo White Shell Woman, she lives in a house in the western ocean. Her house is a kiva, which the Sun enters each night through a hatch in the top in order that he may travel under the ocean and rise in the east again. Huru'ingwuuti and the Sun dry the land after the emergence and make it habitable. Together they create the birds, animals, water creatures, and humans by covering effigies of them with cloth and singing over them. And, like White Shell Woman, Huru'ingwuuti creates humans, then Hopis and Navajos and, finally, the Hopi clans. After these creations, Huru'ingwuuti leaves to live forever in the western ocean, telling the people:

"You remain here; I am going to live, after this, in the midst of the ocean in the west. When you want anything from me pray to me there." Her people regretted this very much, but she left them. The Hurúing Wuhti of the east did exactly the same thing, and that is the reason why at the present day the places where these two live are never seen.

Those Hopi who now want something from them deposit their prayer offerings in the village. When they say their wishes and prayers they think of those two who live in the far distance, but of whom the Hopi believe that they still remember them. (Voth 1905, 4)

Like Changing Woman or White Shell Woman, Huru'ingwuuti is sometimes presented as a duality, a deity of the east as well as the west.

References to her changing nature are few, however: In the myth of the Summer Snake ceremony the hero comes to Huru'ingwuuti's home and spends the night with her as a beautiful young woman, but in the morning she is an aged hag (Voth 1903, 349–351).[16]

Female creator goddesses appear almost exclusively in the myths of matrilineal societies and are especially prominent in Pueblo myths: Huru'ingwuuti of the Hopi, the older and younger sisters of the Keresans, Blue Corn Woman and White Corn Maiden of the Tewa, and the Pueblo Spider Grandmother.[17] The Navajo Changing Woman or White Bead Woman appears to be the embodiment of Pueblo matrilineality, who appears after the emergence and, in the company of the masked gods, the *Haashch'ééh dine'é*, supersedes the supernaturals of the First Man group who came from the underworlds.

The Twins are also derived from Pueblo myths. Despite the fact that myths of brothers or twins are distributed far beyond the Pueblo world, the story of the Navajo pair most closely resembles the Pueblo both in detail and in plot.[18] Hamilton Tyler has summarized the Pueblo myths (1964, 209–220). The mother of the Pueblo Twins, like the Navajo, is impregnated by the Sun; she conceives either when a ray of sunlight falls on her while she sleeps, or when a drop of water falls upon her. Often both events combine to create the children—sunlight for the elder and water for the younger. In fact, the Hopi name for the elder is *Pookong Hoya* (Son of the Sun Youth) and for the younger is *Bahonga Hoya* (Water Dripping Sun Youth). Their birth and subsequent development are magically rapid. In four days her pregnancy is visible, and in twelve days the twins are born. The precocious boys soon inquire after their father and are told that he lives in the east. They go in search of their father, the Sun, despite the fact that the Spider Grandmother doesn't wish

16. Voth was told this myth by a priest of the Snake clan, who was in the "hostile" faction at Orayvi during the years before the split. Because the "friendly" faction glorified Huru'ingwuuti in their narration of the creation myth and demonized Spider Woman, it is probable that the narrator here was denigrating Huru'ingwuuti in a like manner. If it were not for the fact that this is a story about a creator who is essentially good, one would accept Huru'ingwuuti's transformation as an example of the evil female motif that is ubiquitous in Navajo myth: the beautiful seductress is found to be an aged witch in the morning. Here, the transformation is more likely a reference to Huru'ingwuuti's "changing" nature.

17. The Tewas, of course, were not matrilineal but had bilateral descent.

18. In the eastern part of the area occupied by the northern Athabascans, many tales relate the deeds of the so-called Two Brothers, who are usually providers rather than deliverers (Bierhorst (1985, 68–69). These tales do not replicate the Navajo Twin story as closely as do the Pueblo myths.

them to go.[19] Like the Navajo Twins, the Pueblo pair is tested by their
father before he believes that they are his children. Following this, they
kill a variety of monsters who have been killing people. The Twins are
the war gods of the Pueblos, and they also represent war in Navajo ceremonials. Despite the fact that they are the children of Changing Woman
and must be mentioned by all singers of Blessingway, their exploits are
to be found in the Enemy Monsterway, a war ceremonial. And like the
Pueblo Twins, they are born in the present world rather than being a
part of the emergence. Unlike the Pueblo Twins who descend into the
underworld to guide the people to the surface, the Navajo Twins have
no association with the underworld.

After recounting the wanderings of various Navajo clans, Sandoval
relates the story of Mountainway and the Fire Dance and then tells several unrelated stories. Among these are the story of the beggar's son and
the story of the two maidens and the white butterfly, which, although
not labeled as such, are major episodes in the myth of Frenzy Witchcraftway (O'Bryan 1956, 143–166). The Sun gives the hero of these two
stories the "medicine that the Gambler had used and taken up into the
sky with him," thus connecting the myth of the Gambler to that of
Frenzy Witchcraftway. This is the only account of the creation myth that
includes myths of Frenzy Witchcraftway.

Goldtooth's creation myth also includes a story not included by other
tellers, that of "Chap Man," which is a version of the widely spread myth
of the hiding and release of game. These atypical inclusions are important for arguments presented in subsequent chapters because they pose
the question whether they and similar variations represent the individual narrator's style or diverse traditions.

We have seen that many of the differences among the narrators are
random. The number of beings created in the First World, for example,
varies not only from narrator to narrator but from one telling to another
by the same narrator, depending upon the audience. Sandoval seems to
have been especially concerned with the formal structure of the myth
when he worked with O'Bryan. Major events take place in the odd numbered worlds. The even numbered worlds have little action and seem to
satisfy a desire to have four underworlds rather than to further the plot.

19. In Pueblo myths, the mother of the Twins is not very important; it is their grandmother who cares for them. Spider Woman is, along with Huru'ingwuuti, a great female
creator. It would appear that the Navajos made a female creator patterned after the Huru'ingwuuti after developing matrilineal descent.

The other narrators are less concerned with accounting for all of the underworlds. Indeed, one could argue that the most important division
for these narrators is between the underworlds and the present, surface
world. It may not be important that First Man appears only in Torlino's
Fourth World, whereas all the others have First Man and First Woman
appear in the First World. What might be far more important is that,
whereas all the others present First Man and Coyote as the prime creators, Torlino demotes both to more subservient positions: he depicts
First Man and First Woman as creations of the *Haashch'ééh dine'é*, and
Coyote as wholly despicable and sharing his birth with Badger. The question arises whether these differences have greater significance than personal taste would seem to suggest. Do they, in fact, indicate different
theological approaches?

Goldtooth, we recall, maintains that there are two ways of learning:
"One was the Bego Way and the Begochidi with Witchcraft. The other
is the Good Way and the Good Way with Witchcraft. The Bego Way and
Good Way are the same except that in the Bego Way, Bego does everything while in the Good Way, White Bead Woman, First Man and Talking God are the important gods" (Fishler 1953, 2–3). Goldtooth identifies First Man, First Woman, and Coyote as the first beings created by
Wind. He also names Talking God, Black God, and Begochidi as creators. Begochidi creates insects, seeds, mountains, and game animals.
First Man and First Woman create plants. The Holy People—Talking
God, Calling God, and others—create the domestic animals, but Begochidi has to demonstrate how to bring them to life. Coyote is a god
but occupies an ambiguous position: according to Goldtooth, Coyote
has knowledge but not power.

Klah also makes Begochidi preeminent. Begochidi creates First Man
and First Woman after creating the birds and animals. There is a persistent conflict between Begochidi and Black God, the fire god, who destroys many of the things Begochidi creates, and it is Begochidi who
leads the people from the underworld into the present world. In the present world, Begochidi makes the first sweat house and creates humans
as well as the Holy people, including Talking God.[20]

---

20. The antagonism between Begochidi and Black God is interesting. If Begochidi is
a later transformation of an earlier. Athabascan trickster, his antagonism to Black God is
a replication of the trickster's antagonism to the Raven trickster of the Northwest Coast.
But because Black God has come to be perceived as a version of Masau, the Hopi god of
fire who owns the surface world, the conflict between Begochidi and Black God also represents that between the shamanistic and agricultural traditions.

Gishin Biye' makes First Man the major creator in the underworlds and emphasizes his witchcraft as well as the fact that the Evilways begin in the underworlds. Coyote is among the first beings and, although he is not a creator, people go to First Man and Coyote to ask for guidance. First Man and Coyote are also the first ones to speak and act. Despite the importance Gishin Biye' gives to the First Man Group, he keeps Changing Woman and the masked gods separate from those who emerged from the underworlds. Changing Woman represents all that is good, even to the extent that her promiscuous mating with the Sun is ascribed to another woman entirely. In contrast, all the beings of the underworlds are described as being evil.

According to Torlino, First Man and First Woman, instead of being the original deities, are created out of corn by the *Haashch'ééh dine'é*. This presages the creation of humans in the present world. Throughout Torlino, the *Haashch'ééh dine'é*—Talking God, Water Sprinkler, Calling God, and Black God—are the preeminent deities. The Pueblos are also found in the lower worlds, where they are already practicing agriculture, living in houses, and cutting their "hair straight in front" (Matthews 1897, 67–68). They invite the newcomers (the First Man group and the Mirage and Insect People) to live with them. The *Haashch'ééh dine'é* teach First Man and First Woman as well as their children to wear masks and to pray for abundant rain and crops. When the people plant, they get their seeds from the Pueblos. During the separation of the sexes, First Man invites the Pueblos to join the men. Six of the Pueblo clans do so, "but they took their women with them" (Matthews 1897, 71).[21] Coyote is born very late and plays a role only in the separation of the sexes and the theft of the Water Monster's child that causes the flood. The inclusion of the Pueblos and the preeminence of the *Haashch'ééh dine'é* distinguish this version from the others.

I have used Sandoval's narration on the presumption that, because he was not a ceremonialist, he was uninfluenced by the perspective of any particular ceremonial point of view and would, therefore, have been free to include materials that might have been excluded by singers of ceremonials. For example, his depiction of Coyote is difficult to place in any ceremonial tradition. On the one hand, Sandoval gives Coyote pride of first place, allowing Coyote to claim that he was created even before First Man, which suggests a connection with the Evilways in

---

21. Paul Zolbrod changes this to "They too had allowed their women to anger them" (1984, 61).

general. On the other hand, Sandoval describes two distinct aspects of Coyote: one the good creator, the other a marplot. Sandoval's treatment of Coyote differs from that of the other narrators, none of whom make Coyote more important than First Man. Unfortunately, we do not know from which strand of tradition he drew his inspiration.

In *The Navajo Hunter Tradition* (1975), Karl Luckert suggests that Coyote represents the creator-trickster god of an older hunter tradition who was "defamed" by the Navajos after they came into contact with the Pueblos and adopted agriculture. Coyote's role as creator is omitted, whereas his chaotic and evil characteristics are retained. If Luckert is correct, one must ask whether these traces of the hunter tradition are to be found in the myths of some ceremonies and not others. And can one account for the persistence of an older tradition in these ceremonies despite the fact that virtually all sings have both an evil and a blessing side and that even a sing done according to Evilway must be concluded with Blessingway songs? Certainly, all singers know the myths of the Blessingway and must take them into account when narrating a myth to an anthropologist. In the same manner, a Blessingway singer may recount episodes of the underworlds even though they are not part of the Blessingway, which starts at the place of emergence and not in the underworlds.

In order to examine Luckert's hypothesis in more detail, chapter 5 traces the development of Navajo myths from their homeland in the Athabascan north to their arrival in the Pueblo Southwest to determine whether there is evidence of an older hunter tradition that may be at odds in important respects with the Blessingway tradition. Chapter 6 examines the Blessingway myth in detail to determine how Blessingway singers other than Torlino characterize Coyote, First Man, and Begochidi. Following that determination, chapter 6 demonstrates, first, that myth motifs as well as myths representing the early hunter tradition are found in some sings but not in others and, second, that the distribution of these early elements represent an old tradition that adapted as the Blessingway emerged as the core of Navajo religion.

5

Tricksters North and South

Several authors interpret the development of Navajo religion as an attempt to incorporate the communal values borrowed from the Pueblos into the persisting, individualistic orientation of the Athabascan immigrants' hunting and gathering worldview. David Brugge believes that the Blessingway ceremonial began to assume its contemporary form as "the core of a nativistic re-assertion of the Athabascan way of life" during the later years of hosting Pueblo refugees, between 1750 and 1770, and that "Blessingway now holds a central position in Navajo religion and the Navajo way of life, giving both a unity in spite of a complex diversity" (1963, 22, 25; 1983, 494–495). Bert Kaplan and Dale Johnson have suggested that "Navajo culture comprehends two historically distinct traditions, one based on the Apache hunting and raiding past and a second based on comparatively recent Pueblo contact. Each tradition has its related set of values, which not only are different from each other but are in important respects opposed and conflicting" (Kaplan and Johnson 1964, 204). Over time, according to these authors, the Pueblo tradition came to dominate and repress but not altogether eradicate Athabascan values, which find current expression in patterns of deviance and psychopathology.

Similarly, Karl Luckert propounds the notion that the Coyote of Navajo myth is a "defamed" hunter god (Luckert 1975; 1978; 1979). In Luckert's view, Coyote was never an important trickster figure in Navajo culture and his "defamation" consists not only in denying him the role of a mediator of game but also by referring to him only in negative terms. In my opinion, this interpretation fails to consider the long period of time it took for the ancestors of the Navajos and Apaches to reach the South-west after leaving their homeland in the subarctic. If, as Luckert suggests, the nearly extinct Coyoteway was once a hunting ritual (1975, 170–171), one must ask where and when the Navajos switched from Wolf as a hunting deity and adopted Coyote in his stead. With the exception of the Pimas and Papagos, Coyote is certainly not the Southwestern trickster figure par excellence. Among the Pueblos, Coyote occupies a minor position, and there is little evidence that either the Navajos or the Apaches absorbed much of the traditions of the Pimic speakers. Coyote is, however, the pre-eminent trickster in the Great Basin, the Plains, and parts of the Plateau and California. In the Basin, Coyote is a trickster-creator who is even credited with the creation of the world and humanity.

The myths of the hunting societies of North America favor trickster cycles. The farming societies, in contrast, favor emergence myths that symbolize pregnancy and delivery and the agricultural cycle of germination and growth. The trickster figure has been said to represent the shaman who heals but is also feared as a witch (Ricketts 1966, 338). At their worst, American Indian tricksters pose as babysitters and eat the babies, or they disguise themselves as women in order to marry men (Bierhorst 1985, 12). In one of the best known stories of the western hemisphere, told from California to the Great Lakes and south as far as Tierra del Fuego, the trickster falls in love with his own daughter and pretends to die, advising the young woman that as soon as he is dead she will meet a stranger whom she must not fail to take as her husband. After digging out of his grave, or rolling off his funeral pyre, the trickster reappears in disguise and marries the daughter. If he has two daughters, he marries them both (Schmerler 1931).

Paul Radin has written that the trickster is among the most archaic figures of human mythology. Among the North American Indians:

Trickster is, at one and the same time, creator and destroyer, giver and negator, he who dupes others and who is always duped himself. He wills nothing consciously. At all times he is constrained to behave as he does from impulses over which he has no control. He knows neither good nor evil yet he is responsible for both. He possesses no values, moral or social, is at the mercy of his passions and appetites, yet through his actions all values come into being. (1956, xxiii)

And John Bierhorst adds that:

Since the trickster's antics have a way of leading to acts of creation, he is susceptible of being treated as a god, even if he has the personality of a devil.

As if to clarify the situation, some tribal mythologies distinguish between two kinds of Coyote. . . . In other tribes there is a tendency to give the trickster a companion so that we have stories about Coyote and Skunk, Coyote and Wolf, or Coyote and Fox. In some cases the two personalities recall the modern distinction between good and evil. (1985, 14).

This chapter identifies those myths the Navajos brought from their original home in the subarctic and characterizes the figure of the northern Athabascan trickster. As the Navajos moved south, they came into contact with tribes of the Plateau, Great Basin, and Plains. By tracing one hunter myth from the subarctic to the Southwest, I show how the trickster figure has been transformed by the Navajos from the time they left their homeland until their contacts with the Pueblos and the development of their myth corpus as we know it today. This exercise allows us to identify other trickster figures found only in the Southwest, which were utilized by the Navajos after their adoption of agriculture. In chapter 6, I locate the myths of these trickster figures among the myths of the Navajo healing ceremonies to determine whether they appear randomly or are usually found in certain ceremonies rather than others.

The efforts of Luckert and Kaplan and Johnson to identify the remnants of the Apachean past in Navajo religion and life contrast sharply with the majority of scholars, who describe Navajo values almost exclusively in terms of the Pueblo tradition.[1] Despite this difference, all of these investigators present Navajo cosmology, values, and religion as a single, integrated whole, rather than a tradition that embraces a continuing conflict between what I have called the Blessingway and Trickster traditions. This and the succeeding chapters must demonstrate that two identifiable traditions exist and that a continuing conflict between them can be identified and traced over time.

From North to South

Several myths of the Canadian Athabascans have been carried south by the Apacheans. One of these, the Bird Nester, is distributed across the entire continent and is thought to be very old because

---

1. For scholars who describe Navajo values in terms of Pueblo tradition, see Clyde Kluckhohn and A. Kimball Romney (1961), John Ladd (1957), John Farella (1984), and James McNeley (1981).

it is also found in South America. It is most prominent among hunters and gatherers and therefore probably predates the origin of agriculture (Bierhorst 1985, 10). Most anthropologists label it "Sky Rock" among the Navajo; it is part of the Navajo myths of Evilway, Beadway, Red Antway, and Big Starway. Other northern myths found among the Navajo are the Visit to the Thunderbird Nest, which is usually a sequel to the Sky Rock episode, and the Attack on the Giant Elk. The Giant Elk is one of the monsters slain by the Navajo Monster Slayer. Another widespread story among hunters and gatherers is the Release and Hoarding of Game. This myth, too, is remarkably old and occurs in both the Old and New Worlds (Thompson 1989, I:225–226).

The myth of the hoarding and release of game animals can be traced from the Athabascan north through the Plateau, Great Basin, and Plains into the Apachean Southwest. Neither Coyote nor Raven was the supreme trickster of those Canadian Athabascans most closely related to the Apacheans. Instead, Raven was always the adversary of the Athabascan transformer-trickster, and Coyote was adopted as preeminent trickster during their migration south. In these northern myths, Wolf appears neither as the Master of the Game nor as the Trickster.

Among the myths of the Canadian Athabascans, there is a shift away from Eskimo and Northwest influences. These myths contain both a manlike transformer and Raven, the trickster-provider-creator of the Northwest Coast. Raven tends to be cast as a marplot among those tribes not adjacent to the Northwest Coast, and is only infrequently found east of the Rocky Mountains. The transformer, known as Old Man, Navigator, or Beaver, travels from place to place by canoe and is usually concerned with ridding the world of monsters who eat people. In the central part of the area, Raven is portrayed as an adversary of the transformer, who has trickster tendencies (Bierhorst 1985, 65–72). An antagonism between Raven and a transformer-trickster recast as Coyote may well have originated prior to the Apacheans entry into the Southwest but after their southward migrations began.

The northern Athabascan Kaska say that Raven hoards the game animals, and the transformer has to release them (Teit 1917). The Beaver tell how Crow hid the game animals: The people attacked and freed them, but Crow covered them with bone shell so they could not be killed, and everyone, including Crow, went hungry. The Chipewyan say that a man painted Crow black. This made Crow angry, so he fenced in the deer on barren grounds. Two white foxes succeeded in getting past Crow to release the deer. Crow then hardened the deer's skins so they would be hard to kill, but he softened them again when the hunters promised to leave the liver and fat for him (Lowie 1912). The Tahltan, neighbors of the Northwest Coast Tlingit, cast Raven in the role of the hero who releases the game. In one tale, game was hoarded by a few people so that most were starving. Raven created the tides to expose underwater sources of food and make them available to the people (Teit 1919, 201). Another tale relates how Raven was able to release eulachon, a species of smelt, by trickery (Teit 1919, 213). A similar tale is told by the Tsimshian of the Northwest Coast: The owner of eulachon kept them away from Raven, who caught a fish and smeared the scales on his canoe and clothing. So disguised, he was able to enter the compound where the eulachon were kept. When the owner realized he had been outwitted, he released the eulachon (Boas 1916). Yet another Tahltan story tells that Game Mother owned all the animals who could run fast and were difficult to hunt. She called them home, and people began to starve. Raven made them less elusive so that they were easier to hunt, but Game Mother could still call them home, and thus there are still periods of game shortage (Teit 1919, 216).

These myths, similar in plot, differ in the identity of the game hoarder and the one who releases the game. In the interior, the Athabascan transformer is at times the hero and Raven is the hoarder. On the Northwest Coast and among the adjacent Athabascan tribes, Raven is the hero. It is instructive to see how this myth has been influenced by the tribes with whom the Apacheans came into contact on their journey to the Southwest.

Coming into the Plateau, they would have had contact with the interior Salishan speakers—the Shuswap, Kutenai, Flathead, Coeur d'Alene, and the Sahaptin-speaking Nez Perce. The southern and eastern tribes of the Plateau emphasized Coyote as a trickster-transformer-creator: "He is the advocate of death and the steadfast champion of sexuality, yet by accident or design he is also the bringer of food and sometimes the creator of the world. Usurping the role of the Transformer, he even slays an occasional monster," as in the Athabascan homeland (Bierhorst 1985, 141–142).

The Kutenai tell how Raven was hungry and hid the buffalo. Beaver feigned death, caught Raven's leg, and helped people to capture him. Raven escaped but was tracked. Jackrabbit transformed himself into a puppy, Hare became a stone, and both were taken into the tent of two old women. Hare and Jackrabbit freed the buffalo and escaped by holding on to the testicles of a buffalo bull (Boas 1918, 303–304). The

Table 2 *The Hoarding and Release of Game*

	Hoarder	Releaser	Puppy
SIBERIA			
Koryak	underground	Raven	
NORTHWEST			
Tsimshian	owner of eulachon	Raven	
ATHABASCAN WEST			
Tahltan	people	Raven	
Tahltan	people	Raven	
Tahltan	Game Mother	Raven	
ATHABASCAN CENTRAL-EAST			
Kaska	Raven	Transformer	
Beaver	Crow	people	
Chipewyan	Crow	two foxes	
PLATEAU			
Kutenai	Raven	Jack Rabbit and Hare	+
Thompson	Raven and others	Bluejay, Pinejay	
Sanpoil	two women	Coyote	
BASIN			
Shoshone	Crow	Weasel	+
Shoshone-Comanche	people	Coyote	+
Western Shoshone	Wolf	Coyote	
PLAINS			
Gros Ventre	old woman	Nixant (trickster-creator)	+
Kiowa	White Crow	Sendeh (trickster)	+
Wichita	Raven	Coyote	+
Comanche	old woman and cousin	Coyote	+
SOUTHWEST			
Lipan	Crow	Coyote	+
Jicarilla	Raven	people, medicine men	+
Chiricahua	Crow	Enemy Slayer and Coyote	+

Table 2 (continued)

	Hoarder	Releaser	Puppy
Mescalero	Raven	Monster Slayer (but Coyote tried)	
White Mountain	Raven	Monster Slayer	
White Mountain	Ganiskidi	Raven	
Navajo	Black God-Crow	a hunter	+
Navajo	Black God-Crow and Talking God	people	+
Navajo	Black God	people	+
Navajo	Black God-Crow	people	+
Navajo	Deer Raiser	Self Teacher	
Zuni	people	Fathers of the Katsinas	
Zuni	Yellow Woman	Hero Twins	
Keresan	Yellow Woman	Hero Twins	
Hopi	a girl	a boy	

transformation of the releaser into a puppy is a detail found on the Plateau, among the tribes of the Great Basin and Plains, and in the myths of the Apacheans. Raven appears as the game hoarder on the Plateau as well as in the north. He, too, travels south with the Apacheans. According to a Sanpoil version, Coyote freed the salmon from two women who had impounded them. He then followed the salmon, giving them as gifts to villagers as he traveled. Wherever maidens rejected his amorous advances, he created waterfalls that kept the salmon away (Boas 1917, 101). The Thompson say that Raven, Fisher, Marten, Wolverine, and Lynx hid the game animals, who were then freed by the tricksters, Bluejay and Pinejay, dressed in the clothes of Raven's servants (Teit 1912).

Reaching the Great Basin, the Apacheans would have had most contact with the Eastern Shoshone and the Ute as well as those Shoshoneans who were later to be known as Comanches. According to Bierhorst:

The most persistent figure in Basin stories is the trickster-creator Coyote. . . . In company with his elder brother, usually Wolf, Coyote creates the earth by pouring sand on the primeval waters, creates light, steals fire, steals pine nuts, and releases impounded game animals. . . . One of the most striking incidents in the numerous recorded tales of Wolf and Coyote is the motif of the human race spilled from a jug. (1985, 124–126)

This story of the human race spilled from a jug often includes the *vagina dentata* motif. Coyote comes upon a beautiful woman living with her mother. He discovers that the woman, and sometimes the mother as well, has a toothed vagina. Using wood or horn, he manages to destroy the teeth. The woman then gives birth to many small babies, which she puts into a jug; she tells Coyote to take the jug to his own home but to be careful not to look inside. Of course, Coyote looks inside, and the babies spill out to become the people of this world.

A Shoshone tale tells how Weasel transformed himself into a puppy in order to free the animals that Crow had impounded. After they had been freed, Crow had to be satisfied with the remains of the hunted animals (Lowie 1924). The Comanche tell how Coyote sent a small animal to where the buffalo were kept by an old woman and her younger cousin. The small animal howled and frightened the animals so that they broke down the gate and escaped (St. Clair and Lowie 1909, 280–281). The western Shoshone say that Coyote liberated the game animals (Steward 1943, 298).

The story of the hoarding and release of game is widespread on the Plains, and Coyote, the trickster-creator, is often the one who finds and releases the animals, although he may be known by other names (see Dorsey 1904, 191–194; Kroeber 1907, 65–68; Parsons 1929a, 21–26). Here, too, the trick of transforming someone into a puppy in order to gain access to the game is widespread.

Arriving in the Southwest, the Apacheans came into contact with societies whose myths were concerned more with agriculture and ceremonial and social matters. Hunting, however, had not disappeared entirely, and many myths deal with the hunt and with animals. The hoarding and release of game is also found among the agricultural tribes of the Eastern Woodlands as well as in the Southwest. It is still a sacred text among the Iroquois, in a myth that features twin creators (Hewitt 1900, 519–521). The myth is also told as a secular tale among the Seneca; in this version, deities play no role and no motivation for the hiding of the game is proffered (Curtin and Hewitt 1911, 519–521). The Biloxi tell how hunting was easy because the "One Above" kept the animals in his house and gave access to those who wished to hunt. A "bad boy" opened the gates, the game escaped, and now the animals must be hunted in faraway places (Dorsey and Swanton 1912, 47). A Cherokee myth says that an adopted "wild boy" and his brother freed the deer their father kept beneath the ground (Mooney 1888, 98–100).

All of the eastern tribes relied on hunting more than did the Pueblos of the Southwest, where we find only one unequivocal example of the myth. According to the Zuni, the game animals were hidden in a canyon by people who lived to the southeast. They were released by the Fathers of the Katsinas and pursued by the prey animals of the cardinal directions (Cushing 1883, 21–24). The myth accounts for the directional locations of the prey animals and not, as in the hunters' myths, for the difficulty of hunting the game. In another Zuni story, a beautiful huntress has hidden all the animals on Yellow Mountain. She tells suitors that she cannot marry them unless they bring her deer, which, of course, they are cannot do. Finally, the Twins, disguised as ugly midgets, discover where the game has been hidden and so are able to marry the maiden and allow humans to hunt (Cushing 1901, 104–131). Hamilton Tyler equates this huntress with the Zuni katsina, Chakwaina, who is the mother of both game and childbirth, as well as with the Keresan Yellow Woman, whose brother is the spirit of game and who is so lazy that Yellow Woman must be a huntress (1964, 188–189).

The Hopi have grafted the release of game motif onto the Zuni story about the killing of Paiyatemu by an evil woman (Voth 1905, 136–141). In the Hopi version, it is a human youth who is killed. When his family find and restore him to life, the clothing of all the youths slain by the woman turn into game animals and escape.

Apachean myths are directly comparable to those of the Basin and Plains and have no details in common with the Pueblo versions. In all the Apache accounts, Raven or Crow is the game hoarder, which retains the Beaver and Chipewyan preference for Raven as adversary. Among the Lipan, Coyote releases the buffalo (Opler 1940, 125), and in a Chiricahua account, Coyote and Slayer of Enemies together free the animals (Opler 1994a, 15). Pliny Goddard notes that in a Mescalero version Coyote tries but fails to release the animals, whereas Monster Slayer succeeds (1911, 212–214). The releasers of the game, or buffalo among the Jicarilla, are either two youths, medicine men, or the people in general (Opler 1994b, 256–258; F. Russell 1975, 259–262; Goddard 1911, 212–214). The White Mountain Apache cast Monster Slayer in the role of releaser (Goodwin 1939, 86–88). In another White Mountain version, it is Raven who frees the deer hidden by Ganiskidi (Goddard 1919, 126–127).

The Navajo versions of the myth usually cast Black God in the form of Crow as the hoarder, but with the exception of one version, it is the mythic prehuman people who release the game (Luckert 1975; 1978). In one tale, the hoarder is a witch named Deer Raiser who keeps an underground game farm. The animals are released by an "earth surface" person named Self Teacher who has married Deer Raiser's daughter. Whereas Deer Raiser is a master of game animals, Self Teacher is a successful grower of corn. In no myth does Coyote figure as a leading character.

From this distribution of the myth, we see that those Apachean tribes with the most Pueblo contacts—Jicarilla with Taos; Western Apache and Navajo with Hopi and Zuni—are the ones that denied Coyote the role of the hero who releases the game. Thus, even in the preserved myths from the hunting past, Coyote was expunged as the agriculturalists' culture gained in importance.[2]

While hidden, animals were easy for the hoarder and his family to hunt because they were almost tame. When the animals were released, the hoarder or his wife did something to make them difficult for humans to hunt. There are several methods of making the animals difficult to hunt: among these, a White Mountain Apache myth tells how Raven's wife touched the deer's noses with clothing from between her legs so that they could smell danger a long way away (Goodwin 1939, 86–88), and a Navajo account says that the escaping animals were made to smell Deer Raiser's wife's vagina (Fishler 1953, 126–128). This motif is perhaps derived from the belief that hunters must not come into contact with menstrual blood prior to the hunt. Why it is found only among the western Apacheans and not among the hunting tribes is unclear.

The story of Deer Raiser, minus the release of game motif, is part of the Navajo Plumeway myth. The Navajo hoarding and release of game myth is part of the Deerway hunting ceremonial. Deerway myths have been collected by Karl Luckert and Berard Haile (Luckert 1975; Haile, referred to in Luckert 1975, 6). A sister who has four brothers is transformed into a deer. Before she leaves them to live as a deer person, she teaches the brothers various hunting rites. After she has gone, the game disappears. The brothers discover that the game has been hidden by Black God, who, along with Talking God, Begochidi, and other Holy People, created the animals. These deities taught the people all the hunting rituals, but people hunted improperly, and so Black God hid the animals. The brothers—or the people—make a small puppy who releases the game.

Claus Chee Sonny, the singer who gave Luckert the Deerway myth, later told his version of Deerway *Ajiłee,* that is, Deerway Frenzy

2. Monster Slayer and Killer of Enemies are Apachean versions of the elder of the Twin War Gods of the Pueblos.

Witchcraftway (Luckert 1978). The only change in the hoarding of game myth is the addition of Frenzy Witchcraft medicines as the means by which the animals were protected from hunters. Talking God and Black God hide the game animals inside Black Mountain, the home of Black God. Talking God and Black God put poisonous plants out to protect the game from hunters such as Coyote, Lynx, Mountain Lion, and Wolf. The people transform one among them into a puppy, who follows Black God into his home and frees the game. As the deer depart, they eat the poisonous plants (*ch'l agháanii*, locoweed and jimson weed) and become crazy.

So the young man and the young woman (young deer people) became crazy, and they began living with one another as crazy people. As brother and sister they began having sexual intercourse with one another. They became crazy because of the poisonous plants. It was decreed that if humans were to eat these plants or the meat of animals that had eaten them, they would become crazy. As Talking God and Black God were responsible for *ajiłee* craziness in the first place it is up to them to also cure the people who are so affected. (Luckert 1978, 28)

Although the use of jimson weed and the other plants connects this form of Deerway to the Frenzy Witchcraftway, the inclusion of sibling incest is found in the Mothway.

This shifting of emphasis away from Coyote parallels Pueblo myths, where Coyote plays a far less important role than he or other tricksters do in the myths of hunters and gatherers. Chaos and unpredictability are given far less leeway, and the creative aspects of Coyote are sharply separated from his "evil" actions. Many of the more archaic Coyote themes are retained, but they are usually placed in less pivotal positions. According to the Keresans, Coyote brought fire, but instead of doing it of his own accord, he was a well mannered messenger who delivered the fire that the underground creator Mother wrapped in his tail (Parsons 1974, 194, 211). For all the Pueblos, he is a guard who warns of enemies, sights game, and, at Taos, forecasts the weather (Parsons 1974, 194). At Zuni, where the hunt animals are given special importance, Coyote is the hunt god of the west and the hunt society is named after him (Parsons 1974, 188). But he is expunged entirely from themes of sexual conflict such as the conquest of the *vagina dentata*, which, in the Hopi version, is accomplished by a medicine society (Stephen 1929, 28). Although still associated with witchcraft and death, he seems not to be the major symbol of either in any of the Pueblos, and he is not associated with any of the shaman societies. Nor is the coyote avoided but may be hunted and even eaten when game is scarce at Hopi and Jemez (Stephen 1929, 22).[3]

Black God has also been transformed; in Navajo myths, he is one of the masked gods along with Talking God and Calling God. He is the Navajo fire god. Gladys Reichard describes him as phlegmatic, slow moving, modest, and sometimes very old (1963, 399–403). In the creation myths, depending on the teller, he is either a beneficent creator or an evil doer.

According to Klah and Goldtooth, who give Begochidi preeminence, Black God is an adversary of Begochidi who burns Begochidi's creations. Gishin Biye', an Evilway singer, says that Black God has the power of divination along with Gila Monster and various birds. He also associates Black God with witchcraft. And yet Gishin Biye' also says that Black God forces the release of a man held by Dark Hail Man and gives to the Evilway the fire drill songs that counteract witchcraft. Torlino, the Blessingway singer, includes Black God with the Holy People who create First Man and First Woman.

In the myths of Deerway, Black God hoards game only because people have been hunting improperly, and he, along with Talking God, use the Frenzy Witchcraft plants to protect the game from hunters. In Red Antway Evil, he starts a conflagration so that the people must flee. In Big Starway, Black God, Talking God, and Water God restore the hero. In all the myths of healing ceremonies where Black God appears, he plays a minor role and is one of the masked gods.

Black God has undergone an almost complete transformation from the marplot Raven-Crow to the god of fire—a clear identification of Black God with Masau, the Hopi god who is not only the terrifying god of fire and death but also a trickster and a god of fertility (Tyler 1964, 3–48). Even though Evilway singers may associate Black God with evil—an association that retains some of his earlier character—he is no longer a trickster and thus cannot be used to identify the persistence of a hunter tradition in the myths of the healing ceremonies. Coyote is another matter, however: not only does he appear as a trickster but also as a master of witchcraft. Indeed, the motifs in which Coyote is the main character fit well with Luckert's characterization of him as a defamed deity—until we recall that Coyote is also a creator and the first created in some creation myths.

3. For other references to Coyote and witchcraft and death, see Elsie Parsons (1974, 64, 66n, 89, 193–194).

Coyote Motifs

COYOTE TRANSFORMATION

Desiring to seduce the hero's wife, Coyote transforms the hero into a coyote and, taking the form of the hero, proceeds to trick the wife. The Male Red Antway Evil describes the process:

But the Coyote from somewhere cherished a desire for this woman, and many were the ways in which he began his schemes. All sorts of things he tried on the young man to deceive him, but always failed. Now this man was exclusively occupied with the chase. He was an expert at it and never returned empty handed. . . . In his accustomed manner he had one day not gone very far before he came upon the tracks of a deer, which he began to track. . . . In the meantime, while he was following it, Coyote had waylaid him and without being aware of it, he was running parallel with Coyote. Thus it happened that he (Coyote) blew his own voice, his entire interior, his breath, and his entire exterior, exactly as he was in appearance upon the young man. This caused a change to come over him, he began to stagger and in time fell over. . . . He then lay there in the form of a coyote, while Coyote walked away in the form of a man. This they call, he struck him with a coyote's dried skin. (Wyman 1965, 129–130)

This is described as a transformation achieved by throwing a coyote skin on the victim, who is then left senseless in the form of a coyote. But, by blowing his "breath," that is his wind or soul, on the man, Coyote has possessed the hero's body with his own soul. The displaced or lost soul of the man is left behind in the form of a coyote. It is important to note that he is left senseless. He is not in possession of his own soul, nor is he in possession of Coyote's soul. Likewise, a mindless person who is discovered wandering about aimlessly is thought to suffer from soul loss. The restoration rite involves passing the patient through a series of hoops to remove the coyote skin.

Nevertheless, a Red Antway Holy singer may present Coyote in a positive light. At the end of his Holyway myth, one narrator remarked to Berard Haile, "The witchcraft side is corrected by Coyote who transforms people who get into trouble" (Wyman 1965, 74). Haile then added, "Several legends of chants use at least part of the Reckless Coyote story to rationalize their Ghostway (Evilway) rituals, but never include it in their Holyway legends." But this motif is not as restricted as Haile thought: there are two Coyote transformations in one recording of Red Antway Holy, and the motif is found in myths of Waterway,

Shootingway, Frenzy Witchcraftway, Beadway, the various Evilways, and the Stargazing rite.

BAD SMELLS

After Coyote takes the hero's place, he sleeps with the wife:

Then after dusk she laid robes for him. While the young man had been backward and reserved with his wife, this one was not so, he bothered her constantly all night long. . . . On the morning of the fourth night he left again. So she entered her mother's home. But when she warmed up, she clearly smelled of Coyote urine. "So it is Coyote doing this I see! Where is the place in which he has not yet schemed!" (Wyman 1965, 130–131)

The smell of coyote urine is strong, and at times hungry coyotes will urinate on their food before eating it, although why this is done is not understood (Young and Jackson 1978, 63, 98). The smell of Coyote is referred to in both the Holy and Evilway myths of Shootingway and Red Antway. Not only is the Coyote's presence discovered by his smell, but after the hero is restored by the hoop ceremony, the smell remains and is thought to be so contaminating that the hero has to undergo four purifying baths, one of which contains an herb with the odor of field rat urine (Haile 1950, 79–82).

The Navajo word for coyote is *mą'ii*. *Mą'* is the stem and *ii* is "one who" or "which." Haile translates this as "roamer": "It appears that coyote would occasionally visit here with talking god, the inner form of dawn. Here it seems he would remark that he wanted to be called holy young man, and this (change of name) probably was the purpose of his frequent visits, because he was ashamed of the name roamer by which he was known" (Haile 1950, 139–40) Yet words beginning with *mą* are exceedingly rare in Navajo. Besides the nine entries in the Navajo dictionary for words derived from *coyote—coyote food, coyote trap*, and the like—there are only four other entries, three of which are loan words from Spanish or English (Young and Morgan 1980, 520). There are, in fact, only twenty words listed that begin with an *m*. Herbert Landar (1961) believes that *mą* had a proto-Athabascan ancestor with another meaning altogether. Noting that in Chipewyan there is a verb stem— *mą́*, which means "stink" (Li 1933), Landar concludes that the Navajo word for *coyote* is probably a noun derived prehistorically from an expression meaning "the one who stinks."

Even when Coyote is not mentioned by name, references to bad smells are used as euphemisms for mental disorders. Informants often mention the Mountainway ceremony as the preferred treatment for anxiety, fainting, temporary loss of mind, delirium, violent irrationality, and insanity, but also recommend it for rheumatism, swollen extremities, and arthritic pains. The myth describes the physical symptoms in detail: As the hero or heroine flees the tormentors, his or her feet, ankles, knees, and wrists become so sore that the protagonist can hardly continue and is unable to sleep because of the pain. By contrast there are only two passages that seem to refer to mental disorders: "But to him the odors of the lodge were now intolerable and he soon left the house and sat outside" and "The ceremony cured Dsilyi' Neyáni of all his strange feelings and notions. The lodge of his people no longer smelled unpleasant to him" (Matthews 1887, 410, 417).

CHANGING BEAR MAIDEN

In Sandoval's creation myth, the story of Changing Bear Maiden is told after the immediate postemergence events and the appearance of the monsters but before the birth of Changing Woman and the Twins, Monster Slayer and Born for Water. The story tells of Coyote's marriage to a beautiful young woman with twelve brothers.[4] This woman has refused all suitors and, when Coyote courts her, says that he must first kill the giant, Gray Big Ye'i, before he can be her husband. This he does through a ruse, after which she kills him four times; each time, he revives because he has concealed his vital organs. After passing these tests, he marries her, and her brothers leave home when they smell Coyote urine in the firewood. Coyote teaches his wife how to hide her vital organs and kills her four times. He then joins the brothers on the hunt but is killed on his way home by cliff swallows and spiders. At this point, Coyote's wife changes into a bear and avenges Coyote's murder, killing all her brothers except the youngest, who has learned of her evil. This brother kills her with the help of Wind: he finds and shoots her vital parts and, by keeping her blood streams from joining, prevents her revival. He then dissects her and changes her parts into useful things. Her limbs become bears, and her nipples become pinyon nuts. The Holy

---

4. In Goldtooth's version, there are only five brothers (Fishler 1953, 110). This and the changing number of siblings in Plains and Apache versions suggest that the actual number is shaped to fit the needs of the story. For example, the number of siblings may change to match the number of stars in the constellation that the escaping siblings become. And Goldtooth says that four of the brothers are killed, each in a different cardinal direction.

People help him restore his brothers, who then return home. This myth belongs almost exclusively to the Evilways (Wyman and Bailey 1943, 8–9; Wyman 1962, 33).

The story explains why bears are dangerous and provides a female counterpart to Coyote. The Mountainway is an important antidote for mental illness caused by bears, yet Changing Bear Maiden is only referred to tangentially in the myth (K. Spencer 1957, 128, 129, 133), and the only indication of mental loss is the reference to bad smells. Because Mountainway includes the masked Ye'is on the final night and is in the Holyway group, my guess is that the Blessingway emphasis has, over time, succeeded in expunging the myth of Coyote witchcraft.

The story of a woman who turns into a bear and attacks her family has a wide distribution in North America, extending from the prairies westward to California, the Plateau, and the Northwest Coast (Thompson 1966, 345, n244). The versions closest to the Navajo myth are found among the tribes of the western Plains as well as the Jicarilla and White Mountain Apache.

In the Blackfoot story, a young woman with seven brothers and a little sister refuses all suitors because she has taken a bear for her lover (Wissler and Duvall 1908, 68). The younger sister discovers her secret and tells their father, who kills the bear. Angry, the older sister takes flesh from the bear's paws and, by so doing, becomes a "powerful medicine woman." She turns into a bear and kills many people, after which she returns to human form. She then attempts to kill her sister, who escapes and flees the country along with her six brothers. As they try to escape, the brothers are killed one by one, but they are later revived by the youngest brother. Finally, they escape into the sky, where they become the constellation, Ursa Major.

The Jicarilla version speaks only of a girl who changes into a bear and kills the children she is playing with. Her younger sister escapes and, with six hunters, ascends into the sky, where they become the Pleiades (Opler 1938, 113). But in another Jicarilla story, Coyote woos a maiden and wins her brother's approval by helping him to hunt successfully. The girl says that she will marry Coyote only if he can come back to life four times. Coyote agrees and manages to come back to life because he divides his heart in two and puts one part at the tip of his nose and the other at the end of his tail (Opler 1938, 319).

Grenville Goodwin recorded a White Mountain Apache version that has even more details in common with the Navajo Changing Bear Maiden (1939, 174–178). A young girl manages to escape from Big

Owl, who has killed all of her people. When she comes to Coyote's camp, she promises to marry whoever kills Big Owl. Coyote goes to Big Owl's home and, by trickery, breaks his legs and steals his cap, but does not kill him. Seeing the cap and believing Big Owl dead, the girl marries Coyote. The people go hunting but give nothing to Coyote, who retaliates by turning the deer antler, which had been soft and edible up to this time, into hard bone. The people try to kill Coyote by having him fall into a canyon, and Coyote's wife turns herself into a bear and takes revenge by killing the people. Chipmunk tells her little brother not to let her delouse him. "Watch her shadow," Chipmunk tells him, "and if it turns into a bear, jump up and kill your sister." The brother does as he is told and kills the bear.

The Apachean myths differ from those of the Plains by making Coyote a major character. In other respects—the woman who changes into a bear, the role of a younger brother or sister, and the bear's attempt to kill the brothers—the Apachean stories appear to be the same. That the Jicarilla have two stories, one like those on the Plains, the other like Changing Bear Maiden of the Navajo, suggests that Bear as a dangerous being became a part of Navajo mythology as they moved south and, in order to explain the nature of Bear, they made a connection with their major trickster, Coyote.[5]

In Sandoval's version of the Changing Bear Maiden, Coyote cuts Gray Ye'i's leg but doesn't kill him (O'Bryan 1956, 40–48). In Haile's Evilway myth, Coyote kills Gray Big Ye'i (1928, 210), and in another version, Coyote kills Big Ye'i himself (Haile 1984, 69–77). In some versions of the Monsterway, the Twins kill both Big Ye'i and Gray Big Ye'i. The Evilway myth places the story after the slaying of the monsters by the Twins. Sandoval, however, has it precede the birth of Changing Woman and the Twins, as well as the slaying of the monsters. In addition, Big Ye'i is the first monster to be killed by the Twins. The coexistence of two Big Ye'is suggests that, although the task of slaying monsters has been given to the Twins, Coyote retains, in some myths at least, the same role as the early trickster-transformer of the northern Athabascans.

5. Tracing the mythology about bears is a subject in its own right and beyond the scope of this book. Suffice it to say that bear ceremonialism and shamanism were prominent among neither the northern Athabascans nor the tribes of the Great Basin. They were, however, important among the Keresan Pueblos, from where they spread to the Tanoans and Zunis. They were also prominent on the Plains and in North Central California (see Levy 1994).

Changing Bear Maiden is killed by her youngest brother, who is often confused with the younger twin, Born for Water, just as Changing Bear Woman is often confused with Tracking Bear (Haile 1984, 22). When Changing Bear Maiden is killed by her youngest brother, he turns her limbs into bears and her nipples into pine nuts. Similarly, Tracking Bear is dissected by the Twins. In one version, Tracking Bear's nipples become pine nuts, one half of a piece of fat from the tail becomes bears, and the other half becomes porcupines. In another version, Monster Slayer cuts the head into three pieces: one becomes broad-leaved yucca; one becomes narrow-leaved yucca; and one becomes the mescal (Reichard 1963, 74). Again, it appears that the children of Changing Woman, the central deity of Blessingway, appropriate earlier Coyote themes.

SKY ROCK

Sky Rock is the bird nester motif, which is one of the oldest stories on the continent. The typical story found across North America tells of a father who strands his son on a high rock so that he may seduce the woman they both desire. The son is rescued by a supernatural helper and takes his revenge on the father. In the Big Starway and the Evilways, Coyote strands the hero on an inaccessible rock pinnacle so that he may seduce the hero's wife. After a variety of adventures in the sky, the hero learns the ceremony and is helped back to earth by supernaturals, then finds and kills Coyote, who is living with his wife. In the Beadway, which also contains a Coyote transformation, the hero is stranded on an inaccessible rock ledge by Pueblos variously identified as coming from sites in Chaco Canyon (Kintyel or Pueblo Bonito), Canyon de Chelly (White House), or Jemez. Kintyel and Pueblo Bonito are the locations where the contest with the Great Gambler takes place. White House is where the first Mothway is performed. And Jemez is where the Coyote Pass clan originated. Thus, although Coyote is not involved in this episode of the Big Starway myth, connections with the trickster figures are implied.

It is interesting that, as with Tracking Bear, the elder Twin slays the monster Giant Birds in a manner that parallels the Sky Rock motif. One of the Giant Birds drops Monster Slayer on his rock aerie for his youngsters to feed upon. Feigning death, Monster Slayer is able to kill both the father and mother but spares the two young birds, whom he changes into eagle and owl. After this, Bat Woman carries him back to earth.

INCEST

The Navajos have included the story about Coyote committing incest with his daughter in the origin myth of Coyoteway Holy. Many of the other old Coyote tales are told in secular contexts. More often, the theme of father-daughter incest involves a witch father-in-law who tests the hero before he can wed the daughter. Witchcraft and incest are intimately connected, although the type of witchcraft is not specified (Kluckhohn 1962, 25). Specific reference to sibling incest is more directly connected with Begochidi in the Mothway, though Coyote medicines are used to cure the resulting seizures.

Coyote is the source of all sexual deviance and excess. He crosses the river to reach the women during the separation of the sexes in the underworlds. There he is in such a sexual frenzy that he commits cunnilingus and, according to Goldtooth, even copulates with his sisters and his mother's sisters (addressed in Navajo as "mothers") without recognizing who they are. Goldtooth emphatically insisted that all conditions referred to by the *tsi* prefix imply generalized convulsions caused by incest, are characteristic of Coyote, and may ultimately be traced to him. The thematic prefix *tsi* connotes extreme behavior of all sorts including drunkenness, violence, convulsions, and irrational behavior. *Tsi* means the manner in which one walks in all directions—that is, aimlessly and chaotically (Young and Morgan 1980, 470). Lack of direction as well as going to extremes is exemplified by Coyote the "roamer," who lacks constraints and direction.

WITCH ARROWS

In Male Shootingway Evil, the hero is transformed into a coyote but restored. Later, while attempting to revenge himself, he is bewitched by Coyote. Bird people shoot ritual arrows at Coyote; the arrows enter his anus and kill him. Afraid that he will bewitch them in turn, the birds restore Coyote. Nevertheless, Coyote bewitches the hero a second time by possessing him. The ceremony is performed by which the "ghost" of Coyote is killed and the hero is restored (Haile 1950; K. Spencer 1957, 208–211).

Begochidi

As we have seen, Begochidi figures prominently in the creation myths of Goldtooth and Klah, where he is a primary creator. Yet neither anthropologists nor Navajos agree as to his identity or character. Gladys Reichard describes him as "a creature of versatile and conflicting characteristics" (1963, 386). Paul Zolbrod notes that Begochidi has been identified as a trickster, a supreme deity, and the father of the monsters and believes that he is "a deity that enters the pantheon of Navajo supernaturals fairly late, reflecting Christian and European influences in one way or another" (1984, 373, n33). W. W. Hill also notes that his informants could not agree on Begochidi's role (Hill 1938a, 99). One of Hill's informants thought that all the animals were under Begochidi's control. Another said that Begochidi created the game animals but that Talking God and Black God controlled them. Yet another said that Talking God and Black God controlled the game but that Begochidi was more important, that he was the god of game and taught the game songs to men. Begochidi is one of the creators of game, in contrast to Black God, who hoards game in the Deerway myths recorded by Luckert.

Washington Matthews also notes that Navajos do not agree on all the characteristics of Begochidi (1897, 226, n78). If a Navajo wants a fine horse, he prays to Begochidi. Some say Begochidi made all the animals not otherwise specified in the myths; others say that he and Sun made the animals together. Still others say he only made the larger game animals and the modern domestic animals. Some say he carries the moon. Some say he was born when Sun impregnated a certain flower. Others say he has the power to bring game to those hunters he favors and can spoil the aim of those he dislikes. All agree that he is a great mischief maker among the gods but that he often takes pity on those who fall on hard times, even if their problems are caused by their own "disorderly" behavior. Quoting from Matthews' notebooks, Zolbrod reports, "The name [Begochidi] signifies 'He tried to catch it.' He got his name while he was out hunting" (Zolbrod 1984, 373 n33). And Reichard says, "He was also in charge of insects, called them at will, and even sometimes appeared as a worm or insect" (1963, 386–390). Insects, we recall, were the first people of the underworlds and are always associated with witchcraft.

Begochidi is also the tutelary spirit of the Butterfly People, who turn into moths after committing sibling incest in the Mothway. In the myth, his status as a hermaphrodite is of key importance, but he is neither good nor evil. When he leaves the Butterfly people to their own devices, it is to pursue game. He appears in five of the eight episodes of Hailway as a helpful deity. Despite his positive role, he is described as a trickster and hermaphrodite in one episode:

On their way to the peace ceremony they are puzzled by meeting a boy who, laughing, throws dirt up in the air; he appears first in their rear, then ahead or amongst them in the form of a yellow worm and other transformations. The people want to kill him. . . . When they catch him all kinds of stinging insects swarm out of his mouth, ears, face, and nose, attacking and rendering them unconscious. They beg this creature to stop, addressing him as grandfather, and he sucks the insects in, "laughing inordinately he rolled around like a ball." He has gray eyes and red hair and is dressed like a woman. He specifies his prayerstick and says that he is to blame if earth people get sores around the mouth, ears, face or on the body. He continues with the peace party. . . . To their amazement they discover this is Begochidi. (K. Spencer 1957, 104)

In one version of the Plumeway there is a possible reference to Begochidi:

Wheelwright's informant traces the activities of Deer Raiser, the witch father-in-law in the foregoing versions, to the general Navaho origin myth. Under the name of He Who Can Change into Anything, he and Coyote are the offenders in the seduction that precipitates the separation of the sexes. . . . There follow the events of the emergence. . . . He who changes is at this time placed in charge of game and renamed One Who Raises Deer. (K. Spencer 1957, 174)

The story of Deer Raiser was told by Goldtooth as a part of the creation myth. Matthews says it is the myth of Plumeway (1897, 160–194). In both accounts, it is the story of Self Teacher who became the son-in-law of Deer Raiser. Neither identifies Deer Raiser with Begochidi. Goldtooth, however, says that Self Teacher released all the game in Deer Raiser's underground "deer farm" so that they could be used by the Earth People. This story is, then, a form of the hoarding and release of game myth. In Matthews's version, there is a game farm but no mention of their release by the hero. Instead, the story concludes with Self Teacher curing Deer Raiser of his witchcraft by the use of what came to be known as the Plumeway medicines.

Wheelwright's informant, Klah, would be expected to feature Begochidi; the name "He Who Can Change into Anything" may be derived from the fact that Begochidi is a *nádleeh* (he repeatedly becomes, or changes).[6] If this is in fact a reference to Begochidi, we find him closely connected with Coyote and with sexual excess as well as with the game animals. And as the witch father-in-law, he is associated with father-daughter incest, as is Coyote. Hill quotes one of his informants:

Begochidi was the son of the sun. The sun committed adultery with every-thing in the world. This was how so many monsters were born. After this, the sun was put a way off so that this could not happen again. But as the sun came up he touched a flower which became pregnant and gave birth to be'gochidí. He was the youngest son of the sun, and the sun spoiled him. He was put in control of many things, such as game and domestic animals. He was a berdache and the first pottery maker.

He could also move about invisibly and change into different forms at will: a rainbow, wind, sand, water, etc. He was named be'gochidí because he would make himself invisible and sneak up on young girls to touch their breasts, shouting "be'go, be'go" (breast). He especially annoyed men who were hunting. When a hunter had taken aim and was ready to shoot, be'gochidí would sneak up behind him, grab his testicles and shout "be'go." This spoiled the hunter's aim every time. The worst was when a man and woman lay down to have intercourse. He was always touching one or the other and shouting "be'go." (1938a, 99)

There are a number of healing ceremony myths that contain episodes that do not mention Begochidi by name but that are clearly references to him when his true identity as a Pueblo deity is recognized. These myth motifs are Butterfly Seduction, White Butterfly, and the Great Gambler.

Begochidi represents sexual excess as well as game animals and sexual as well as hunting magic or witchcraft, and he is a trickster, as is Coyote. The question arises, why was there a need for Begochidi, when Coyote was already a perfectly adequate trickster figure? The answer proposed here is that, as the Pueblo influence increased in Navajo religious thought, those practitioners who still adhered to the hunting tradition adopted a trickster figure from the Pueblo pantheon that could not be as easily "defamed" as Coyote. This figure was the Pueblo Paiyatemu.

BEGOCHIDI-PAIYATEMU

The association of the butterfly and a bisexual fertility god with incest and seduction is derived from Pueblo, especially Zuni and

6. Goldtooth and Washington Matthews both note that the hero's name changes dur-ing the story. According to Goldtooth, it changes from "Chap Man" to "Self Teacher." Matthew's hero was called both "Self Teacher" and "He Who Has Floated." In a note, Matthews says that the hero's name changed after the story but does not reveal what that name was (1897, 243, n201).

Keresan, myths. Awonawilona, the creator god of the Zunis is a "He-She" bisexual life-giving power (Stevenson 1894, 22). His first act of creation is to turn himself into the sun. Subsequently he impregnates a human, who gives birth to a son called Paiyatemu. Before this, however, while the first humans are searching for the Middle Place where the Zunis are supposed to settle, a brother and sister are sent to help with the search. They commit incest and give birth to children who are the proto-types of the Koyemsi, or Mudhead, clowns. The incest is done while the brother is "crazed for love" (Stevenson 1904, 22; Cushing 1896, 32). After this, the pair become hideously ugly and grow great knobs on their heads. Ten children are born of this union. The first born is an her-maphrodite with the form of a woman but the stature and strength of a man. The other children are remarkably ugly and malformed, without sense and, although male in appearance, without sex.

Paiyatemu is a handsome clown who bears the shield of the sun on his journey and at times entertains him by playing his flute. A foil of the sun, he is funny and senseless and is allowed to do as he pleases (Tyler 1964, 142–143). He is also the fertilizing and sexual power of the sun. Born of a mortal woman and the sun, he uses music to seduce women; he is always surrounded by a myriad of butterflies and playing his se-ductive flute, from which the butterflies emerge as objectified musical notes. At Sia and Acoma, he is the Koshare clown patron; at Zuni, he is the father of the Newekwe clowns as well as the patron of the Koyemsi. He is an archetypal trickster who, in his "daylight mood and appear-ance," is gross and funny. His jokes are "reversals," and he is thought-less, loud, and uncouth. At the same time, he is the god of dew, dawn, and fertility (Cushing 1896, 439).

At Zuni, Paiyatemu lusts after the Corn Maidens, which causes them to leave. Later, however, he is sent to find them and bring them back to Zuni. They are sisters and represent the different colored varieties of corn. Tyler believes that they are sisters of Paiyatemu himself and, just as the cycle of germination, birth, and death causes them to die in or-der to be reborn, so also must Paiyatemu die and be restored. Paiy-atemu's death is told in the story of evil sisters who kill him and hide his heart and head. As the god is running along, he comes upon the oldest sister, who challenges him to a hiding contest that, according to Tyler, is a transparent echo of the disappearance of the Corn Maidens. The sister hides in a cloud and Paiyatemu fails to find her. But when he hides behind the sun, she draws a drop of milk—clear rather than milky, because she is a maiden—from her breast and sees the tip of his headdress reflected in it. Because he loses the contest, his life is forfeit and he is beheaded.[7]

Restored in the form of a butterfly, Paiyatemu seeks revenge. He "entered the room where they were weaving baskets. Wishing to copy the designs on his wings they pursued him, throwing various articles of their clothing in an attempt to net him, until they were all naked and fell asleep. Paiyatemu then took off his butterfly disguise and blew upon his flute, whereupon each of the evil maidens came out as a crazily flying butterfly, flying without direction" (Tyler 1964, 148–149). This story is the Butterfly Seduction of Navajo myth.

Tyler believes there is an incestuous relationship between Paiyatemu and his sisters, both the Corn Maidens after whom he lusted and the "evil" sisters whom he seduced, although none of the Zuni myths that I have identified make this explicit. Nevertheless, Paiyatemu is connected with sibling incest as well as with love magic and sexual excess. Paiyatemu is not only the patron of the Newekwe clowns but also of the Koyemsi clowns, who represent the offspring of the first incestuous union.

The bumps on the heads of the Koyemsi are filled with all kinds of seeds, and the Koyemsi possess the most potent love magic. Moreover, the Koyemsi are the most dangerous of all katsinas. If anyone touches a Koyemsi while he has his paint on, that person will surely go mad. They carry the sacred butterfly, Paiyatemu, in their drum to make people follow them, and anyone who does follow will go crazy. The butterfly love charm affects everyone but especially young girls, who must go after anyone who has it (Bunzel 1932, 871–872, 947; Tyler 1964, 198, 200).

Paiyatemu's connections with the hunt and hunt magic are less pronounced, as might be expected among the agricultural Pueblos. These connections are found in ritual activities rather than in myth. Paiyatemu causes the flowers to grow, especially the *tenatsali* plant, whose blossoms are said to be in the colors of the six directions. The Newekwe combine the hearts of butterflies and dragonflies with the blossoms as a medicine, and the hunt society uses this medicine without the hearts for their ceremonial hunt. No woman may have any of this medicine

---

7. See Ruth Bunzel for the story of how Sun Youth is beheaded, revived, and later gets revenge (1933, 248–262). The revenge episode is the Navajo Butterfly Seduction motif. A Hopi story, "The Youth and Maiden Who Played Hide and Seek for Their Life," is virtually the same except that the actors are human (Voth 1905, 136–141, 293–294). Three Keresan tales, "Turkey Woman," "Sun Youth," and "Sunrise," are versions of the Butterfly Seduction and the relationship of Paiyatemu, or Sun Youth, with the Corn Maidens (Boas 1928, 82–102, 255–256).

because, if married, she would commit adultery, and if single, she would be filled with "amorous desires" (Stevenson 1904, 569 note a). At Zuni, the skulls of the prey animals are kept in a cave shrine with offerings to Paiyatemu, and initiation into the hunt society at Sia uses an image of Paiyatemu (Parsons 1974, 480, 606).

Paiyatemu, then, is not only a trickster representing sexual excess and possibly incest but also a god of fertility and growth intimately connected with corn. As a trickster, he appears to be the model for the Navajo Begochidi, and as a god of fertility, he has a central position in the creation myths of Goldtooth and Klah. In the Acoma origin myth, it is Paiyatemu who seduces a young woman and fathers the War Twins (Stirling 1942, 92). However, unlike Coyote, he is not associated with witchcraft, and in Navajo myths, his witch powers—although present—are not emphasized.

BUTTERFLY SEDUCTION

Frenzy Witchcraftway (*'Ajił'ee*), called Prostitutionway by Haile and Excessway by Leland Wyman, is used to counteract sexual witchcraft as well as witchcraft used to defeat hunters and gamblers. Hunting and seduction are intimately connected: the hero is given love magic to acquire a woman and an outfit in which to stalk deer, which enables him to pay for her, and the hero is transformed by Coyote while he is out hunting. In addition to the Coyote transformation, the myth of this ceremony contains the butterfly seduction and White Butterfly motifs.

In order to seduce two "non-sunlight-struck" Pueblo maidens, the Hero transforms himself into a beautiful butterfly, flutters into their chamber, and attracts their notice. The girls want to catch the butterfly to copy its pattern in their weaving. Chasing it, they are enticed out of their room. Although one of the sisters realizes they are being tricked, they are incapable of resisting.

Navajos believe that Mothway and Frenzy Witchcraftway are closely related. In part this is because they both originate at Riverward Knoll, the hill where the fertilization of the medicinal plants occurs and where Begochidi is conceived. However, despite the prominence of the butterfly symbol and sexual themes in both myths, Navajos associate these stories more with Coyote and believe that the ceremonies are closely related not only to each other but also to Coyoteway and Mountainway. Coyote medicines are used in Mothway and are, quite likely, the same as those used in Frenzy Witchcraftway. A Coyote episode that duplicates one involving White Butterfly is inserted into Frenzy Witchcraftway. Some Navajos even think of Mothway as the "Rabid Coyote branch of Coyoteway," although, in my experience, this ritual is used as a substitute for the now-extinct Mothway ceremony (Kluckhohn 1962b, 230).

WHITE BUTTERFLY

Sometime after the Butterfly Seduction in Frenzy Witchcraftway, the hero's Pueblo wives are stolen. The hero use his flute to trace them to the home of White Butterfly. He then engages in a contest with White Butterfly to regain his wives. Ultimately the hero is victorious and kills White Butterfly by striking him on the head. The head splits open and from it emerges a flock of butterflies, which are returned to the sky to become rain. In one version there is no seduction, instead the hero has a contest with the Great Gambler who is considered to be the equivalent of White Butterfly (K. Spencer 1957, 134–148). Waterway includes all of the themes found in Frenzy Witchcraftway. In neither ceremony is Begochidi mentioned by name, but the image of butterflies escaping from the head of White Butterfly parallels the cure for moth madness in the Mothway, and in both accounts the butterflies are sent to the sky to become rain. The association of sexual frenzy with hunting is also characteristic of Begochidi. He is a child of Sun and a flower, as is the hero of Frenzy Witchcraftway, whose siblings are also born of the Sun and various butterflies. The association of Begochidi with White Butterfly and the butterfly seduction episode seems clear.

THE GREAT GAMBLER

After the appearance of the monsters in the present world but before the birth of Changing Woman and the Twins, the people in their various forms flee the monsters and build a great dwelling at Aztec, Colorado (O'Bryan 1956, 48–63). They then build Blue House above Farmington, New Mexico. The people of Blue House come to gamble with Nááwíiłbįįhí (He Always Wins). Afterwards, they go to Chaco Canyon and build a dwelling there. They bring many goods with them from the place where the two rivers crossed (in the third world). The Sun becomes jealous of their chief because he has all the jewels. Sun impregnates an old, poor woman who gives birth to a youth whom the

Sun trains as the Great Gambler.[8] The gambler plays against the people and wins all their goods and makes them his slaves. But when the Sun asks for the great turquoise that the people have, the Gambler refuses and instead challenges Sun to gamble for it. Sun becomes angry and goes to the Mirage people, where he impregnates a woman who gives birth to a boy whom the Sun trains to beat the gambler. When, after seven games, the young man wins the foot race, all the people blow their flutes because the gambler has forfeited his life.

Gambler brings out an axe and tells the youth to kill him with it. But Sun tells the youth not to kill Gambler because Gambler is his older brother. Instead, Gambler is shot into the sky, calling out as he rises that he was born in the center of the earth and wishes to return there. As he rises to the upper worlds, the last thing they hear is "adios."

In Matthews's version of the story, before the people arrive at *Kin nteel,* a gambling god descends among the Pueblos who are living there (1897, 81–87). He challenges the Pueblos to all sorts of games and wins their goods and women. He orders them to build the Great Pueblo and in return gives them back things they have lost. The story then follows the same plot as Sandoval's. When the gambler is shot into the sky, he comes to the home of Begochidi, "the god who carries the moon, and who is supposed by the Navahos to be identified with the god of the Americans. He is very old and dwells in a long row of stone houses." Begochidi makes for him "pets or domestic animals" of new kinds. He is now the god of the Mexicans (Matthews 1897, 86).

The identification of Nááwíiłbįįhí with White Butterfly and, therefore, with Begochidi rests primarily on the fact that both White Butterfly and Nááwíiłbįįhí are defeated in a contest with the young hero. In the Waterway, which contains the Butterfly Seduction as well as other motifs from Frenzy Witchcraftway, Nááwíiłbįįhí is specifically equated with White Butterfly: "Yonder is the one from whom you have won his legs, the former (notorious) winner [Nááwíiłbįįhí]. Into the form of a white butterfly he has gone" (Haile 1979, 51, 115).[9] In Coyoteway Evil, the episode replicates the Great Gambler as it appears in Matthews's account (Luckert 1979, 221–222).

8. A Keresan gambler story is related by Boas (1928, 76–82, 253–254). In that story, Sun Youth is not the Gambler but the hero who defeats and finally slays him.

9. Sandoval starts his story of the defeat of White Butterfly by saying that the youth was given the medicine of the Great Gambler (O'Bryan 1956, 143). This, as well as the description of the medicine, suggests that the Great Gambler's medicine was the same as that in Frenzy Witchcraft.

White Butterfly is killed by a blow to his head, out of which come many butterflies or moths that the hero turns into rain. Nááwíiłbįįhí, however, is shot into the air, where he finally comes to the home of Begochidi, who creates domestic animals for him and makes him god of the Mexicans. The myth of Coyoteway Evil says only that he was shot into the air and, although he said something, the people could not understand what he said. The idea that Begochidi is the god of the Mexicans or the Anglo–Americans will be discussed in chapter 6.

DEER RAISER

Klah's version of the myth of Plumeway raises the possibility that Begochidi may be identified with Deer Raiser, the hoarder of game. This would be an important association, because any connection with the hoarding and release of game motif would strengthen the link between Begochidi and early hunter trickster figures, as well as his already recognized connection with the game animals. According to Klah, Deer Raiser is also called He Who Changes, which suggests that he is the *nádleeh*, Begochidi. Klah also associates Deer Raiser with Coyote and incest in the underworld and says that his name was changed to Deer Raiser only after he was placed in charge of the game animals.

Reichard describes Deer Raiser as a sorcerer whose witchcraft power is associated with father-daughter incest and wealth (1963, 429). She also says that he hid the game animals so he alone could use them, and that the hero released them for everybody. The witch father-in-law is found in Eagleway, Enemyway, Plumeway, Evil Moving Upwardway, Coyoteway Evil, and Chiricahua Windway.

The Deerways that include the hoarding of game motif do not refer to Deer Raiser. There is no hoarding of game in Eagleway, Plumeway, Chiricahua Windway, or Enemyway. The elderly couple in Chiricahua Windway control the game and release some animals so that the hero may hunt successfully. However, the association of Deer Raiser with Begochidi and even the association of the witch father-in-law with the hoarding and release of game is not a motif that can be used to identify early trickster or hunter traditions with any certainty.

The question, then, is whether the Coyote and Begochidi motifs are found in the myths of some ceremonies but not others and whether Blessingway represents a qualitatively different philosophical position from that found in the ceremonies that contain myths of the old hunter tradition.

6

Two Traditions

If the hunter tradition is nothing more than a remnant from the Navajo past, we might expect to find the motifs and actors we have identified scattered randomly among the healing ceremonies' myths. In contrast, if some ceremonialists continued the tradition despite the Pueblo agricultural influences represented by the Blessingway, we might expect to find these motifs and actors clustered among a limited number of ceremonials. In the latter case, each tradition would have to take the other into account and continually make adjustments to achieve a general accommodation.

Navajo ceremonies may be arranged along a continuum between two opposed concepts, *hozhǫ́* and *hóchxǫ́'*. According to Leland Wyman, "The Navajo term [*hozhǫ́*] includes everything that a Navajo thinks is good—that is, good as opposed to evil, favorable to man as opposed to unfavorable or doubtful. It expresses . . . such concepts as the words for beauty, perfection, harmony, goodness, normality, success, well-being, blessedness, order, ideal, do for us" (1970, 7). *Hóchxǫ́'*, by contrast, is most often glossed as "evil" and presented as the polar opposite of *hozhǫ́*. However, John Farella shows that a dualist view that pits good against evil is far too simplistic (1984, 31–39). The simplistic nature of the dualist view is an important issue and one to which we shall return. For the moment, arranging ceremonials along a "good" to "evil" continuum is a helpful way to think of them. We note in passing that Wyman and Clyde Kluckhohn (1938) have used two very different criteria—modes of performance and etiological factors—to group the numerous sings into four major and two minor categories. Because this classification is used widely, it is presented in the appendix.

The Blessingway (*hozhǫ́ǫ́jík'ehgo*) "is concerned with peace, harmony, and good things, and should exclude all evil. . . . It is not a curing ceremonial such as we find in chantways, no medicines are administered, and medicine songs are absent" (Wyman 1970, 4). Blessingway ceremonials are not intended to cure illness but to invoke blessings in order to avert possible misfortune, and from them various songs and procedures may be abstracted to constitute rites such as the girl's puberty rite, the House Blessing rite, and the Seed Blessing ceremony.

The Holyways (*diyink'ehgo*) include all chants that utilize sandpaintings, paintings of anthropomorphic figures on the body of the patient, and beads of turquoise and white shell given to the patient during the ceremony. This group is characterized by these and a number of procedures rather than by any single etiology. It is the largest of all of Wyman and Kluckhohn's classes and is further subdivided into the Shooting, Mountain, God Impersonator, Wind, Hand Trembling, and Eagle Trapping subgroups.

The Lifeways (*'ináájík'egho*) are specifically for injuries from accidents, sprains, strains, fractures, and so on. In cases of stubborn or critical illness, a Lifeway may be tried in conjunction with other ceremonies. The ceremony lasts at least two nights but may continue for many nights until relief is obtained or hope is given up.

The Evilways (*hóchxǫ'íjí*) are used against illness caused by the ghosts of the dead. All Evilways are exorcistic, and the chief symptom is fainting. Because witches use "ghost powder" to affect their victims, these sings are also used to counter the effects of witchcraft. Moving Upway (*haneelnéhee*) is the principle ceremony of those sings used against the ghosts of dead Navajos. The ceremonial is the only one to originate in the underworlds and to use the preemergence period in its myth of origin. The name "Moving Upway" seems to refer to crawling out of the lower worlds to the present one. The Enemyway (*'anaa'jí*) is used to counter the ghosts of aliens, and its function against ghosts is the only reason it is included in the Evilway group. It is not properly a sing because, like Blessingway, it does not use a rattle. Nor does its myth of origin have anything in common with the Evilways. At one time, it was probably a war ceremonial used to purify warriors when they returned from a raid.

It is important to recall that this classification is tentative, that no single principle is used to provide the logic of the classification, and that

Navajo singers themselves are unable to agree on which ceremonies are to be included in each group. There is widespread agreement, however, that Blessingway controls all the sings; every sing is concluded with at least one Blessingway song. There are singers who claim that Evilway is the oldest ceremony, along with Hailway and, perhaps, Beadway. Over the centuries, ceremonies have multiplied and been elaborated. There are male and female branches, and a sing may be done according to Holyway or to Evilway. There are even divisions according to Angry and Peaceful Ways. In sum, it is not possible to learn much about the development of the ceremonial system from examining the various ceremonies, their modes of practice, or the uses to which they are put.

The Shamanistic Substrate

If there is a stratum of shamanism surviving in Navajo ceremonialism, it may perhaps be identified by finding, along with the trickster figures and motifs identified in chapter 3, what the shamanistic hunter-gatherer societies of North America thought were the major causes of disease.

"The quintessential North American shaman was someone who received supernatural power from one or more spirit helpers during a vision experience and who effected cures by communicating with these supernaturals while in a trance. It was the trance that distinguished the shaman from the ceremonialist or priest" (Underhill 1948). Disease theory held that sickness was caused by intrusive objects, loss or possession of the soul, and violation of taboos. Of these causes, soul loss and possession were the most feared. Just as the shaman's soul traveled to the realm of the supernatural in order to work cures, so also could witches and supernatural beings possess and displace the souls of humans.

Contemporary Navajos never attribute their illness to soul loss or possession, despite the importance of the soul concept. At death, the soul (*nitch'i*, wind) leaves the body but lingers for a few days before proceeding to the underworld. During this time it is referred to as a ghost (*ch'įįdii* or *nitch'i*) of the dead and is dangerous because it may take the souls of the living with it when it finally leaves this world. Fainting is often thought to be the first symptom caused by contact with a ghost. It is contact that is mentioned, however, and not soul loss. Yet, when we read the origin myths of the healing ceremonies or talk with ceremonialists, we find the principal diseases described in terms of posses-sion. The myth of Waterway, for example, tells of the hero who is cured when he is made to vomit the Coyote food he has eaten, and descrip-tions of the Mothway say that the patient will spit out moths that have lodged themselves behind the eyes. The Coyote transformation motif is also a description of possession.

Some fifteen healing ceremonies feature Coyote or Begochidi as well as associated motifs in their myths of origin. In table 3, the ceremonies for which we have myths of origin have been arranged along a contin-uum from *hozhǫ́* to *hóchxǫ́*, according to whether they include episodes of possession or Coyote or Begochidi motifs. Positioned toward the *hozhǫ́* pole represented by the Blessingway are the ceremonies that lack such motifs. Depending on the account, Coyoteway may include Coy-ote or Begochidi motifs or lack them altogether.

Chiricahua Windway, Hand Tremblingway, and Suckingway entered the repertory of ceremonials in the nineteenth century, presumably while the Navajos were incarcerated at Fort Sumner and shortly thereafter (Wyman and Kluckhohn 1938, 28; Haile 1950, 296–297). There is no recorded myth for the Suckingway; thus I do not include it in the analy-sis. Although Hand Tremblingway has no episodes of possession in its myth, those who become hand tremblers are said to be possessed by Gila Monster while in a trance, during which they diagnose an illness.

Enemyway may lack shamanic motifs because it is thought to have originated as a war purification ritual that was transformed into a heal-ing ceremony after the cessation of warfare, sometime during the reser-vation period. We have already seen that it is not like the other healing chants, and it takes place during the warm months, in contrast to the other healing ceremonies, which can be performed only in the cold months between the first and last frost.

SINGS WITH COYOTE MOTIFS

Given that Coyote is the symbol of all that is evil, it comes as no surprise that the Evilways contain many Coyote motifs. Witchcraft originated in the underworlds, and Coyote, First Man, and First Woman were its practitioners. Coyote was also the one who decreed that death should be permanent. Moving Upway is the only ceremonial whose ori-gin myth begins in the underworld. With the signal exception of Coy-oteway, all sings containing Coyote motifs include an episode of pos-session. They may be thought of as representing the shamanic element

Table 3 *Coyote and Begochidi Motifs in Navajo Sings*

	Number of themes		Possession Soul loss	Wyman-Kluckhohn Classification
	Coyote	Begochidi		
Blessingway Tradition, Hozhǫ́				
Blessingway	0	0	–	Blessingways
Flintway	0	0	–	Lifeways
Monsterway	0	0	–	War Ceremonials
Nightway	0	0	–	God Impersonator, Holyways
Plumeway	0	0	–	God Impersonator, Holyways
Coyoteway I	0	0	–	God Impersonator, Holyways
Beautyway	0	0	–	Mountainway, Holyways
Mountainway	0	0	–	Mountainway, Holyways
Enemyway	0	0	–	Alien Purification, Evilways
Chiricahua Windway	0	0	–	Windway, Holyways
Hand Tremblingway	0	0	–	Hand Tremblingway, Holyways
Eagleway	0	0	–	Eagleway, Holyways
Hóchxǫ́				
Navajo Windway	0	0	+	Windway, Holyways
Beadway	1	0	+	Eagleway, Holyways
Shootingway	3	0	+	Shootingway, Holyways

Table 3 (continued)

	Number of themes		Possession Soul loss	Wyman-Kluckhohn Classification
	Coyote	Begochidi		
Hóchxǫ'				
Red Antway	3	0	+	Shootingway, Holyways
Big Starway	4	0	+	Shootingway, Holyways
[Star Gazing]	2	0	+	not classified
Coyoteway II	3	0	−	God Impersonator, Holyways
Moving Upway	4	0	+	Native Purification, Evilways
Shootingway Evil	4	0	+	Native Purification, Evilways
Red Antway Evil	5	0	+	Native Purification, Evilways
Begochidi-Coyote Tradition				
Deerway	0	1	−	Gameways
Deerway, Frenzyway	0	1	−	Gameways
Hailway	0	1	−	Shootingway, Holyways
Waterway	1	3	+	Shootingway, Holyways
Frenzy Witch	1	3	+	Mountainway, Holyways
Mothway	1	1	+	Mountainway, Holyways
Coyoteway Evil	1	1	−	not classified

surviving in the ceremonial system. The majority of these episodes are accounts of a Coyote transformation in which the hero is possessed by Coyote and assumes his shape while Coyote, in the form of the hero, seduces the hero's wife. Big Starway has several Coyote motifs but lacks the Coyote transformation; it substitutes two episodes of snake transformation and possession and restores the victim by a hoop ritual similar to that used to restore the hero from Coyote possession.

Navajo Windway lacks any of the typical Coyote motifs but includes a snake transformation caused by Coyote People, and a hoop restoration. In this myth, after Talking God and Calling God cannot restore the hero, it is discovered that "prostituting Coyote people" have possession of his mind, and he is restored only after the mind is stolen from them (Wheelwright 1946). The hero is given a medicine to cure "Coyote madness," and "prostituting Coyote" is one of the supernaturals the hero encounters during his travels (K. Spencer 1957, 183; Wyman 1962, 72–74). The presence of an episode of possession as well as the references to Coyote stealing the hero's mind suggest that this sing might best be placed in the Coyote category despite the absence of Coyote motifs.

The resemblance of several Shootingway sings to the Evilways makes one wonder why the Shootingways are included in the Holyway group. Although the Evilways contain possession motifs, the Evilway ceremonies cure contact with ghosts usually brought about by a witch administering "corpse powder" to the victim; therefore other possession etiologies might have to be treated by other ceremonies. If so, the Shootingways would cure other ailments thought to be caused by possession and classed separately from the Evilways along with Red Antway, because ants were among the original witches in the first underworld.

The Shootingways—which feature lightning, arrows, and snakes as disease etiologies—and the "stinging" insects of Red Antway suggest themselves as ceremonies used to cure illness caused by intrusion of foreign objects. This etiology, however, is nowhere mentioned in their myths of origin. The sucking cure was ubiquitous among hunting societies and has been retained by some Pueblos. Rejected by the Navajos, it was reintroduced during their incarceration at Fort Sumner in the nineteenth century (Haile 1950, 296–297). Kluckhohn also notes that ʻadagą sh, the form of witchcraft used to introject foreign objects, is a recent development (1962, 34–35).

SINGS WITH BEGOCHIDI MOTIFS

Ceremonies that refer to Begochidi have elements of possession only if Coyote motifs are also present. Waterway and Frenzy Witchcraftway have Coyote transformations. In Mothway, the Butterfly People, who were once led by Begochidi, are possessed by moths that lodge behind their eyes—"It was found, however, that Coyote alone had medicine for (incest) cases of this kind" (Haile 1978, 88). This medicine is made from the plants of the Frenzy Witchcraftway combined with the male and female genitalia of sibling coyotes, yellow and blue foxes, badgers, and bears, all associated with sexual excess either starting during the separation of the sexes or through Changing Bear Maiden's marriage to Coyote.

Because Hailway, Deerway, and Deerway Frenzy (*'ajiłee*) use Begochidi in much the same way as Blessingway does, I discuss them with other ceremonies that are heavily influenced by the Blessingway tradition.

Blessingway

Blessingway is said to control all Navajo ceremonies. Long Mustache, one of Berard Haile's informants, said that "Blessingway is representative for them, it is the spinal column of songs" (Wyman 1970, 5). According to Farella, Blessingway "is the backbone of Navajo philosophy. . . . Navajos commonly conceptualize and refer to their philosophical and ceremonial system as a corn plant. The junctures where the plant branches are at the branching off of the major ceremonials" (1984, 20). The roots of the plant extend into the underworld, but the myth of Blessingway starts in the present surface world at the place of emergence. Thus, although Blessingway singers know and may narrate the events of the underworld when telling the creation myth, there is a tension between the First Man group and the major creative deities of the Blessingway—Changing Woman, Talking God, and Calling God. Evilway is the only ceremony with origins in the underworld, and thus its myth properly starts with the initial creation.

Blessingway is not a curing ceremony; it lack medicine songs, and neither sandpaintings nor prayer sticks are used in its rituals, Nonetheless,

Blessingway has precedence over chantways and these acknowledge their indebtedness to it. They close with a song taken from it. No other ceremonial can make similar claims of control. At the end of every performance of a chant the singer lays aside his rattle and sings at least one Blessingway song to justify the chant, to ensure its effectiveness, to correct inadvertent omissions of essential song and prayer words, to correct errors in sandpaintings, and in cutting and coloring prayersticks, "just for safety" as natives put it. (Wyman 1970, 5)

Gladys Reichard's Navajo informants told her that "ideally chanters should learn the entire Hozhǫ́ǫ́jí lore before they take up the study of a particular chant" (1963, 325).

Some scholars believe Blessingway to be "a nativistic re-assertion of the Athabascan way of life" (Brugge 1963, 22, 25). In a number of ways, however, Blessingway is the most Pueblo-like ceremony of all Navajo sings. Just as Hopi ceremonies are owned by specific clans, so the mountain soil bundle of Blessingway may be owned by the kin group, probably the coresident matrilineage, and is not necessarily the sole prerogative of singers (Wyman 1970, 22). Just as Pueblo ceremonies are intended to promote life through fertility and group well-being, so also Blessingway emphasizes life-giving supernatural power in all its forms, on the happiness of long life (sǫ'a naghái bik'e hózhǫ́), the home, and the creation of living things. And, although an individual patient is treated, Blessingway rites are thought to benefit the social group the patient represents. Blessingway is also especially concerned with the uses of pollen and the creation and care of corn. Moreover, it lays special emphasis on the masked deities Talking God and Calling God. Two closely related ceremonials, Nightway and Big Godway, set aside an entire night that is devoted to feeding the masks used by impersonators of the yé'ii and to singing Blessingway songs. In Hopi ritual, too, the katsina masks are fed with pollen. Thus, Blessingway comes closest to replicating the Pueblo communal ceremonies.

Whatever changes there were in Navajo shamanistic practices during the period of most intense Pueblo contacts between 1669 and 1777, the shift to a system comprised primarily of community-based ceremonies stopped when the Navajos dispersed and became more dependent on pastoralism than on agriculture. The dispersal of the Navajo population meant that sedentary communities like those of the pueblitos were no longer possible and that families lived in isolation for much of the year. The result was an amalgamation of the two religious approaches. Shamans became chanters (hataałi) who, like Pueblo priests, obtained their power from learned rituals rather than from a spirit helper while in a trance. But, like shamans, their rituals were primarily for curing individual patients. Divination and diagnosing disease were still done in a trance state but by lesser practitioners known as stargazers, listeners, or hand tremblers. Only Blessingway retained the Pueblo-like features mentioned previously.

Even the process of divination and diagnosing changed. Initially, stargazers and listeners were male. Their powers, although not obtained directly from Coyote, were considered very dangerous (*báábádzid*) because, first, it was Coyote who could see, hear, and know everything; second, the medicine the stargazers used was an effective antidote for Coyote infection; and third, their trance was caused by Coyote possession (Wyman 1936a; 1936b). Over time, the number of stargazers and listeners declined as they were superseded by hand tremblers who obtained their power from Gila Monster. Hand trembling is thought to have been borrowed after 1860 from the Apaches (Wyman and Kluckhohn 1938, 28–29). All diagnosticians are said to be in a trance state while practicing their art and may, therefore, be thought of as shamans. Today, in my observations, most hand tremblers are women.

The girls' puberty rite, carried south with the Apachean speakers and thus ancient, is an exclusive Blessingway feature and prerogative, although Blessingway has changed it considerably. In former times, a girl was completely segregated and feared or taboo for the duration of her first menses. "A small shelter of brush was made for her. Her hair was untied, her hands were covered, and a scratching tool was tied to her fingers to give her relief in case of itching, She could not come into contact with her skin. Food was brought to her as she must avoid touching dishes" (Wyman 1970, 9).[1] Today most of these practices are no longer followed.[2] In the Blessingway myth, the second menstrual period of Changing Woman is the occasion for the third Blessingway rite. Father Berard thought this second ceremonial was introduced to wean Blessingway from every influence of the First Man group and place it under the direction of Talking God so that he and Changing Woman would control the entire rite in the future.

Blessingway is also especially concerned with the hogan and the sweat bath, also of Athabascan rather than Puebloan derivation.[3] The hogan is

1. For a description of puberty rituals in North America, see Harold Driver (1941).
2. For further discussion of these changes in menstrual practices, see chapter 8.
3. The early Navajo forked stick hogan is a southwestern version of northern structures. The steam sweat bath is also common among the hunting tribes of the continent, whereas the Pueblos practiced direct fire sweating in the kivas (Driver and Massey 1957, 314).

"the center of every blessing in life: happy births, the home of ones children, the center of weddings, the center where good health, property, increase in crops and livestock originate, where old age, the goal in life, will visit regularly. . . . Those reaching old age in it have nothing to fear, not even death" (Wyman 1970, 10). That the Athabascan emphasis on the hogan and the sweat bath figure prominently in Blessingway is probably why Brugge thought the ceremonial was a nativistic development designed to counter Pueblo influences. It seems more likely that associating these ancient Athabascan features with Blessingway served to give it the imprimatur of Navajo tradition and thus make it more acceptable.

If Blessingway represents the core of Pueblo values retained by the Navajos, references to Coyote and Begochidi in the origin myth of Blessingway and Enemy Monsterway ought to differ from the treatment of these supernaturals by singers like Klah and Goldtooth, and perhaps by Evilway singers as well. Unable to omit references to these deities entirely, Blessingway singers would make Coyote and Begochidi as unimportant as possible and leave it to Evilway to treat Coyote as the very antithesis of Changing Woman and the masked gods.

Coyote in Blessingway. Father Berard recorded three versions of Blessingway, which have been published by Wyman (1970). The first version was dictated by Slim Curley of Crystal, New Mexico, in 1932. Father Berard preferred this version because he felt it was closest to the traditional account. Slim Curley had worked with Haile for many years and was the author of many recorded texts.

The second version was obtained from Frank Mitchell of Chinle, Arizona, between 1930 and 1932. Frank Mitchell not only details Coyote's actions more than the other narrators but also spends more time and detail on the immediate postemergence events.

Haile received the third version from River Junction Charley of Chinle between 1929 and 1932. This version differs from the other two in including the myths of Monsterway and Enemyway, an inclusion considered so unorthodox by Haile that he left the manuscript unfinished. But, because the Twins were the children of Changing Woman and perform their task of ridding the present world of monsters so that their mother and the masked gods can proceed with the task of creating corn and the Navajos, it would have been logical for River Junction Charley to have told the myths even if they are not a part of Blessingway.

Coyote appears in all three versions as a significant but minor character. During a ceremonial or a council to make plans, Coyote bursts in and begins to give advice, suggests himself for important posts, interferes with procedures, and acts obnoxiously. He is ridiculed and told to leave, but by sheer persistence he has his way in the end. In Slim Curley's narrative, for example, Coyote intrudes: "Now it seems that for the entire time that this Blessingway was in the making, the intent had been to exclude everything mean from it. Instead, Coyote had now taken his stand next to [Talking God]" (Wyman 1970, 174). Coyote is also mentioned as the messenger of the Holy people who watches Huerfano Mountain "very closely" before the Sun comes to mate with Changing Woman (Wyman 1970, 195).

In the third version, River Junction Charley makes a number of enigmatic references to Coyote. Although he admits to Coyote's early origin and great knowledge, he refuses to give Coyote credit for any positive acts. Speaking of the origins of Talking God and Calling God, he mentions in passing that Coyote had come up from the underworld with the others so that they could witness the no-sleep ceremony of Blessingway (Wyman 1970, 503). It is not clear whether it is Coyote who plans that they should witness the ceremony or if it is the general plan of those in the underworld. In another episode, "there were some monsters being born, they say. So when they were born, they dispersed with First Man, First Woman, Salt Woman, and Coyote, making four, up to Huerfano Mountain. . . . Talking God [and Calling God were] also present at the Emergence. When they entered the water First Man instructed them. . . . Coyote was not spoken to nor was he mentioned" (Wyman 1970, 507). Yet, when the Holy People discuss what Talking God and Calling God should be named, it is Coyote who already knows the names. Coyote repeatedly appears to have foreknowledge of the details of Blessingway, yet at no point is he welcomed or given credit.

Coyote is also cast in the role of an evildoer: After the twins are born, Coyote, Crow, Magpie, and Turkey Buzzard spy for Big Ye'i, the first and most powerful of the monsters. And when Black God is asked to perform the Enemyway over Monster Slayer, he claims that Coyote is his partner: " 'If you really must tell and cannot keep your knowledge to yourself, notify my partners roundabout for me!' These happened to be man-eating ones, the Buzzard and Coyote and all others [of that sort]." These partners sing the sway songs at the ceremony (Wyman 1970, 603–604). In this instance, Black God is performing a desired ceremony and his partners are helping, yet at the same time they are identified as man-eaters. Although the message is not explicit, I get the impression that these Blessingway singers would have liked to erase Coyote from consideration entirely, but because he was a figure of long-standing importance in Navajo cosmology, they could not omit him entirely and had to accord him some measure of power. Even when they portray him as an evildoer, they do not mention the great witchcraft power ascribed to him in other sings. The status of Black God is also somewhat ambiguous. He is one of the masked gods, yet because he was once Raven, he is still associated with Coyote.

In contrast to the other two Blessingway narratives, Frank Mitchell's narrative has Coyote not only win arguments but also give extensive and valuable advice based on astute reasoning. According to Haile, the individual philosopher puts his own words into Coyote's mouth. Father Berard believed Mitchell's use of Coyote in this manner was significant because an effort was made to exclude every shade of meanness from Blessingway, and Coyote is the prime exponent of meanness. Wyman thinks that Mitchell may have introduced Coyote so that even Blessingway will have a modicum of an opposite quality and thus fulfill another important and all-embracing Navajo theory—namely, that to achieve harmony or balance in the universe, Blessingway must be an all-inclusive unity containing both good and evil as complementary components. It is Coyote who argues compellingly and logically for the necessity of opposites, deciding that there will be day and night, sun and moon, birth and death, slow and rapid growth of plants, property and poverty, food and hunger, warmth and cold, summer and winter, and so on.

In fact, Mitchell not only details Coyote's actions more than the other versions but also spends more time and detail on the immediate postemergence events. In Mitchell's version, the establishment of agriculture, usually a preemergence event in most narrations of the creation myth, takes place after the emergence to emphasize agriculture's association with Changing Woman. Mitchell's version is also unique in having Coyote cooperate with Changing Woman. In one instance, Coyote even distances himself temporarily from First Man and First Woman, taking the side of Changing Woman against them.

When earth and sky are placed, Coyote argues against planting vegetation in orderly rows:

"Therefore what you say, [that is,] setting [plants] in rows, you can see, will not be a good thing since if at any time one [of the plants] or likewise one of those that give birth should die there would be [conspicuous] gaps and passageways between them," he said. "And if at any time in the future all should reach old age together, a regrowth [that was expected] would be impossible," he said. "And only where the rows are to be would something exist, while between them nothing would grow up. Make it so that they exist everywhere on [the earth's] surface without any special order!" he said. (Wyman 1970, 346)

This is an argument for the preservation of randomness or chaos: If planted in cultivated fields only, plants can easily be destroyed all at once, but if scattered about, they will be harder for enemies to find and can more easily survive. It is also a means by which the creative or good side of chaos is retained as part of Blessingway.

When corn was created, Talking God was told to sanctify it but failed. Coyote, in company with Begochidi, was then asked to perform the sanctification:

"Go ahead, old man, you must be of use here," [Coyote] was told. "You will get a name, a name will be made for you," he was told. "Besides from now on, any plans which you propose to add to those of others will not be overlooked again," he was told. "Then too, over such various things of which the powerful [Holy] People are in charge you will partly share their authority," he was told. "You too will be in the same position," that Begochidi was told. "And, as time goes on in the future, you will partly be in authority over things which are going to be made on the surface of this earth," he was told. "Now that is the way people ought to talk to a person," Coyote said, and Begochidi said likewise. (Wyman 1970, 367).

Because First Man was doing the planning, it was he who thwarted the efforts of Talking God and let Coyote and Begochidi do the sanctifying:

And now it seems Coyote got ready. He then sanctified the Sun, the Moon, the grand [twelve-eared original] corn and the plants which had been placed in position. . . . This it seems had occurred just as First Man himself had it in mind, Coyote I suppose, alone being aware of it.

On that account Talking God, for some hidden reason, had failed. That was due to First Man who, being aware that Coyote had no name and that the Holy People particularly engaged in this had exclusively assumed most of the authority, had therefore let this happen. He strove therefore to put Coyote partly in charge of it and to get him a name. . . . " Besides as time goes on in the future, after man has come into being, whenever you realize that a particular bad thing is about to occur to him, you will immediately give him warning. (Wyman 1970, 368)

Dreams are a means of warning people of what is to come, and Changing Woman was thinking about how to bring dreams into being and how to use them in Blessingway (Wyman 1970, 427). Despite Coyote's association with First Man and First Woman, from whom Changing Woman and the Twins had withheld the visit to the Sun and Changing Woman's plan to go to the west, Changing Woman talks freely with Coyote and engages his services.[4] Coyote steals dream from sleep and gives it to the Talking Gods of White House in Canyon de Chelly. These gods are "somewhat mean in disposition," and, associated with the site of Mothway, they serve as intermediaries between the polarities. By this device a direct transaction between the polarities is avoided while what was heretofore the domain of the shamans comes under the control of the *hataałi* priests.

Finally, when Changing Woman is planning to go to the west and, at last, tells First Man and First Woman, First Woman becomes angry and tells Changing Woman to leave without Blessingway. Talking God, however, reassures Changing Woman that she and not First Woman is in charge of Blessingway and that, because First Woman is being mean, none of her songs or prayers will be a part of Blessingway. First Man then says that he and First Woman will also leave. Before leaving, however, First Man says:

"From here may it always happen whichever way I may think! May epidemics come time and again, and may fatal events happen time and again! By no means should people live comfortably! May I be in control of disease! May I be in control of fever! May I be in control of everything that kills time and again! May death occur regularly as I wish." (Wyman 1970, 441)

Unexpectedly, Coyote objects to the malevolence of First Man:

"From way back yonder, as you know, we started out together, and came along together from there. We arrived up here without ugly thoughts towards one another and without ugly words with one another," he said to them. "That being so, what is the reason for being differently disposed toward one another? Why should there be actions like these when people are engaged in things that always make us feel happy? There is no sense in acting that way! If you continue this what will be the outcome?" he said to them.

"As for me I cannot take sides with one of you!" he told them. "Because all are my relatives I have a [loving] feeling for all," he said. "Therefore whose mind is directing your actions in this? I want to find out whose mind directed what happened here," he said. (Wyman 1970, 442)

---

4. Dreams are one of the major reasons Blessingway is performed today, and Changing Woman wished to get the matter of dreams into Blessingway.

Ultimately, Coyote leaves with First Man and First Woman after accusing the Sun of poor planning. Thus it appears that Coyote remains a connecting link between the First Man group, Changing Woman, and, presumably, Talking God and Calling God. Frank Mitchell admits that a polarization of forces has taken place but, unlike the other two Blessingway singers, uses Coyote to find a less dualistic middle ground. Blessingway singers make Coyote acceptable by turning him into a corn and rain deity. Frank Mitchell, in contrast, seeks to retain the creative aspects of Coyote's chaotic qualities.

BEGOCHIDI IN BLESSINGWAY

As we have seen in chapters 3 and 4, Goldtooth and Klah differ from other narrators in according Begochidi a prominent position in the creation myth. Similarly, the three narrators of the Blessingway myth do not agree on Begochidi's role.

Slim Curley holds that Changing Woman created horses and sheep and put Begochidi in charge of them, whereas Talking God was put in charge of wild game. In Slim Curley's version, Changing Woman describes Begochidi as one whom "the sun never leaves, who time and again transforms into sunlight, into sun ray, into wind, who is found absolutely everywhere" (Wyman 1970, 244, 246).

River Junction Charley concurs: Talking God is responsible for the wild game, but Begochidi is responsible for the domesticates. Talking God speaks to the wild game: "I made you so that you will be Holy People. You will be wild and you will live only in holy places. You will roam on the top of mountains. You will always be important. You will be useful. . . . The Gameway plants will be used as medicine. The sheep will be treated with them, the horses will be treated with them" (Wyman 1970, 629).

Begochidi then gives names to the domesticates, each time asking the other Holy People present whether the name is appropriate. And Begochidi only assumes responsibility for them after the others have refused. The masked gods have appropriated the game animals from the hunter tradition and restricted Begochidi to the agricultural period by associating him with domesticates. This restriction is in sharp contrast to Begochidi's role in Klah's narrative, where Begochidi is a mediator and creator of game.

Frank Mitchell attempts to embrace both extremes: he pairs Begochidi with Coyote when First Man has Coyote sanctify corn instead of Talking

God; this simultaneously maintains Begochidi's connection with the underworld and associates him with agriculture. In addition, he says that Begochidi was in charge of the game (Wyman 1970, 401, 409, 435). This seems to put his view at odds with that of the other Blessingway singers, including Torlino, although Begochidi is not an important being in any of the Blessingway myths and is subservient to Changing Woman, who created the animals over which he is put in charge.

Frank Mitchell may have been more attuned to a monistic philosophy that seeks to unite opposites, or he may have been reluctant to abandon the older tradition entirely. Unfortunately, we do not know from whom Mitchell gained his ceremonial knowledge other than those singers who taught him the Blessingway.[5] It is also possible that, because he had more off-reservation experience than the other Blessingway singers, he was more sensitive to the growing uncertainties of reservation life as the wage-work economy became increasingly important. In any event, his views stand in contrast to the dualism of other Blessingway singers who keep Changing Woman and the *Haaschch'ééh* separate from and superior to the other Holy People, especially Coyote and First Man.

SINGS ASSOCIATED WITH BLESSINGWAY

The ceremonies most closely related to Blessingway should give prominence to Changing Woman and the masked gods, place less emphasis on the First Man group, and not attribute the diseases they aim to cure to possession. The sings in the God impersonator subgroup of Kluckhohn and Wyman—Nightway, Big Godway, and Plumeway—appear to fulfill these expectations, as do Beautyway, Monsterway, Eagleway, and, perhaps, Mountainway.

Nightway and Big Godway. The Navajos consider the sings of the God Impersonators subgroup, especially Nightway, to have been derived from the Pueblos (Kluckhohn 1962, 74).). The myth of Nightway tells the story of the hero (the Visionary) who is rejected by his family because they do not believe his visions and because he is something of a ne'er do well. The hero is taken by supernaturals disguised as mountain sheep. He attends ceremonies and is watched over by Talking God. He is abducted by one of the Holy People and, in one version, Coyote. These supernaturals are denied entry to the ceremony and cause

5. On the singers who taught him the Blessingway, see Frank Mitchell (1978).

trouble. Later, they have to be propitiated. In the version that includes Coyote, he is promised that he will be named god of daylight, darkness, the rain, the rainbow, the corn, and all vegetation. This episode also occurs in the Blessingway, and I suspect that it represents the means by which Coyote is "tamed" and made acceptable by the Blessingway tradition. A god of rain and corn is certainly an agricultural deity with little resemblance to Coyote the trickster.

The second myth thought to be a part of Nightway is that of the Stricken Twins. However, Matthews's account is the only one to include this myth as a part of Nightway (Matthews 1902), and it is better thought of as the myth of Big Godway, *Hashch'éétsohee* (Faris 1990, 32–35).[6] The Stricken Twins were parented by Talking God and the daughter of a poor family. In a way, this seems to parallel the Twins born to Changing Woman and the Sun, except that these twins become blind and crippled and need to be cured by a performance of Nightway.[7] In this story, the importance of the twins' kinship with the Masked Gods is stressed and, "although such a relationship occurs in other chantway myths, it does not assume such central importance for the plot" (K. Spencer 1957, 156).

Plumeway. Plumeway is recognized as a separate sing, although it is closely connected to the Nightway. It comprises two narratives: the Hollow Log Trip and the Witch Father-in-Law. A Nightway singer gave two versions of the Hollow Log Trip to Matthews, claiming that one was part of the Nightway and the other was the myth of Plumeway (1897, 53).[8] The Hollow Log narrative accounts for the coming of agriculture and, in particular, corn. The Witch Father-in-Law episodes deal with game. The two-part division of the myth opposes agriculture to hunting: the hero, an agriculturalist, must overcome the dangers of hunting. That witchcraft is mentioned only in connection with game does not indicate that hunting is evil but that special powers are needed to cope with the unpredictability of the hunt. The hero obtains these powers by overcoming the witch. Sings of this subgroup are used to treat diseases caused by deer infection (Wyman and Kluckhohn 1938, 27).

6. Big Godway has not been included in table 3 because it was probably a branch of Nightway.

7. Parents of twins either value or devalue them according to whether they are seen as representing the Hero Twins or the Stricken Twins (Levy 1964).

8. James Faris also notes that the Hollow Log Trip is a subsidiary myth of the Nightway (1990, 31).

In Matthews's and Klah's versions, the witch is identified as Deer Raiser, and, in Matthews's version, he lives in an incestuous relationship with his daughter.[9] Klah omits mention of incest but, as we have seen, says that Deer Raiser is also called He Who Changes, which suggests that he is the *nádleeh,* Begochidi. Klah also associates Deer Raiser with Coyote and incest in the underworld and says that his name was changed to Deer Raiser only after he was placed in charge of the game animals.

The story of Coyote's incest with his daughter is one of the oldest trickster tales on the North American continent, and I cannot help but wonder whether Coyote was once a prominent actor in this ceremony. Because this is a ceremony in which the masked gods appear, I believe the Blessingway influence has expunged reference to Coyote and hunting themes and transformed them into an uncomplicated account of witchcraft that the hero must counteract. It is also worth noting that the first episode in the myth is the Hollow Log Trip, one of the most popular episodes among Navajo ceremonial myths, during which the hero learns agriculture. This story is modeled on similar Hopi and Zuni tales, which strengthens my belief that Nightway and Plumeway are centered in the agricultural tradition.[10] The retention of associations with Coyote, incest, and the hoarding and release of game is found only in Klah's and Goldtooth's versions, which strengthens the view that these devotees of Begochidi resisted the tendency to expunge all the old hunting tradition from these sings of the God Impersonators subgroup.

Beautyway. Like Mountainway, Beautyway continues the experience of the two sisters who were seduced by Bear Old Man and Snake Old Man at the conclusion of Enemyway. The Beautyway story follows the adventures of the younger sister as she flees her snake husband. She continually disobeys instructions and must be rescued from a variety of predicaments and restored from Toad's witchery by the snakes. She spends four years with the Snake People, learning the Beautyway, which she then takes back to her people. After she teaches the ceremony to her younger brother, she returns to live with the Snake People as a supernatural.

9. For a summary of several versions of Plumeway, see Katherine Spencer (1957, 164–176).

10. For the myth of the Hopi Snake clan, see H. R. Voth (1905, 30–36). Fred Eggan has collected a longer and more detailed version (Eggan, personal communication with the author). In a Zuni story, "The Box Boat," Paiyatemu-Newekwe befriends the hero, who is an addicted gambler journeying in a hollowed log (Bunzel 1933, 199–210).

There are several aspects of this story that connect it to Blessingway philosophy. First, Beautyway is one of the few ceremonial myths in which a woman rather than a man is the central character. Second, the elements of anger and resentment are absent. Despite Snake Old Man's magical seduction, the heroine's escape, and her repeated disobedience to their instructions, it is the Snake People who teach her the ceremony and it is her snake husband who performs Beautyway over her. The Snake People appear to be good rather than bad, and, at the conclusion of the story, she returns to live with them.

Flintway. Haile (1943a) recorded two versions of Flintway, which, although associated with the Holyways, borrows more heavily from Blessingway and approximates it better than any other sing (Wyman and Kluckhohn 1938, 9). Many ceremonies have both male and female sides, but only the female side must be mentioned specifically, otherwise reference to the male side is assumed.[11] This order is reversed for the Flintway, where the female side is assumed and the male side, if performed, must be mentioned specifically (Haile 1943a, 4). This assumption perhaps reflects Flintway's closeness to Blessingway and the importance of Changing Woman. It is also possible that Flintway developed during a late period of ceremonial elaboration and proliferation.

Monsterway. Like Enemyway, Monsterway occupies an ambiguous position among the healing ceremonies. On the one hand, it shares with Blessingway the account of the birth of Changing Woman and the birth of the Hero Twins. On the other hand, because nothing fearful or disturbing can be included in Blessingway, the slaying of the monsters by the Twins can be included only in Monsterway and Enemyway, and the birth of the twins is included in Blessingway only to round out the story of Changing Woman and to provide the motif of the Twins' visit to their father, the Sun (Wyman 1970, 50). Despite this difference,

11. Many Navajo sings may be performed according to their male or female "sides" as well as according to different "branches" or "phases." There is a general tendency to classify phenomena according to whether they are thought of as male or female. For example, male rain refers to sudden violent downpours that create flash floods, female rain to the slow and steady rainfall that sinks into the ground and benefits plants. This tendency is extended to ceremonies, although the differences between a sing's male and female sides is often minimal. Haile thought that the distinction referred to the sex of the protagonist of the myth. Two myths of the Mountainway are similar except for the sex of the principal actor. The female side's version of the sing utilizes the portion of the myth that features the heroine.

Wyman and Kluckhohn include a Blessing form of Monsterway in the Blessingway group. Coyote and Black God (in the form of Crow) are two of Big Ye'i's spies, along with Turkey Buzzard and, in some versions, Bluejay or Owl. In Monsterway, Big Ye'i and Gray Big Ye'i are killed by the Twins, not by Coyote as in the story of Changing Bear Maiden. Thus, Monsterway is a complementary feature of Blessingway that displaces and defames Coyote.

Eagleway. The Eagleway myth traces the travels of Changing Woman's daughters, White Shell Woman and Turquoise Woman, in their efforts to avoid the monsters.[12] Talking God and Calling God give them each an ear of corn, which they are never to give away. They are helped by and ultimately marry Monster Slayer, for whom they grind the corn that they were supposed not to give to anyone. Two identical maidens arrive and also grind corn for him. They leave, but he goes in search of them. When they return, they defeat White Shell Woman and Turquoise Woman in a corn-grinding contest and subsequently marry Monster Slayer, returning with him to their home, where he faces a series of trials devised by his witch father-in-law. Having passed these trials, which include the slaying of several monsters, he is taught the eagle-trapping ceremony by his father-in-law. Finally, Monster Slayer returns to his first two wives before those wives depart for the sacred mountains and he leaves for Shining Water.

Like the account of how Changing Woman gained possession of dreams, the Eagleway myth enables opposing deities to interact in a disguised manner. Instead of Changing Woman herself, two "daughters" who are corn maidens marry (their brother?) Monster Slayer. He, in turn, is deceived by two look-alike Pueblo corn maidens, who take him to their witch father, from whom he gains supernatural power. Reichard calls these two look-alikes "wily pueblo girls," who could only be distinguished from the Navajo girls by their "bold manners" (1963, 496). In Klah's version, the witch father is Game Chief rather than Cornsmut man as in other versions (Wheelwright 1945, 1–10). Klah tends to identify the Game Keeper with Begochidi, who is the Navajo version of Paiyatemu. And, like Paiyatemu, Monster Slayer not only goes in search of the corn maidens but also plays his flute for his Navajo wives. In ef-

---

12. In some situations, White Shell Woman and Turquoise Woman are other names for Changing Woman (Reichard 1963, 494–497). At other times, White Shell Woman is the sister of Changing Woman. Here, they are her daughters.

fect, Blessingway protagonists Changing Woman and Monster Slayer have obtained necessary power from the opposing shamanistic tradition.

Mountainway. We have seen that Mountainway mentions bad smells to indicate the hero's insanity. Mountainway refers to Changing Bear Maiden, but her story is not a part of the plot. Commenting on the absence of this motif, Wyman notes that it properly belongs to Evilway ritual and, as "Mountainway, at least today, is never performed according to that ritual, there is no reason to include her story in its myths" (1975, 138). But, because the ceremony aims to counter illness caused by bears and because the motif was well known, some reference to it is made. Some tellers mention Coyote in two episodes: the Hero Feigns Death, and its sequel, Raised by Owl.[13] Wyman believes that these references belong to the secular trotting-Coyote cycle and are independent explanatory myths extraneous to the myth proper (Wyman 1975, 148–149). Although not included in the God Impersonators subgroup by Wyman and Kluckhohn, the masked gods appear on the last night of this major nine-night ceremonial. These Holy people are the *ye'iis* (masked gods) of the Nightway, who visit and are not a part of the myth itself. It is possible that a bear ceremony once existed that used the Changing Bear Maiden story as a central part of the myth and that it had close connections with the Coyote of the Evilways; both ceremonies seek to dispel mind loss and insanity. I believe that, over time, this ceremony has been brought under the influence of the Blessingway tradition, especially because the bear, as a dangerous being, was not a northern Athabascan character but was adopted through contact with the Plains tribes.

The Transition

As Puebloan values gradually asserted their ascendancy over those of the shamanistic past, ceremonial myths transformed and ceremonies arose that lacked the old trickster motifs and possession.

---

13. The Hero Feigns Death is the story of Coyote's incest with his daughters. It is only told by Klah. The story's protagonist feigns death so that he may marry his wife's sister (Wheelwright 1951, 1–16; K. Spencer 1957, 228, n157). Klah is also the only narrator to include mention of Changing Bear Woman and Thin Woman, another dangerous female.

Myths in which Begochidi is a major actor represent a transitional stage because Begochidi is a less potent trickster figure than Coyote and may safely replace him. Songs that couple Coyote motifs and possession with Begochidi, however, were still considered dangerous and remain closer to the Coyote pole. The most vivid example of a ceremony that has not found its final resting place is that of Coyoteway, which we have in three versions, each of which differs radically from the others.

COYOTEWAY

Coyoteway is included in the God Impersonators subgroup by Wyman and Kluckhohn, which immediately suggests the presence of Blessingway characteristics. The oldest version we have was told by Yoo' Hataałii to Mary Wheelwright in 1931 (Luckert 1979, 191–202). He learned the myth from a ceremonialist from Rainbow Bridge and the ceremony from a singer from Keams Canyon. The myth is a Holyway version referred to as Coyoteway I in table 3.

The myth is introduced by telling the creation of the Coyote clan by Changing Woman at her home in the western ocean. The clan members were originally known as Bead People because they were made of white shell and white corn.[14] The first people were made of white corn, then people of yellow corn were made. Changing Woman tells them to travel to the east, and from then on they are called White Corn People and Yellow Corn People. The White Corn headman dreams that he is the originator of the Beadway. The Yellow Corn headman dreams he receives power from the Rainbow. They perform the Blessingway and make offerings to Changing Woman while on their journey. Then White Corn headman dreams he is to become one of the Mountain Lion People, and Yellow Corn headman dreams he is to become one of the Coyote People. Finally, the two groups separate, the White Corn People going to the Lukachukai Mountains, the Yellow Corn People going to Canyon de Chelly.

This introductory section firmly places the setting of the story with humans rather than supernaturals and starts with the creation of two clans by Changing Woman. Whatever else may occur, the two groups

---

14. The clan's original name, the "Bead People," explains the connection between Beadway and Coyoteway. Beadway also contains an episode of possession, as well as the Sky Rock and Coyote Transformation motifs. It is more than likely that Yoo' Hataałii was also a Beadway singer, because that is the meaning of his name.

are created from corn, the one group to start the Beadway, the other, ultimately to become known as the Coyote clan and to start the Coyoteway.[15] These elements join what is to follow with the Blessingway tradition, although Karl Luckert also points out the shamanic character of the two headmen's dream visions.

In Canyon De Chelly, the headman sings the first Coyote songs and appears to the people as a *yé'ii*. It appears that the headman has been selected by the Holy People to give the Coyoteway. He deposits all that Changing Woman had given him and sings a song of Talking God at a place that is to be holy and where people will pray for rain. Coyoteway is to be a rain ceremony, and during droughts, coyotes will call the rain for the people. Dressed and masked as Talking God and singing *yé'ii bicheii* songs, the headman walks into a rock and disappears forever. Again, we see a firm connection with the masked gods and Changing Woman.

After the headman leaves, his nephew is selected as leader, marries the headman's widow, and fathers children. While hunting, the oldest child comes upon coyote tracks, which he follows until they disappear into a lake. Guided by the spirit of the first headman, now called Messenger Wind, he descends into the lake, where he finds fields of corn of different colors. Coming to the home of the Coyote People he is addressed as son-in-law, told the story of the origin of the clans, and told that the Coyote People will make him holy. With the Coyote People, he eats Coyote food, receives corn to take back to the surface world, marries eight Coyote Girls, becomes a Coyote-person, and learns Coyoteway. In this nine-night ceremony, the patient is treated by a masked god and, on the last night, three *Haashch'ééh dine'é*—Talking God, Coyote, and Female God—come to the patient.[16] The hero then returns to the surface world, where he teaches the ceremony to his younger brother before leaving to go back to his wives and the Coyote People.

---

15. Canyon de Chelly is said to be the original home of the Coyote Pass clan (*Ma'ii deeshgiizhnii*), descendants of people from Jemez pueblo who intermarried with the Navajos in historical times. The canyon is also where the original Mothway took place. Upon their arrival in Canyon de Chelly, the Yellow Corn People found many berries and bears, and ate *ma'iidą́ą́*, or coyote bush. Thus, connections are also made between coyotes and bears. Whenever the canyon is named as a central place in an origin myth, one may look for connections with Coyote and, in consequence, witchcraft and incest. Kluckhohn notes that Canyon De Chelly (Chinle) is one of three locations, the others being Black Mesa and Cañoncito, where witches are thought to be particularly numerous (1962b, 47, 233 n3).

16. The nine-night Coyoteway witnessed by Luckert featured three *yé'ii* impersonators: Talking God, Blue Coyote Carrier, and Female God. The last two wore identical blue masks of Female God and were identified as Coyote Girls. Blue Coyote Carrier, however,

This version clearly belongs to the Blessingway tradition. Coyotes are rain deities made of corn, and Coyote himself is a masked god. Other than the echoes of shamanic vision experiences noted by Luckert, the only feature that differs from other ceremonies of the God Impersonator subgroup is the fact that the Coyote People and the ceremony come from the underworld rather than from visits with the Holy People in the upperworlds.

The second Holyway myth was told by Tséyi'nii from Canyon de Chelly in 1934, when he was seventy-five years old (Luckert 1979, 203–216). Although a Holyway myth, it contains the most trickster Coyote motifs of all the versions. The hero follows coyote tracks to a lake, which he enters, to find himself in the underworlds. Here, as in the first version, the land is fertile and corn is growing by houses placed at the four cardinal directions. He meets Coyote People who inform him that there are good and bad Coyote People. The bad Coyotes bring all the illnesses of the world to human beings, but the good Coyotes call up rain and have clouds on the ends of their noses and flowers edging their mouths. While he is with the good Coyote People, a witch in a coyote skin comes but does nothing. The good Coyotes teach the hero Coyoteway, which he takes back to the surface and teaches to his brother. Talking God and Calling God live nearby and have fathered coyotelike dog children.[17] The hero returns to the underworld to obtain more ceremonial knowledge, including the prayerstick used to cure insanity.[18] He is given four sacred ears of corn, which he takes back to the surface world.

The story then traces the adventures of "bad" Coyote and *hastói*, an unnamed holy person according to the text, who steals the hero's corn.[19] *Hastói* gets caught but blames the trouble on Coyote and is released. Coyote visits Horned Toad, claims he has his corn, and swallows him. Horned Toad kills Coyote by cutting his throat but is reprimanded by Talking God because, with Coyote dead, there would be no more rain. These

---

was dressed as a male and carried a stuffed animal, Blue Coyote, under his arm. The third *yé'ii* was impersonated by a woman and dressed in a skirt and blouse (Luckert 1979, 160, 167, 170). One wonders why Coyote himself was not impersonated but only carried in effigy by a Coyote Girl. Luckert says, "Quite obviously, the Coyote Carrier and his Blue Coyote together constitute one being." Perhaps, however, this indicates that Coyote cannot be represented directly even in his own ceremony but must be carried in effigy.

17. Luckert avers that the two gods "exceed the Coyote People in authority," although the story does not make this explicit (1979, 203).

18. This harks back to mind loss caused by Coyote possession and transformation, although possession is not mentioned.

19. This person is not identified. *Hastói* is the plural of *hastiin* and means "elders" or "menfolk." It is not, as far as I am aware, used to refer to supernaturals.

episodes are followed by traditional stories of trotting and adulterous Coyote, including the story of Coyote's incest with his daughter and his being shot by magic arrows that enter his anus and kill him. The last episode relates Coyote's marriage to Changing Bear Woman in detail.

Luckert claims that Tséyi'nii tries to disassociate this "bad" Coyote from the origin of Coyoteway by saying that "Coyote was not the person who brought the *ma'iijí hatáál* to men" (Luckert 1979, 204, 215). Despite this disclaimer, we are left with a myth of a Holyway ceremony of the God Impersonators subgroup that includes a major Evilway motif as well as stories from the secular Coyote cycle, which are in general not included in ceremonial myths. In this respect, this version is like Mountainway, which according to one narrator includes stories taken from the secular Coyote cycle.

The third published Coyoteway myth is that of William Charlie of Smith Lake, recorded by Maude Oakes in 1942 or 1943 (Luckert 1979, 217–223). It is the only evidence we have of an Evilway version of Coyoteway. The introductory passage directly connects what is to come with the underworlds, hunting myths, and myths of Great Gambler and White Butterfly. The hero is the grandson of First Man and First Woman and lives at the place of Deer Raiser, the Master of Animals, during a time when many people who are great gamblers are living at Pueblo Bonito. While hunting, he comes to the home of Coyote People and meets Coyote-out-of-Mind, or Coyote-Who-Changes-Around, who wears skins of many different colors and who is also a hunter.[20] The hero watches Coyote dodge lightning by twirling about. He learns hunting techniques from Coyote and watches Coyote cure Lightning Man and Black Thunder, who fainted when they were trying to attack him. Coyote gets power from Lightning Man to be chief of all rains and water. The patient smokes wild tobacco, and medicine is put into his eyes so that he can see and hear. The medicine comes from prayerstick powder, the dirt in a badger's ear, and from liquid from the watery part of a live eagle's eye.[21] Bits of a poisonous herb are eaten by both singer and patient.[22] This sing is used if a person goes insane, is bitten by a coyote or mad dog, misbehaves sexually, or is too anxiety-ridden to work or do anything else. This sing is also useful for men who go hunting.

20. An important connection between the hunter Coyote called Coyote-Who-Changes-Around is made in the context of the Gameway myths discussed subsequently.

21. This is the medicine used by stargazers, which associates Coyoteway Evil with the stargazing ritual.

22. This is most probably jimson weed used in Frenzy Witchcraftway and Gameway Frenzy.

Having learned Coyoteway, the hero leaves and travels to Pueblo Bonito. There, with Bat and Snake People, he decides to beat the Great Gambler who is the chief of Pueblo Bonito. Then follows the story of Great Gambler's defeat as found in Waterway and Frenzy Witchcraftway, which ends: "The Gambler was shot up into the Sky World by the bow. They heard him say something as he went but could not understand what he said" (Luckert 1979, 23). After this, the hero returns home, to the Place of Deer Raiser.

Although in the Evilway Group, this myth is unlike the other recorded Evilways: it includes Frenzy Witchcraftway themes of Begochidi and the Great Gambler and presents Coyote as a powerful healer rather than an evildoer. It is also associated more with hunting than the Holyway versions, which prompts Luckert to observe that this myth is closer to the Navajo-Apachean hunter stratum (1979, 217). The connection to Frenzy Witchcraft and Begochidi also suggests that a somewhat later Pueblo development has been added.

With only the evidence presented thus far, it would be permissible to dismiss Tséyi'nii's inclusion of Coyote cycle tales as individual additions made, perhaps, for informational purposes. It is also possible that he was not a Coyoteway singer but was knowledgeable and wished to include much of what was known about Coyote whether properly part of the ceremony or not. However, the contemporary material given to Luckert by Man with Palomino Horse and Luke Cook in 1974 cautions against this interpretation (Luckert 1979, 15–22).

Man with Palomino Horse, a Coyoteway singer according to Holyway, maintained that only the hero's visit to the Coyote People under the lake was the true myth of the ceremonial. In contrast, Luke Cook also included the Witch Arrows and Coyote Visits Toad episodes, as does Tséyi'nii. Man with Palomino Horse learned Coyoteway from Many Whiskers (Bidághaa' Łání).

The reproductions of Coyoteway sandpaintings also show considerable variation in the subjects depicted (Luckert 1979, 224–233). One group of paintings was collected from Big Mustache, who may have been the same as Many Whiskers. These paintings depict Coyote Girls, corn plants, Coyote's home, and rain. A second set, by *Bit'ahnii Bidághaaí*, includes "the first sandpainting of the Coyote Chant," which depicts four Coyotes of the cardinal directions and four butterflies; this replicates the Mothway association of Coyote with Butterfly People. One sandpainting by William Charlie depicts Thunderbirds with flint caps and lightning alternating with birds and clouds and, at the east side, Bat,

Big Fly Messenger, and Yellow Bird Messenger. This sandpainting appears to illustrate the episode in which Coyote is attacked by Lightning and Thunder. We must conclude that the Coyote motifs most often associated with Evilway ceremonies were often included in the Holyway versions of many singers. The ceremony seems to be in a state of transition, with some singers reluctant to expunge Coyote's evil side entirely. Yet it is significant that none of the three myths includes an episode of possession.

GAMEWAY

Gameway has been recorded in a number of versions, two by Berard Haile in 1929, and two by Carl Luckert in 1971 and 1976. All versions are from the Deerway subgroup (Luckert 1975; 1978). I have placed them in the transitional category because, despite their strong connections with the Blessingway tradition, their central theme is the hiding and release of game, which, we have seen, is one of the old myths that migrated south with the Apacheans from their northern Athabascan homeland.

According to one narrator, Begochidi, Talking God, and Black God created the game animals. In another version, it is Talking God, Calling God, Begochidi, Black God, and Game Grower (Deer Raiser?) who create game. However, later in this second narrative, "Talking God became master of all game, they say, and Black God, too, became their master, and Wind and Sun and Begochidi, too, with Coyote, these and no more" (Luckert 1975, 102). Coyote insists that he is the master of all game, although Black God disputes this. Coyote scatters the game so that hunters cannot kill them, because the hunters refuse to offer prayers to him as the master of game (Luckert 1975, 105, 114–115).[23] W. W. Hill's informants also gave varying accounts: the animals were under the control of Begochidi; Begochidi made the game, but their control was in the hands of Talking God and Black God; Talking God controlled the bucks, and Black God controlled the does, and these two taught the songs used in hunting; Talking God and Black God controlled the game, but Begochidi was more important. He was the god of game and taught the game songs to men (Hill 1938a, 99). Begochidi appears to vie with Talking God for preeminence, and Coyote is totally absent except for

23. This version told by James Smith to Berard Haile is the only one to make explicit Coyote's claim to being a master of game.

the one instance in which he is paired with Begochidi. Despite Talking God's importance, however, the Talking Godway of hunting was the most informal of all Gameway rituals. "It could be indulged in by a single individual or by a group" (Hill 1938a, 121). It was not necessary to make a separate hunting camp, and although skinning and butchering were performed in a ritual manner, the more important rituals of the hunting camp were eliminated.

The myth proper starts with the hiding and release of game. In one version, this is preceded by the teaching of Gameway to humankind. A young woman who has four brothers is transformed into a deer. Before she leaves them to live as a deer person, she teaches her brothers hunting rites. After she has gone, the game disappears. The game has been hidden by a person who was dark like coal. "That person was Crow. . . . He is the Black God. He had captured all the game animals, from all the four directions" (Luckert 1978, 24). On the one hand, Black God is the marplot who hides the game as in the northern myths: "'The Crow which usually flies to us, as you say, is really Black-god. He is feared as one not to be trifled with. He is mean,' my Granduncle Talking-god said to me" (Luckert 1975, 88). On the other hand, he is an ally of Talking God, who hides the game because they have been hunted without the proper ritual and respect.

The Blessingway tradition has put Talking God in control, turned the trickster marplots Crow and Begochidi into masked gods, and has Black God hide the game to protect the animals from disrespectful hunters who do not perform the hunt rituals. Yet Black God may also hide the game out of spite and remain dangerous and mean, and Begochidi, Coyote's trickster replacement, may retain his role as creator of game and teacher of ritual and still be paired with Coyote, while Coyote continues to claim precedence as master of game. It is also important to mention that, although now a masked god, Coyote's mask has nowhere been observed, and in the Nightway only an effigy of Coyote is used (Faris 1990, 158–162, 195). Moreover, in none of the creations myths is Coyote identified as a masked god.

Finally, there is one last, although cryptic, retention of Coyote as the master of animals. We recall that Coyote is *ma'ii* and that wolf is *ma'iitsoh*, or Big Coyote. According to the Gameways, the animals believed to be in partnership with the hunters are referred to by their ritual names (Hill 1938a, 104; Franciscan Fathers 1910, 141). Just as Navajo and Apache may extend *ma'ii* as a generic term to wolves and foxes and even to other predators, so the ritual name used for predators and hunters may also be an extension of another name for coyote.[24] Luckert's informants always mentioned an identification with Wolf rather than Coyote, which led him to conclude that Wolf was the original master of game before Talking God and Black God appeared on the scene (1975, 67, 145, 169, 170, 172–174). The ritual name for wolf is *naatł'éé tsoh;* for coyote it is *naatł'eéi t'sóóz.* And as *t'sóóz* (shaggy) is a play or pun on *tsoh,* so, in my opinion, are *naatł'éé* and *naat'leéi* (the one who does *naat'léé*) plays on *nádleeh* (to become, revert to a previous state *and* he repeatedly becomes, he changes) and on *tł'ééh* (trots). Translations of Coyote's names have included "trotting coyote" as well as "Coyote-Who-Changes-Around" (Luckert 1979, 219). If I am correct in my inference, Coyote remains the master of animals and the hunt, and human hunters are still identified with him in the Gameway, but because of Coyote's defamation, they prefer to speak about Wolf, whose ritual name also refers to Coyote.[25]

MOTHWAY AND FRENZY WITCHCRAFTWAY

Mothway and Frenzy Witchcraftway ceremonies also pair Begochidi with Coyote. Both include episodes of possession, and I have placed them close to the Coyote pole. They do not, however, have their origins in the hunting tradition but deal with concerns that arose after the period of Puebloization and only bring Coyote into their myths to satisfy the need to connect with Coyote's unbridled sexuality.

Mothway ceremony and myth differ considerably from the usual pattern. There is no single protagonist who gains knowledge and power through exploits. Moreover, the illness it aims to cure is punishment for a forbidden act and not, as is more generally the case with breach of taboo, the result of contact with a dangerous supernatural. The cure is also unusual in that the "original sin" must be reenacted in the ceremonial setting. Mothway and Frenzy Witchcraftway, which reproduces the patient's *'ajiłee* madness by the ingestion of the datura medicine, are the only ceremonies I know to use this direct form of sympathetic magic in working a cure.

24. See Karl Luckert for the extension of *mą'ii* and the Chiricahua Apache *mbai* (1979, 7).

25. There may even be further ramifications of the pun—*tł'eestooz* = loin cloth (crotch + a flat flexible object), which perhaps refers to Coyote's uncontrolled sexuality. *Tł'eeh* also means "night," and hunters say that while identifying with the great animal hunters, they have the skills of predators, including night vision (Luckert 1975, 67)

The story relates how the Butterfly People (*K'aalógii dine'é*) are led by the hermaphrodite Begochidi, who was born at Riverward Knoll, the place where plants and butterflies originated and where the Sun fertilized both the male and female plants. In like manner, Begochidi fertilizes the male and female Butterfly People so that they never need to marry aliens (Haile 1978). He puts his hand on their genitals and says "bego bego." He also does this to hunters, thus making them miss their mark, as well as to people who are about to urinate or have intercourse. Begochidi eventually deserts the Butterfly People, leaving them for a land that has game animals. After this desertion, they move to Hopi country and are forced to consider whether they will allow their children to marry outsiders: "As time passed, in the course of a single day, from fifty and sixty places, useless requests for marriage had come to be made" (Haile 1978, 86). The discussion revolves about the prospect of losing their children, who would go to live with their new relatives. The debate continues after they make camp opposite White House in Canyon De Chelly, where it is pointed out that they never had any alliances or cooperative relationships with these foreigners.

It is finally decided that "this evening your children, those that love each other, shall prepare their bedding for one another. They shall lie together" (Haile 1978, 87). Doing this, however, makes them go wild as though they had drunk whiskey and, like moths (*'iich'ahii*), rush into fires that have been built nearby (Haile 1978, 88). Dawn Boy and Dawn Girl, supernatural siblings who have observed everything, emulate the butterflies and also become sick.[26] And because no one knows a cure for this condition, "there is absolutely a mutual fear of their lower parts between brothers and sisters. The mere thought of such a thing is to be feared" (Haile 1978, 88).

The Mothway is performed over Dawn Boy and Dawn Girl by Big Bear Man.[27] Only Coyote has medicine for their condition. This medicine is made from the genitals of male and female sibling coyotes, yellow and blue foxes, badgers, and bears. There are also four Moth medicines, which are the same plants used in Frenzy Witchcraftway. A kilt of coyote skin is wrapped around each of the patients, after which they

---

26. Although convulsions are not described, present-day Navajos invariably regard the major epileptic seizure to be the condition referred to in the myth because epileptics, like moths, fall into fires.

27. Today, Mothway is extinct; our knowledge of it comes from Haile's published account and from one of our informants, an elderly woman who had the ceremony performed for her in her youth (see Levy, Neutra, and Parker 1987).

drink the medicine concoction. Then, with their buttocks touching one another, they vomit the moths that are inside them, and these in turn are thrown into the fire.

In a first-person account, a patient describes this ceremony, which was performed over her around the turn of the century:

A white curtain was put up inside the ceremonial hogan and around both patients. Within this curtain the patients had sexual intercourse as part of the curing ritual. Both wore fox skins representing their tail similar to a Nightway dancer. While the patients were copulating, they howled like whirling coyotes. When intercourse was over, the singer caught some of the semen of both patients which was then applied to the prayer stick prepared for an offering. (Levy, Neutra and Parker 1987, 47–48)

Finally, they were bidden to drink the Coyote and Moth medicines and then to face away from each other while inducing vomiting.

Navajos think of the Mothway myth as an explanation of the prohibition against sibling and clan incest, and moth madness is still the apical Navajo disease producing the dramatic signs and symptoms of the grand mal epileptic seizure and destroying the lives of those suffering from it. But why incest is the focus of such anxiety and concern, and why there is no complementary belief about father-daughter incest, remains to be explained.

Incest within the family is universally abhorred in North America, and societies with unilineal descent invariably practice clan exogamy. If, as Isadore Dyen and David Aberle believe, the Navajos already had matrilineal descent groups upon their arrival in the Southwest, they would hardly need to make the taboo more forceful than it already was; nor would there be a need to borrow Pueblo symbols (Dyen and Aberle 1974). And if they had only developed matrilineal descent after their arrival and needed to give added salience to the prohibition against clan incest, one would expect the matrilineal Western Apaches to have emphasized sibling and clan incest as well.

The Apaches, however, treated incest as a civil crime and did not believe that it caused either seizures or other illness. There was no ceremony against it or its aftereffects, and the offenders' kin were in no way tainted by it (Goodwin 1969, 309, 416–424, 427; Opler 1965, 59–61, 249–251). The offenders were thought to be witches, and if discovered in the act, they could be killed by their kin on the spot. Otherwise, they were brought before the chiefs for trial. Most often the man was thought to be the witch and the woman his victim. There was no distinction made between sibling and father-daughter incest, except that siblings were often too young to have knowledge of witchcraft. Among the matrilineal Western Apaches, clan and phratry endogamy were also forbidden. If people of the same clan married and refused to divorce, it was thought that they would give birth to deformed or insane children. The parents, however, suffered only ridicule. There was also the belief that incest offenders would not be able to have children by a later marriage.

There is, however, evidence that Northern Athabascans may have looked upon sibling incest with special abhorrence. The Kaska of western Canada believed that witchcraft and incest caused insanity. "Overwhelmed by shame and guilt, an unhappy man might tear off his penis or leap into the fire. Most grievous of all was incest between brother and sister" (Honigmann 1954, 90–91).

Although abhorring incest, most North American Indian societies did not think of it as a major cause of disease or other form of supernatural sanction. Despite the fact that these people lived in scattered encampments that were isolated for much of the year, recorded accounts do not suggest that incest was a source of much anxiety.[28]

Except for the Zuni, most Pueblos had no specific beliefs about the causes or consequences of either clan or sibling incest. As we have seen, a Zuni myth tells of how the original act of sibling incest created hermaphrodite and asexual, infertile children. Clan incest was believed to cause earthquakes that might release wild animals from underground (Parsons 1974, 53). Neither familial nor clan incest were thought by the Hopis to do any harm to the participants, and when asked why one should avoid such relationships, the average Hopi could give no specific reason beyond "they are of the same blood"; when pressed on the subject, they "appeared baffled and could not understand how one could seriously raise the point" (Brandt 1954, 165, 206–210). Tewas believe that there was no punishment for incest, either social or supernatural, other than the bad reputation the family would have (Levy, Neutra, and Parker 1987, 52).

A more plausible explanation of the origin of Mothway is that the original intent was to encourage intermarriage with the diverse groups of Pueblos who joined the Navajos after the Pueblo Revolt by extending marriage prohibitions beyond the rule of clan exogamy. In the myth of Mothway, the potential for conflict raised by requests for intermar-

28. On attitudes toward incest, compare North Alaskan Eskimo (R. Spencer 1959, 76) and Cheyenne (Llewellyn and Hoebel 1941, 178–181).

riage with Pueblos precipitates the problem, and although phrased in terms of sibling incest, resistance to intermarriage brings about madness. Some of the larger *pueblitos,* as well as the early Navajo populations in Canyon de Chelly that included Hopis and Jemez, must have contained a number of exogamous descent groups.[29] Recall that, as shown in chapter 2, the need to keep people from marrying back into father's clan and phratry required the development of marriage prohibitions that forced individuals to seek mates from clans not already allied by marriage in the immediately preceding generation. The prohibition against marriage into father's clan and phratry has persisted to the present time, and Navajos are not unanimous in believing that sibling and clan incest are the only causes of moth madness: Many insist that it is also caused by marriage into father's clan or phratry.

Familial incest would have become more of a problem after the dispersal of the population and the shift to pastoralism, when many families were isolated for much of the year and so dispersed over the countryside that social controls were weak. In addition, the shift to pastoralism increased the importance of males. This latter transition would have fostered ambivalent feeling toward the opposite sex that suffused the incestuous impulse, making it more anxiety provoking than it was among tribes whose way of life had been stable for longer periods of time.

The efficacy of social controls is an important factor in determining the amount of attention paid to the problem of incest. Pueblo communities were tightly structured and so densely populated that clandestine acts stood little chance of going undetected. Supernatural sanctions may not have been necessary, especially when we consider that the western Pueblos had been matrilineal for many centuries.

The Western Apaches also lived in what Grenville Goodwin has called "local groups" composed of several "family clusters"—that is, extended families corresponding to the Navajo camp (Goodwin 1969, 123–192). Local groups had recognized leaders who were formally chosen, installed, and instructed. Families living apart from a family cluster were rare, as were family clusters that were not part of a local group. Although the Apaches were more mobile than the Pueblos, they rarely did anything alone. People seldom traveled, hunted, or went gathering alone, not only because of enemies but also because of possible accident and

29. Pueblo and Navajo clans are grouped into phratries, or clan groups, which are also exogamous. Thus, although there are more than sixty Navajo clans, there are only nine phratries.

injury. Goodwin found mature men who had never spent a night alone, and even the less sedentary Chiricahuas had a special treatment for loneliness (Opler 1965, 37, 429).

How different were the pastoral Navajos, who spent much of the year in relative isolation in residence groups composed of one extended family, from which nuclear families might separate for a variety of purposes and for varying lengths of time? As often as not, isolated family groups were small nuclear families. During the 1930s, almost half of Navajo families were nuclear, composed of a married couple and their dependent children; the remaining half lived as members of slightly larger extended families (Aberle 1961, 187). Sheepherding is often a solitary occupation, and there are many stories telling of chance encounters between traveling men and single women who were tending sheep. The chance of discovery, in our opinion, was far less for the Navajos than for the Apaches, and the fear of community reaction correspondingly weaker. Under these conditions, there would be a greater need for supernatural sanctions.

Clyde Kluckhohn believes that the isolation of Navajo families created many tensions that could be relieved only by witchcraft accusations, which released hostilities generated within the group by displacing and projecting aggression onto persons outside the immediate kin group (1962b, 93). Kluckhohn also notes that it was always a sibling who was mentioned in Navajo accounts as the relative killed by the witch initiate (1962b, 102–104). When informants told of were-animals, they often mentioned that the witch was recognized as a real or clan sister. In sum, changing conditions led to a reinterpretation of moth madness as a consequence of sibling and clan incest rather than as the result of community endogamy.

The story of Frenzy Witchcraftway follows the adventures of a human hero who is given love and game magic by the gods (Haile 1978; Kluckhohn 1962b, 36–42, 158–174, 177–188; K. Spencer 1957, 134–148). Begochidi is not mentioned by name but is represented by White Butterfly, who as we have seen is Paiyatemu and the Great Gambler. After some preliminary adventures that include flirtation with and ridicule by Hopi women, a ceremony is performed by means of which the hero is given love and game magic.[30] Thus armed, the hero proceeds

---

30. The 'ajilee medicines are datura, marsh plant, yellow thistle, and loco weed. Haile believes their power is conferred by the Sun. In Kluckhohn's account, the conferer is Cone-towards-Water Man (1962b, 158–174). Sandoval maintained that the Sun wished the hero to obtain the Great Gambler's medicine power (O'Bryan 1956, 143).

to seduce and marry two Hopi virgins. In Haile's version, Coyote transforms the hero and, taking his form, seduces the hero's wives. After his
restoration by a hoop ceremony, the hero seduces two more Pueblo virgins while disguised as a butterfly. The hero's wives are, in turn, seduced
and stolen by White Butterfly. In the final episode, the hero retaliates by
overcoming White Butterfly, now in the role of the Great Gambler, in
a contest and killing him with a blow to the head from which "moths
spread out up to the sky like ashes and (produced) a (dark) shadow"
(Haile 1978, 78).

Frenzy Witchcraftway is used to cure the effects of the use of love or
game magic by witches. All informants stress the point that no one learns
the ritual by itself because then it is nothing but evil and very dangerous. And some say that if a man learns Blessingway first, he never both-
ers to learn Frenzy Witchcraftway. During the 1960s, I identified ten
practitioners of Frenzy Witchcraftway; each of the practitioners was well
known, although the younger ones were afraid to perform the ceremony
because they feared that if they made a mistake they would get sick or
die. The victim of frenzy witchcraft is believed to lose her mind and to
go into a state of lustful frenzy, tearing off her clothes and running after the man who has witched her. According to Kluckhohn, practitioners of frenzy witchcraft were distinct from witches, wizards, and sorcer-
ers: They did not participate in the "witches sabbath" and did not
transform themselves into were-animals (1962b, 40–41). Nevertheless,
it was as dangerous as other forms of witchcraft: initiation required the
death of a sibling and, according Kluckhohn, there was an association
with sibling incest as well (1962b, 177, 179).

We have seen that there was reason for the creation of severe sanctions for breach of the newly instituted marriage prohibitions during the
time of intense Puebloization. However, the cause of the importance attached to the practice of love magic is less obvious. Although my colleagues and I found many cases of frenzy witchcraft among Navajo
epileptics and hysterics, we found no instances of love magic among the
Pueblo patients (Levy, Neutra, and Parker 1987). Nor does Keith Basso
report any instances in his study of contemporary Western Apache witchcraft (Basso 1969).

That love magic may once have been considered by Pueblo societies
to be especially dangerous is suggested by the belief that the Koyemsi
clowns were, with the butterfly in their drums, able to drive young
women to sexual frenzy. There is also the episode of sexual witchcraft
observed by Matilda Cox Stevenson that demonstrates that this was an

extremely malevolent form of witchcraft as well as the cause of seizure-like activity (Stevenson 1904, 398–402).

The Apaches had love magic very similar to Navajo frenzy witchcraft. The Western Apaches believed that the source of love power was a hill with plants and butterflies (Goodwin 1969, 304–309; Opler 1965, 151–153). The Chiricahua also associated the butterfly with sexual desire but saw it as representing the flightiness of women in general. As among the Navajo, love magic was closely identified with hunt magic. The Apaches, however, did not believe that its practitioners were witches or that the consequences were serious, although an "overdose" could cause insanity. Love magic was linked neither with Coyote nor with incest, and although its practitioners did not often boast openly of their powers, they were not averse to selling their services. Anyone, it appears, could learn enough to practice the magic.

Mothway and Frenzy Witchcraftway are closely related, and many Navajos believe both are connected with Coyoteway. Mothway and Frenzy Witchcraftway originate at Riverward Knoll, the hill where the fertilization of the medicinal plants occurs and where Begochidi is conceived.[31] Both use datura, and both include Coyote either as medicine or as an episode of possession. Nevertheless, the prominence of Begochidi, the inclusion of a Butterfly Seduction, and the use of the butterfly to symbolize sexual excess, suggest that Frenzy Witchcraftway is derived from the Pueblos during the same period as the development of Mothway. Begochidi and the butterfly served to introduce a less dangerous image of excess, and Coyote was later employed to integrate these borrowed materials with older traditions of Coyote's sexual exploits.

Frenzy witchcraft may have become more dangerous after the shift to pastoralism and the dispersal of the population. As moth madness became the consequence of sibling and clan incest rather than of group endogamy, so also love magic may well have become more dangerous as community controls weakened and as women, especially, spent many hours alone herding sheep. There are many accounts of encounters with strangers while herding at some distance from home, and women would have been exposed to sexual exploitation at these times. Older men were thought to practice this form of witchcraft at Enemyway ceremonies, which brought many people together during the warm months and which were famous as opportunities for men to seduce women.

---

31. Kluckhohn's account places the beginning of the story in Coyote Pass Canyon near Jemez Pueblo (1962b, 158).

From Shaman to Diagnostician

Today, the last remnant of the shamanic trance is found among diagnosticians who are said to be in a trance while diagnosing the cause of a disease or divining the location of lost or stolen items. The most common form of diagnosis is hand trembling, which is practiced by both men and women, although women practitioners far outnumber the men. Stargazing, listening, and datura divination are rarely performed today, and although women are thought to be able to perform datura divination, stargazers and listeners are almost invariably men.

As we have seen, Hand Tremblingway was borrowed from the Chiricahua Apaches during the nineteenth century. Not only is its origin myth short and poorly integrated into the larger corpus of Navajo myth, but its supernatural tutelary, Gila Monster, figures prominently in only one other healing ceremony, Flintway. Moreover, gila monsters are found only in the southern deserts and do not range as far north as Navajo country (Wyman 1936a).

Hand trembling is said to be an unsought gift, a sign of possession by Gila Monster, signaled by the shaking of the right arm. After an individual's first episode of trembling, a ceremony must be performed to control the involuntary shaking so that it does not become a disease and, at the same time, to give the individual the status of diagnostician (Wyman 1936b).

Although the trembling (*ndishniih*) is always thought to be involuntary, varying from a fine tremor of the hand to violent and uncontrollable motions of the whole arm, it does not connote wildness or excess. Unlike those suffering form moth madness (*'iicha'ąh*), or affected by frenzy witchcraft, hand tremblers are never referred to by terms using the *tsi* prefix that connote extreme behavior of all sorts and are related to Coyote's extremes.[32] This distinction is consonant with the late introduction of Hand Tremblingway, after the "defamation" of Coyote.

In contrast, stargazing and listening involve possession by Coyote and, although their myths of origin are not well known, the medicine used to enhance the practitioners' powers is that used in Coyoteway Evil

---

32. *Tsi* means "to walk in every direction"—that is, aimlessly and chaotically, lacking constraints and direction. *Tsi'naaɡha* refers to drunkenness, dizziness, or sexual excess (*asdzáni yee tsi'naaɡhá,* going to excess with women). Frank Goldtooth maintained that all *tsi* behavior derived from Coyote.

to enable the patient to see and hear. I was not able to find evidence that these forms are still practiced in the western area of the reservation. I did, however, talk with one former stargazer who maintained that people were afraid to use stargazers because the people thought the stargazers were probably witches. There is evidence that listening and stargazing are being practiced more frequently today as part of Native American Church (peyote) ceremonies (Mitzi Begay and Beulah Allen, personal communications).[33]

Datura divination has been discussed by Kluckhohn (1962b, 39–40, 175–176) and Hill (1938b). It was never widely known and was not mentioned by any of the Frenzy Witchcraftway practitioners I contacted. It seems to have been used only after hand trembling or stargazing had failed. Instead of doing the divination, the singer gives datura to a patient or another person who, while "out of his or her mind," is able to identify the thief or lost items. It may not have been used to diagnose illness.

The changes that transformed Navajo religion and ceremonialism during and after the period of intense Puebloization between 1690 and 1770 involved a suppression of shamanism and visions. A parallel process must have taken place among the Hopi after their acquisition of agriculture, with the result that today the shaman's role is occupied by healers with little status who do not go into trances or possess any great supernatural power (Levy 1994). Exactly how long this process took among the Navajo cannot be known, but by the early nineteenth century, shamanic trances were, in all likelihood, still indulged in only by stargazer and listener diagnosticians. The newly created "singers," like Pueblo priests, obtained their control over supernatural power and their ability to cure through learned ritual and prayer. As soul loss and possession gave way to breach of taboo as the major cause of illness, references to possession were retained only in the myths of the healing ceremonies and diagnosis was made almost always in terms of witchcraft or breach of taboo.

Shamanistic beliefs must have persisted for some time, and the shamans themselves must have resisted the new ideas and beliefs. Al-

---

33. I have not been able to determine whether any peyote Road Chiefs diagnose while in a trance.

though Coyote was demonized by the Blessingway tradition, new dangers such as love magic and breach of the newly promulgated marriage proscriptions called for powerful antidotes. These were provided by adopting a Pueblo trickster, Begochidi-Paiyatemu, and the Pueblo symbol of sexual excess, the butterfly. Whether they, in turn, were connected to Coyote as a means to distance them from the protective power of Blessingway, or were so connected by proponents of the older shamanistic tradition, cannot be determined with confidence. Yet I think it likely that some ceremonialists and diagnosticians continued to believe that the monistic tradition Coyote represented was preferable to the dualistic tendencies introduced by Pueblo influences.

The variations in the several recorded myths of the Coyoteway suggest that the attempt to transform Coyote into an agricultural deity was not entirely successful. The creative side of Coyote was separated from his trickster aspect by creating two Coyotes: one born from an egg, who was in charge of water and fertility, and the other called First Angry, a mischief-maker and creator of confusion and chaos. Coyote's witchcraft was confined primarily to the Evilways, where possession and soul loss are the major concerns. To bring Coyote into the Blessingway tradition, he had to be made into a masked god. Yet this adaptation was not entirely successful, because in the Nightway he only appears in effigy. And in Coyoteway myths, First Angry keeps reappearing and the "good" Coyotes must warn that the "evil" Coyote is still at large.

In the opinion of several singers of Frenzy Witchcraftway with whom I worked between 1964 and 1970, Coyote is the central deity in the creation and maintenance of the Navajo world. One singer maintained that "the whole world rests on Coyote's shoulders" and went on to explain that my interpreter and I could not understand the myths and ceremonies until we thoroughly understood Coyote. One Coyoteway singer believed that all illness came from Coyote, a view that accepts Coyote in his demonized form. But another desired to minimize Coyote's importance and told Luckert that Coyote illness results only from offending actual coyotes (Luckert 1979, 6, 8). There appears to have been an increase in the incidence of Coyote illness during the 1940s, which this singer attributed to the federal government's campaign to eliminate coyotes from Navajo rangelands. He does not mention that the decade from 1935 to 1945 was also the period during which the stock-reduction programs were implemented. Yet this was an extremely stressful and uncertain period that would account for a renewed concern with Coyote.

The monistic trickster-creator tradition is not a petrified remnant of the shamanistic past preserved only in myths, nor does it represent, as Bert Kaplan and Dale Johnson believe, repressed personality traits expressed as forms of psychopathology and social deviance. Rather, it appears as a reasoned theological response to new sources of insecurity and unpredictability consequent upon the development of pastoralism, conquest, and the demise of pastoralism itself in the mid-twentieth century. If the myths merely reflected conflict that took place over two hundred years ago, there would be no clear concentration of trickster-creator elements in only a few ceremonials that have continued to be important even if rarely performed.

Mythmakers faced two difficult tasks during these periods of transition. The first was to give new deities such as Changing Woman and Talking God ascendance over older, well-established deities and, wherever possible, to absorb the older beings into the new tradition. The second was to give the new deities control over the powers once possessed by the older shamanic deities. This latter task was especially tricky as it required that Coyote, for example, would be demonized as a witch at the same time that control over witchcraft had to be put into the charge of Talking God.

Taming such deities as Coyote, Black God, or Begochidi was fairly straightforward. New narratives as well as new names were created. Coyote was created in two guises: First Angry and Born of an Egg. A variety of new names indicating his control over water were also added. The polarization was reflected in the ceremonials, with the Evilways dealing with the angry or evil side. Once this was done, the new Coyote could become a corn deity and the tutelary of the new Coyoteway.

Transforming Raven into Black God was also relatively straightforward. Raven, we recall, was a hoarder of game and, in the north, an opponent of the trickster and, later, of Coyote. In some stories, he is clearly identified as Black God in the form of Raven or Crow and may be an ally of Coyote working as spies for Big Ye'i. As Black God, however, he became the Hopi Masau, the fire god, who is one of the Puebloan masked gods. He still hid the game, but now he did so in order to protect animals from hunters who did not hunt them properly. He used the frenzy witchcraft medicines to protect the game rather than to work hunt magic. But the control of game animals was never settled: Black God, Talking God, Begochidi, and even Coyote all lay claim to them. In one story, Begochidi may be called the controller of game, but only in conjunction with Talking God. In another, he is placed in charge of domestic animals.

How were Changing Woman and Talking God to gain control of the old Coyote's powers? Here the story of the theft of dream is instructive. Initially, Changing Woman speaks directly to Coyote, who agrees to obtain dream for her. We recall that the free soul leaves the body during dreams and trances and that the shaman directs and controls the free soul. Note that we are told not that Coyote controls dream but that he must steal it from Sleep, who is one of the monsters attacked but spared by Monster Slayer (Wyman 1970, 55, 56, table 2). Now Coyote turns dream over to "replica" Talking Gods who are not really Talking God but, coming from Canyon de Chelly, have some quality of "meanness." At this point the story becomes obscure, suggesting that dream was not been stolen from the monster Sleep but from the Holy People (Wyman 1970, 426–432). This sudden switch depicts Coyote in a negative light, and as if to reinforce this depiction, Monster Slayer refuses to take possession of dream because dream was created only to slay monsters. Talking God and Calling God agree to regain possession of the stolen dream. These deities are then able to retrieve dream from the Talking Gods at White House in Canyon de Chelly and return it to Changing Woman and the Holy People, thus making it part of Blessingway.

What began as cooperation between Changing Woman and Coyote has, by the end of the story, become the retrieval of dream by its original owners. The evil, shamanistic side is represented by Coyote, the replica Talking Gods are the thieves, and Changing Woman and Blessingway once again have control of dreams. But dreams are no longer the desired vehicles of the shamanic trance; instead, they may be used to foretell the future. In the case of bad dreams—when the soul has been involuntarily separated from the body as in dreams of journeying to the land of the dead—Blessingway is used to keep them from coming true (Wyman 1970, 224 n168, 337 n236).

The device of substituting replica beings is also used to enable Monster Slayer to obtain the power of Paiyatemu-Begochidi in the Eagleway. Monster Slayer has married the daughters of Changing Woman, who are Corn Maidens given corn by Talking God. Pueblo replicas of the Navajo Corn Maidens take Monster Slayer to their witch father, who teaches him his magic powers. To keep Begochidi at a remove from Monster Slayer, he is known by the name Game Chief or Corn Smut Man.

It is unfortunate that we have no recordings of ceremonialists engaged in discussions about the meaning of various myths. We know that such discussions were common, however, and that there were many points of disagreement. Because myths are the only means by which religion may be shared and transmitted in a preliterate society, a detailed knowledge of the narratives is necessary if new beliefs and ideas are to be woven into the preexisting corpus of knowledge. The means by which this is achieved are both elegant and sophisticated.[34]

34. The view that narrative knowledge is important is contrary to that proposed by Faris, who believes that interest in narrative is a Western quality and that Navajo ceremonialists are more concerned with ceremonial detail (Faris 1990).

PART 3

The Verities

7

The Creation

Christianity, Judaism, and Islam have been set apart from other religions by claims that monotheism represents the highest level of religious evolution. This all-powerful God created the cosmos out of nothing, created man in his image, and is, moreover, a moral god who continues to work in history. It is immaterial whether these beliefs originated in humankind's intellectual search for explanations of mysterious and awesome events and phenomena such as dreams, echoes, visions, and, above all, death, as postulated by Tylor, or were emotional responses to threatening situations. The crucial issue is whether monotheism and its attendant characteristics came after other beliefs and represent a greater degree of sophistication—are, in effect, the result of wider experience and "truer" knowledge. Recall that early evolutionists believed that the mind of the early human was less capable than that of the modern person and that, possessing less knowledge and experience, the early human's beliefs were of necessity naive and, in consequence, less true. This chapter considers Christian, Navajo, and modern scientific ideas of creation, then turns to questions concerning the nature of humankind and its position in the universe.

Myths of creation explaining the origins of the earth or the cosmos are found among most societies and would seem to satisfy the intellect rather than some deep emotional need. The possibilities, however, are rather limited. One can fail to ask the question entirely or be unconcerned, as the Netsilik Eskimo who said, "The earth was as it is at the time when our people began to remember" (Rasmussen 1931, 209).

Alternatively, one can posit that there was a moment of creation either from preexisting inert matter animated by a creating force or of inert matter by a preexisting creator. All of these possibilities are found in North American myths of creation.

Among the arctic Eskimos in general, mythology "reaches its lowest ebb" and "interest is in stories of realistic human situations" (Bierhorst 1985, 58). Yet even if individuals in these small societies were unconcerned about ultimate origins, there were among the Netsilik "a number of disconnected creation myths that point to the following underlying assumptions" (Balikci 1984, 425–426):

First, creation was conceived as a process of increased differentiation from the original chaotic condition. Second, human existence initially was dull and tasteless; following the appearance of suffering and pleasure it acquired meaning. Third, human wickedness seemed to be the source of all evil. Fourth, the creation of the visible world, the supernatural world, and the human moral order took place simultaneously, and in myth the three are considered as a whole.

Nor did Eskimos entirely lack the notion of a supreme deity. The Nunivak knew a great "Universe Being" or "Spirit of the World" who was occasionally heard but never seen, and who was probably the great regulator of the world (Lantis 1984, 220).[1]

A common thread running through North American creation myths is the preexistence of formless, chaotic matter, usually the primeval water. In the Great Basin, it is Coyote who creates the earth by pouring sand on the primeval waters and who then proceeds to create light. Among the Coast Miwok, Coyote shakes his blanket over the primeval waters and causes them to dry up. The Cahuilla myth starts with a primal void where red and white lightning clash to create twin creator heroes who are born in cocoons (Bierhorst 1985, 105, 114, 124). The Pima creation myth tells how darkness gathered itself into a great mass, inside which developed the spirit of the deity who drifted to and fro like a "fluffy wisp of cotton" (F. Russell 1975, 206). In none of these myths is it made clear that the creator god existed prior to matter, although the Zuni creator, Awonawilona, existed alone in the void and from his "thoughts" created mists that fell as rain, which made the ocean (Cush-

---

1. Although Margaret Lantis believes that Sklúmyoa is a male, John Bierhorst identifies the "supreme deity of the Nunivak" as a female creator (Bierhorst 1985, 61). And Lantis notes that the Nunivak had great difficulty in formulating this deity's form and functions.

ing 1896, 379).[2] All these myths agree that the first inert matter was formless and chaotic, dark and wet, and that the act or acts of creation consisted of bringing dry land and light into being before sentient life was created. The progress is from chaos to order, from the inanimate to the animate.

In his discussion of North American beliefs in a supreme being, Åke Hultkrantz notes that "some of the north-central California high gods are distinctly creator figures, and their creative process may furthermore be described as *creatio ex nihilo*." The high god of the Maidu, for example, after "prolonged intense thought, constructed the canoe in which he and his antagonist, Coyote, floated about on the primeval sea at the beginning of time." And the northern Pomo creator "came out on the ocean and turned into a man. He talked, and by the power of his words, the world came into being" (Hultkrantz 1980, 19–21). In neither case, however, is it certain that the god existed before inert matter. Moreover, the high gods of California are not essentially different from other deities, nor do they transcend nature. Instead, they are distant from the other gods and sovereign over them, but once the creation is accomplished, they tend to withdraw from the scene and leave others to work later transformations. These characteristics of the creation and the supreme being seem to be found all over the world. In Japan, for example: "In the beginning was chaos, like an ocean of oil or like an egg, ill defined but containing germs. From this confusion sprang a 'thing' likened to a reed shoot but conceived of as a divinity and given a name" (Saunders 1961, 417).

The Judeo-Christian Tradition

Because Judaism and Christianity have maintained that the *creatio ex nihilo,* the creation out of nothing, was one of the doctrines that differentiated monotheism from paganism, we may ask to what degree the Hebrew God differs from the high gods of North America. The first sentence of the Bible (Gen. 1:1) may be read either as "when God began to create the heavens and the earth" or "in the beginning God created the heavens and the earth." Both translations of

---

2. The creator of the Mbyá Guaraní of eastern Paraguay created himself from the original darkness (Bierhorst 1988, 58).

the original Hebrew are possible. According to Rashi, if the primary intent had been to teach the order of creation, the Hebrew would have been *bereshonah* (in the beginning) and not *bereshit*.[3] It was only later that scholars used the translation "in the beginning" as proof that God created out of nothing (Plaut 1981,18). Thus, depending on the preferred translation, a close parallel with other ancient myths may be claimed: out of formless and therefore chaotic inert matter, God created an orderly world, and water was given priority of existence. But the second account (Gen. 2) makes no mention of darkness and wetness. Instead, the earth and heavens were created without water, after which a mist watered the earth and man was created out of dust. At some point, the first chapter was accepted as the true creation of the cosmos, whereas the second was accepted as the account of the creation of men and women as well as of original sin and death.

Secular as well as religious scholars have claimed that monotheism and the *creatio ex nihilo* not only developed late but represent a higher form of religious thought. For the past century, biblical scholars have held that monotheism developed only slowly in ancient Israel and was preceded by a long period of either polytheism or of monolatry: "Instead of raising the abstract question as to whether or not other gods existed, Israel heard the command that it was forbidden for other gods to lay claim on her allegiance. The commandment does not say, 'There are no other gods,' but '*You* shall have no other gods' " (Anderson 1975, 97).[4] That the world is ruled by a council of gods was a concept common to the ancient Near East, and this concept is often echoed in the Bible: "God has taken his place in the divine council; in the midst of the gods he holds judgement" (Ps. 82:1).

Yehezkel Kaufmann, however, holds that the religion of early Israel was a "cosmic-national monotheism" (1960, 163). Israel knew YHWH as the one and only God who governed the entire world, but he had revealed his name and his Torah only to Israel and, in consequence, only Israel was obliged to worship him.[5] The ultimate expression of this

3. Rashi was a famous French rabbi of the eleventh century whose commentaries on the Torah and the Hebrew Bible are still standard.

4. Although scholars originally thought that the earliest religion was polytheistic, there is no evidence for a belief in polytheism in even the earliest books of the Old Testament.

5. "YHWH" is the Hebrew name of God. See Exodus 3:14–15, where God tells Moses, "I will be that which I will be," and that he should tell the people of Israel "YHWH . . . has sent me to you: this is my name for ever." *YHWH* is the third person singular of the verb *to be,* thus "He is" or "He will be."

cosmic-national religion, according to Kaufmann, was reached in Deuteronomy, where God himself apportioned false gods to the nations:

And beware lest you lift up your eyes to heaven, and when you see the sun and the moon and the stars, all the host of heaven, you be drawn away and worship them, things which the Lord your God has allotted to all the peoples under the whole heaven. (Deut. 4:19)

Then men would say, "It is because they forsook the covenant of the Lord, the God of their Fathers, which he made with them when he brought them out of the land of Egypt, and went and served other gods and worshipped them, gods whom they had not known and whom he had not allotted to them." (Deut. 29:25–26)

According to most biblical scholars, monotheism was made explicit only in teachings of Second Isaiah, and even Kaufmann agrees that prophetic eschatology reached its climax in the vision of the universal kingship of YHWH (Kaufmann 1960, 163).[6] In Isaiah we read:

Thus says the Lord, King of Israel and his Redeemer, the Lord of hosts: "I am the first and I am the last; besides me there is no god." (Isa. 44:6)

Was it not I, the Lord? And there is no other god besides me, a righteous God and a Savior, there is none besides me. (Isa. 45:21)

The distinguishing mark of monotheism, according to Kaufmann, "is not the concept of a god who is creator, eternal, or even all powerful; these notions are found everywhere in the pagan world. It is, rather, the idea of a god who is the source of all being, not being subject to a cosmic order, and not emergent from a pre-existent realm; a god free of the limitations of magic and mythology. The high gods of primitive tribes do not embody this idea"(1960, 29). According to William Irwin, "The great achievement of Israel was not primarily that she asserted the oneness of the world and of God, but rather the character of the God so affirmed. . . . Israel's monotheism was an ethical monotheism" (1946, 224, 227). To this might be added the observation that Second Isaiah advocated an historical monotheism that saw the whole course of history under the control of God, certainly not a trait of other creator gods (Buber 1949, 208–217). In sum, the God extolled by Judaism, Christianity, and Islam is claimed to have existed prior to inert matter, totally

6. The author of the latter part of the book of Isaiah, beginning with chapter 40, was an unknown prophet called Second Isaiah or Deutero-Isaiah who lived during the Babylonian Exile, preaching around 540 B.C.

apart from and in control of the world and the cosmos (despite the fact that Genesis does not make this absolutely clear), to be in absolute control of history, and to be the source of all true morality.

Presumably, the idea that the Hebrew God is free from the limitations of magic and mythology refers to the fact that, as Hultkrantz pointed out, the high gods of North America are not essentially different from other deities and may be compelled to act by the performance of imitative magic formulas. Yet it may also be noted that these high gods are distant from the other gods and, having withdrawn from the world, remain inactive and so may not be enmeshed in the magical rituals of humanity or the subsequent events of their creations. But why, exactly, it is preferable to be free of mythology is almost never explicated.

One such explanation has been attempted by Henri Frankfort, a humanist historian of the ancient Middle East. According to Frankfort, the key to the difference between mythopoeic and modern scientific thought lies in the fact that for the modern person the phenomenal world is primarily an "It" but for ancient and "primitive" people it was a "Thou."[7] That is, so-called primitives have only one mode of thought, the personal. And this animate world, perceived as a "Thou," was expressed directly as an image that must have been "seen in the revelation which the experience entailed." Thus, myths are products of the imagination but not mere fantasy. "Myth does not have the lucidity of theoretical statements because it is concrete with aspects of the irrational" (Frankfort 1946, 3–27).

Frankfort is saying, in effect, that the original, concrete revelation of Coyote experienced by the peoples of the Great Basin or Plains was also experienced directly when the migrating Athabascans passed through their lands and abandoned their trickster-transformer for Coyote. Because they were mentally incapable of abstract thought, the abstract concept best represented by Coyote could not have been borrowed by the Athabascans in order to facilitate communication and understanding. Frankfort does not explicitly claim that mythopoeic thought is prelogical. Nevertheless, he seems to rely on evolutionary theory.

Anthropological approaches to religion have taken for granted that biblical monotheism represents a later and, therefore, more advanced stage of religious thought. E. B. Tylor, for example, believed that religion had its beginnings in the belief in the human soul, which resulted from the universal experience of dreams and visions, or hallucinations

7. See also Martin Buber's *I and Thou* (1956).

(Tylor 1958). The soul concept easily accounted for other experiences. During life, the soul is attached to the body; at death, it departs. Similarly, illness could be accounted for by the temporary displacement of the soul, and the soul could leave the body during sleep, at which time dreams occurred. Once developed, the soul concept formed the basis for ideas about souls of lower grade and of spiritual beings in general, up to and including the supreme being. Moreover, along with this gradual monotheism, there is a progression from an amoral order in which the soul's afterlife does not depend upon deeds performed during its earthly life to an order that includes punishments and rewards for the soul depending upon its lifetime performance.

Evolutionary theory also encouraged the belief in a prelogical, "primitive mentality" that gradually evolved into the superior thought machine of modern, civilized man. The intellectual character of primitive man was based on a direct, unmediated apprehension of external nature: thus, as "mental energies go out in restless perception, they cannot go out in deliberate thought." Moreover, having no "general ideas," the primitive had no idea of causal relationships (Stocking 1987, 225).

The contention that the god of biblical monotheism was also free of the constraints of magic is derived from the proposed evolutionary development of theories of causation: Sir James Frazer saw magic as an early expression of science based on a false notion of the regularity of cause and effect processes (Frazer 1958).[8] Religion was a higher achievement because it substituted uncertainty and prayerful conciliation for misguided notions of causality. Science developed last and returned humankind to the principles of cause and effect, but on the basis of true correlation.

Some anthropologists attacked the evolutionary speculations of Tylor and Herbert Spencer. Andrew Lang disagreed with Tylor's belief that animism was based upon false ideas and that it could not explain the early appearance of high gods (Lang 1898, 66–67, 185). Wilhelm Schmidt used the evidence of hunter-gatherer societies with beliefs in supreme beings to argue that they possessed true monotheism and that later evolution of society was accompanied by a degeneration of religion (Schmidt 1939, 183). Lang's and Schmidt's arguments have been dismissed by Marvin Harris on the grounds that they were founded, not on social science, but on the religious belief that God revealed himself

8. Presumably James Frazer thought that all "primitive" explanatory systems utilizing the principles of "sympathetic magic" were not religions.

to early humans (Harris 1968, 206–207, 390–392). Their arguments have, however, found limited acceptance in the fields of comparative religion and the history of religion but without allowing either that the revelation came from God or that "mythological polytheism is a degenerate offspring" of primitive monotheism (Kaufmann 1960, 29).

Contemporary anthropologists appear to have added little to our understanding of the relationship between monotheism and polytheism. Hypotheses derived from Émile Durkheim's proposition that society is always the real object of religious veneration—that, in fact, humans create god in their own image (Durkheim 1965)—have been tested by Guy Swanson (1960) and William Davis (1971). Both find evidence to support the notion that societies comprising three or more sovereign groups ordered hierarchically have belief in a high god. But it is important to note that a respectable 57 percent of the more simple societies also have a belief in high gods.[9] On other issues, however, Swanson's and Davis's findings are contradictory. In their summary of cross-cultural research on religion, David Levinson and Martin Malone note:

Holocultural research has produced two clear findings about the development of religion: child rearing practices are in some way related to beliefs about supernatural beings; and societal complexity influences religious *practices*. But there is little evidence that social complexity influences religious *beliefs*. And the question of whether specific social organizational factors shape religious beliefs and practices is left unanswered. (1980, 150; italics in original)

The Navajo Creation

As told by Sandoval, the Navajo creation begins with a dark world that floats in water or mist. The clouds are the first things to appear, and they contain within themselves the elements of the world to come. A generalized force energizes the creation. Although no creator

---

9. There are a number of problems involved in selecting the sample, not the least of which is Galton's problem. The reported findings pertain to hierarchies at the national level. When local hierarchies are examined omitting nation-states, there are too few data on belief in high gods. See Robert Textor (1967), who used Swanton's codings as modified in the Ethnographic Atlas (Murdock 1967). In societies where the hierarchy of national jurisdiction has three or more levels, there is a statistically significant tendency for a high god to be present; 85 percent of these societies have this belief. But 57 percent of societies with fewer such levels also have a belief in high gods.

is mentioned, the first creative principles manifesting themselves are the characteristics of maleness and femaleness represented by First Man and First Woman and of chaos represented by Coyote. Sandoval mentions that Coyote disputes First Man's claim to being first; as we have seen, this uncertainty seems to result from the melding of two traditions: that of the hunting past, which gave Coyote precedence as the creator, and that of the agricultural period, which concentrated on the creative power of fertility conceptualized as the coming together of the sexes. Coyote also came to be conceptualized as a duality; the creative aspects of chaos are represented by the Coyote born of an egg, and the destructive aspects are represented by First Angry.

That all the elements of the worlds to come were already contained in the primeval mists is, of course, the agricultural metaphor of birth and growth that informs emergence myths in general. In addition, First Man and First Woman were formed at the same time as white and yellow corn and thus prefigure Changing Woman's creation of humans out of corn in the present world. Because the primacy of male and female principles is continually emphasized in the later stages of the emergence, I believe that primacy is a specifically Navajo response to the changing statuses of women and men after their arrival in the Southwest.

Navajo symbolism of the masculine and feminine principles differs little from what is found in many mythologies. First Man is said to have stood in the east and represents light and life. First Woman is said to have stood in the west and represents darkness and death. Almost all the world's cultures associate blackness with death and evil and associate whiteness with good and life; and when male and female are in opposition, as they most often are in the Navajo creation, the feminine principle often appears inferior or evil. When looking outward to the cosmos, myth equates blackness with chaos; when turned inward to the individual, blackness is the sign of death and the womb, and often black is associated with the west, because of the sunset.

The early introduction of the sexual division of creation found in Navajo myth is not found in Pueblo creation myths, although, according to Matilda Cox Stevenson, the Zuni creator is a "supreme life-giving bisexual power, who is referred to as 'He-She,' the symbol and initiator of life, and life itself, pervading all space" (1904, 22).[10] The Tewas also maintain a unity of the sexual principles by referring to the village chiefs as

---

10. In contrast, Frank Cushing refers to a male, "the Maker and Container of All, the All-father Father," who before the beginning, "solely had being" (1896, 379).

"father-mother" (Parsons 1929b, 109). Alone among Southwestern myths, the Navajo creation pays special attention to the opposition and conflict between the male and female principles, a subject dealt with in chapter 8.

As the emergence proceeds, later creations progress from the more general to the specific, until the present forms of the physical animate world are attained. The creative force is general and unnamed but is manifested in all creation. Although the animate force of creation is present in all things, there is still a conceptual difference between the animate life force and inanimate matter. First Man must place the inner forms of sacred mountains, but it is never made clear whether these "in-standing ones" are to be equated with the souls of animals and humans.

In sum, the Navajo creation is similar to that of Genesis in that the creation proceeds from chaos to order and from dark wetness to light and dry habitable earth. There is no high god: Instead there is an energizing life force that animates the cosmos and all later developments. A discrimination between the animate and inanimate is not made clear in the myth. On the one hand, that the life force is in everything suggests that there is no division, but on the other, that First Man must place an inner being in the sacred mountains indicates that inanimate matter must be animated as it is created at various stages in the course of development.

The direction of events is planned by First Man and those accompanying him rather than by an all-powerful and purposeful deity. Without a guiding deity, the issue of morality devolves on First Man. In the underworlds, evil exists but is controlled by First Man. With the emergence and the coming of Changing Woman, however, a sharp line is drawn between good and evil as the First Man group that emerged from the underworld is repudiated. Finally, the beings of the underworlds who are formless and known only by their inherent characteristics prior to the emergence are given their present forms and may no longer transform themselves at will.

Modern Cosmology

How do these ideas about the creation of the universe and of life compare to what modern cosmologists currently believe about these same topics? Scientific theories about the creation of the cosmos are still unconfirmed, and thus no one theory may be taken as the ultimate truth. As recently as 1950, for example, there were two rival hypotheses concerning the creation of the universe. Astronomers knew that the universe contains many millions of galaxies, each made up of billions of stars. They knew also that these galaxies are moving away from each other as the empty space between them expands. The first and simplest interpretation of these facts, which came to be known as the Big Bang theory, said that everything in the universe emerged from a point, known as a singularity, some fifteen billion years ago, and that all matter was created in one instant. Opposed to this theory was the idea that the universe might have been expanding forever—that as the space between the galaxies stretched, new galaxies were created out of nothing at all to fill the gaps. This would require the continual creation of new matter in the form of hydrogen atoms to fill the space between galaxies.

The dispute shifted in favor of the Big Bang theory during the 1960s with the discovery of cosmic background radiation, evidence of the remnant of the Big Bang fireball. For fifteen billion years, the hot radiation in the original fireball has expanded and cooled. The temperature of this radiation is just under $-270°C$—exactly the temperature it ought to be if the expansion of the universe has proceeded in line with Einstein's general theory of relativity. But if the Big Bang theory was to be confirmed, there had to be "ripples" in the cosmic background radiation, and initial observations could not detect these ripples: the observed radiation was too smooth and uniform for stars and planets to have been able to form.

Today, after observations made by the Cosmic Background Explorer (COBE) satellite, the Big Bang theory has been confirmed. Ripples of exactly the right size were detected in 1992. And these ripples give us a picture of what it was like some three hundred thousand years after the singularity: there were already wispy clouds of matter stretching across vast distances. The universe today is more than 90 percent in the form of dark matter. The confirmed theory has led to a great amount of cosmological speculation. At present, however, it is just that: speculation. In his recent book, *In the Beginning* (1993), John Gribben has summarized our knowledge and placed current theories and hypotheses into a coherent framework from which the following discussion is drawn.

The universe was born in a superdense fireball at a definite moment in time.[11] But the creation of the Universe from the Big Bang is precisely equivalent (within the framework of the general theory of relativity) to the time reversed mirror-image of the collapse of a big object into

11. A tiny split second after the moment of creation—just 10^{-35} of a second later—everything we can see would have been crowded into a volume of space only 1 mm across. That tiny seed would have contained all of the energy that later went into making up stars, galaxies, dark matter, and cosmic background radiation. Over the ensuing fifteen billion years, the seed grew to become the entire visible universe, with a diameter some 10^{28} times greater.

a black hole. The collapse of a previous cycle of a universe toward a singularity *could* have been the collapse of a black hole. The collapse of a black hole—any black hole—*can* lead to a bounce that creates a new universe, which suggests the idea of repeat universes. Moreover, every time a universe is created in a big bang bounce, the laws of physics it is born with are slightly different from those of the parent universe—that is, they mutate. By this reasoning, our universe is just one among a multitude of universes. And in some sense, each universe is competing with others for the right to exist. It is possible that this competition among universes might follow the rules of competition among species: evolution by natural selection.

It seems that we know, more precisely than anybody has ever known before, what the universe is made of, how it came into existence, and how much of the different kinds of matter there are. The universe is so efficient at the job of making stars and turning them into black holes that it could almost have been designed for the job. The ultimate fate of the universe is that the present expansion will first be halted then reversed so that it collapses into a singularity, the mirror image of the one that gave it birth. We actually live inside a huge black hole, one so big that it contains billions of other black holes. And what is more, we have a pretty good idea of what happens to anything that collapses toward a singularity inside a black hole.

The new understanding of cosmology suggests that such a large and complex system as our universe cannot have appeared by chance. Simpler universes came first, and every time a black hole collapses into a singularity and a new baby universe is formed, the fundamental laws of physics are altered slightly so that each new universe is not a perfect replica of its parent. Cosmologists have stopped short of suggesting that the universe is alive, but heredity is an essential feature of life, and this description of the evolution of universes works only if we are dealing with living systems.[12]

But before taking up the issue of the creation of living things, let us compare the ideas about creation and the cosmos discussed thus far. In order to do this, I will take scientific knowledge as a standard against which to gauge the mythical and biblical accounts, not in order to determine

---

12. The best discussions of the hypothesis that ours is a living planet are to be found in James Lovelock (1988; 1991). Lee Smolin, according to Gribben (1993, 260), is the only scientist who has taken the idea of the living universe seriously enough to publish scientific papers on the subject.

how "true" they are, but rather to evaluate their intellectual sophistication. Are the Navajo ideas of an animate universe, of a creation that contained the seeds of its future evolution from the moment of its birth, and of a progression from cold, dark, wet matter to a highly variegated and ordered cosmos, the perceptions of ignorant, primitive intellects in thrall to magic and mythopoeic thought? Or are they, given the paucity of empirically observed facts, nevertheless sophisticated speculations in no wise inferior to the monotheistic theology of Christianity and Judaism?

First, the ubiquitous idea of a creation out of chaotic, dark, and wet matter is at odds with the superdense fireball of the Big Bang. Yet the singularity *was* chaotic. Nor is the notion of the *creatio ex nihilo* unreasonable if one is taking only our own universe into account. If not, and we accept Gribben's speculative universes within universes, the Hindu idea of multiple creations is more in accord with contemporary theories. The question of whether the creative force existed independent of and prior to inanimate matter becomes a nonquestion because, in the Big Bang, matter *is* energy. And in this respect, North American Indian myths, as well as those of other preliterate peoples, agree more with contemporary cosmology than does the biblical idea of God creating inanimate matter first and living things later: The planet and the universe may, indeed, be animate. But much depends upon when one chooses to compare myth and Bible with science.

If this book had been written before 1960, even the steady state of the universe spoken of in the myths of some Eskimos and other forager societies would appear reasonable. And, although the planet and the universe may be considered animate, it is reasonable to argue that Earth was inanimate although not inert before living matter was seeded upon it. Whether, as earlier cosmology proposed, life was originally formed on earth or, as some think today, life was created in the universe, it is still reasonable to see life as a somewhat separate and independent creation that developed later out of preexisting elements.

Before the idea of evolution, it was commonly believed that the only way to explain the existence of so unlikely an organism as a human being was by supernatural intervention. More recently:

the apparent unlikelihood of the Universe has led some people to suggest that the Big Bang itself may have resulted from supernatural intervention. But there is no longer any basis for invoking the supernatural. We live in a Universe which is exactly the most likely kind of universe to exist if there are many living universes that have evolved in the same way that living things on Earth have evolved. And the fact that our Universe is "just right" for organic life-forms like ourselves turns out to be no more than a side-effect of the fact that it is "just right" for the production of black holes and baby universes. (Gribben 1993, 254)

The laws of physics and of evolution do, indeed, explain the cosmos as we know it thus far, and it is not necessary to invoke the supernatural. Nor, however, is it possible to rule out the supernatural. And here lies the difficulty. Once we have come to understand and accept the new cosmology, we will be faced with the same, seemingly eternal questions: Was there a beginning to this process of creation of universes, or is it eternal? If there was a beginning, an ultimate singularity, what came before and what will come after? Are these laws of physics that proceed blindly accidents, or is there some master calculus underlying everything, and, if so, who or what conceived of that calculus and set it in motion?

To the extent that one accepts the authority of the scientific enterprise as the final authority on questions concerning the material universe and how it came to be, the very nature of the monotheistic God is transformed. Many contemporary denominations of Christianity and Judaism have accepted science's authority and believe that "if any conflict develops between the new findings of science and the traditional texts of the faith, then the *texts* are inevitably in error," and although "they need not be revised," they must be understood to have "at best 'symbolic content'" (Klass 1995, 153).

In this conception God is no longer omnipotent. Even if God created the universe, he may no longer interfere with the laws of physics but must become distant and otiose. In this manner, the biblical God has come (or evolved?) in time to resemble the supreme deities of the North American Indians. No longer can God control the destiny of humanity, direct history, or provide absolute guidelines for human behavior. The Ten Commandments may still be adhered to, but they no longer have divine sanction. If a possible God is now distant and otiose, where does humanity fit into the universe, for just as God's domain has retreated to the edges of the universe, so have humans been dethroned, losing their unique place in the creation.

Ecce Homo

The first chapter of Genesis relates how God created, in sequence, the living beings of the water, the air, and the land. Only after he created these did he say: "Let us make man in our image, after our likeness; . . . male and female he created them." Then God said to them, "Be fruitful and multiply, and fill the earth and subdue it; and have dominion over the fish of the sea and over the birds of the air and over every living thing that moves upon the earth" (Gen. 1:26–28). The second chapter of Genesis reverses the order of creation of living things: the male human is created first and placed in the garden of Eden. After this, all other living things are created and, at the very last, the female is created out of the man's rib to be his helper (Gen. 2:6–22).

Man is placed between God and the rest of creation, and although woman is flesh of his flesh and thus, with man, dominant over the earth and life, she is subordinate to him. The man, Adam, is forbidden to eat of the tree of knowledge of good and evil because, should he do so, he would be like God in his knowledge: "The Lord God said, 'Behold, the man has become like one of us, knowing good and evil; and now, lest he put forth his hand and take also of the tree of life, and eat, and live forever'—therefore the Lord God sent him forth from the garden of Eden, to till the ground from which he was taken" (Gen. 2:22–23).

The punishment is severe—woman shall have pain in childbirth and her husband shall rule over her, and man shall toil incessantly for his subsistence, only to die and return to the dust from which he was made. The punishment was for disobeying God's command, not for aspiring to be like the gods. Both knowledge of good and evil and immortality were possible but were not part of God's plan. Presumably, life in the Garden of Eden was to have been one of innocence and ease but not of eternal life. Death was always part of the plan.

For the Navajo, death was not a part of any plan until First Man decided it would not come into existence. Unfortunately, Coyote interfered and saw to it that there would be death. Death was necessary, it was later argued, so that there would be room on earth for future generations. In consequence, death was not an evil willed upon the world by Coyote so much as an unavoidable necessity.

The difference between the Navajo animate universe and the inanimate creation in the Bible is clear, but it is not immediately apparent how the Navajo concept of humanity's place in this creation differs from that of the Bible. Biblical man was close to God and above the rest of creation. Are the Navajo earth surface people also positioned somewhere above the animals and the earth? The answer would seem to depend upon the biblical and Navajo concepts of the soul and whether death was final or only a temporary separation from the source of life—whether that source be God, the Holy People, or supernatural power in general.

Christian and Jewish concepts of the soul developed slowly and always involved considerable controversy. Ancient Israel identified a soul, the breath (*nefesh*) or wind (*ruach*), and a ghost or shade (*shäd*). Shade is usually translated as "ghost" because the word can also mean "demon," perhaps because handling the deceased was defiling. There was no idea of a judgment in the afterlife and death was final. There was also the notion that the ghost, or soul, went to a netherworld called Sheol to sleep, but this idea was ignored by the author(s) of Genesis, where the soul is the breath or wind of God, the body is the earth (*adamah*) out of which the body was made, and death is a return to dust after God has withdrawn the breath (Gen. 3:19; Ps. 104:29).

The problem of the delivery of the soul from death remained unsolved in the Bible. Later Judaism (see Ezek. 37:1–14) and Christianity came to believe in an eternal soul that was rewarded or punished in the afterlife and that could be resurrected whenever God willed. Christian concepts of a body-soul dichotomy originated with the ancient Greeks and were introduced into Christian theology by Augustine and others.

Greek beliefs were also varied. Pythagoras, Plato, and Socrates believed that the soul was of divine origin and existed both before and after death. Aristotle believed that the soul was composed of two parts and that only one, the *nous* or intellect, was immortal, whereas Epicurus believed that both body and soul ceased to exist at death. The early Christians adopted the Greek concept of the soul's immortality and thought of the soul as being created by God and put into the body at the time of conception. The dual soul concept adopted by Aristotle was not an uncommon belief; the Egyptians' dual soul included the breath (*ka*) that survived death but remained near the body while the spiritual *ba* went to the land of the dead.

It is unclear to what degree the ancient Hebrew and Egyptian beliefs parallel North American dual-soul concepts and the resulting problematic identity of the ghost and soul. Navajo eschatology, like that of ancient Israel, is vague, and the creation myths say little on the subject. The soul, or wind (*nitch'i*), enters the body soon after birth and leaves it at the time of death. For four days, the ghost (*ch'įįdii*) remains near the place of death, during which time the ghost is dangerous and may cause sickness or even death.[13] Many Navajos maintain that there is no life after death and, as in the Bible, the only form of immortality achieved

13. *Ch'įįdii* is derived from—*ch'įįd*, lacking (a body?).

is through one's descendants. Other Navajos believe in an afterlife as well as a deity of the underworld.

The soul may also be referred to as *bik'ehgo ntséskeesi*, "that by which I think" (Franciscan Fathers 1910, 87), which serves to equate the soul with the mind, or consciousness. But, with no clear elucidation of the fate of the soul, its relation to the animate universe is problematic. We recall that First Man placed an "inner form" inside the sacred mountains. "By themselves natural phenomena are lifeless, but an inner human form set within them functions as their life principle. This vitalizes and also personalizes each phenomenon" (Wyman 1970, 24). Navajos sometimes equate the inner form (*bii'istíín*) with the wind or soul, which is also called an "instanding one" (*bii'sizinii*), but, according to Father Berard, the inner form and the "instanding one" actually represent a dual concept. Because each inner form is in human form, it also has a wind or soul (Haile 1943a).

Plants and animals are conceived as existing "in man form" (*t'a dinégo*) and can remove their plant and animal form at will; after humans have made use of them, they return to their "man form." "The animal or plant form is merely a cover, or attire, in which the real supernatural appears on the surface of this earth" (Haile 1943b, 67, 69). Presumably this idea derives from the myth time, Luckert's period of prehuman flux, during which the Holy People could appear either as animals or humans and were not yet restricted to their animal forms. Because these beings possessed individual personalities both during the myth time and afterwards, it follows that a human's wind or soul has an inherent nature prior to entering the body at birth. A mean soul may predispose the human it inhabits to commit self-destructive or other mean acts because the soul controls every action and every movement of the body it inhabits (Ladd 1957, 289, 389ff, 417ff, 421ff).

It would appear, then, that the souls of humans, animals, plants, and natural phenomena are all part of the original life force and creative power of the cosmos, and that there is no sharp distinction made between the nature of the supernaturals and the souls of the life forms of the present world. It would follow that souls return to rejoin this supernatural power after death and that humankind does not occupy a special place in the universe either in relation to the deities or to other living species. Should this be the Navajo view, it would be a form of pantheism compatible with the notion of Gaia as well as with current religious concepts such as the Quaker belief that God is in us and in all things. Both John Farella and Gladys Reichard have taken this position.

Są 'a naghái bik'e hózhǫ́ has been called the key concept in Navajo philosophy by Farella, who also provides the most satisfactory description
and analysis (Farella 1984). The concept has two parts: *są 'a naghái* has
been glossed as "long life," and *bik'e hózhǫ́* has been glossed as "happiness." Such translations, however, are too simplistic. The first phrase
refers to repeated rejuvenation and reanimation exemplified by the human goal of growing old. The second phrase refers to the attainment of
the first phrase according to all that is perfect and harmonious. Reichard
renders the two phrases as "according-to-the-ideal may-restoration-
be-achieved" (1963, 45, 47). According to Reichard, these concepts
synthesize all Navajo beliefs, including ideas about the universe, humankind, time and space, creation and growth, and the life cycle. Gary
Witherspoon has identified *są 'a naghái* and *bik'e hózhǫ́* as the "central
animating powers of the universe" that produce the "ideal environment
of beauty, harmony, and happiness" (1974, 56). And Farella enlarges
upon these interpretations:

By saying that one is *sa'a naghái bik'e hózhǫ́* makes emphatic one's direct relationship to the beginning of life in the universe. . . . As part of this I will
die, my life force (*są'a naghái bik'e hózhǫ́*) will return to the Dawn and become part of the "undifferentiated *nítch'i*" that will animate future living
things. . . . The gradual relinquishing of boundary and of ego as one grows
older in the ideal case is again part of this process, as is the absence of *ch'įįdii*
(or a part of one's spirit that holds on to life). (1984, 179)

"If man, like every other conceivable thing, becomes *sa'a naghái*, he
must lose not only his body but even his individuality—the very antithesis of Christian teaching," which strives for "future personal survival and resurrection by trial on earth" (Reichard 1963, 45). Both
Farella and Reichard recognize that other anthropologists and, indeed,
many Navajos do not agree with them:

It is on the fate of this life force or "soul" that there is fairly serious disagreement among Navajo philosophers today. . . . The disagreement cen-
ters on the degree to which the ego or identity is maintained within the
nítch'i bii'sizíinii after death. . . . The view that I prefer has a being's
nítch'i . . . becoming, as it were, a part of a kind of undifferentiated pool of
nítch'i. (Farella 1984, 127)

In contrast to the belief that individuality is lost after death, there
is much evidence to support the view that many Navajos believe in an
afterlife, a continuation of the soul, and a deity of the underworld. Navajos gave Leland Wyman, W. W. Hill, and Iva Òsanai (1942) descriptions

of the afterworld similar to those recorded for other tribes. In my own work on suicide, I found the notion that the souls of suicides went to a different place than those of other humans (Levy 1965). Nor were people sure that witches went to the same place after death as did the majority of souls. Some believed there is a witchery hogan in the underworld, where either the souls of witches and suicides go or, alternatively, where all souls go. There are also myths that tell of a First Death Woman who represents the first person to die after the emergence.[14]

The belief in the persistence of the soul after death may often be inferred from the practice of burying personal possessions with the deceased. According to Mary Shepardson (1978) Navajos bury their dead in good clothes with their jewelry and their personal property because, if property were withheld, the ghost would return to seek it and bother the living. Horses are also killed, but not placed with the deceased in the grave, so that the dead may ride to the afterworld in style. But, according to Haile (1917:31), items of war are scrupulously barred from the grave because "a warrior, upon arrival in the nether world, must not intimidate the spirits there" (1917, 31). Similar beliefs and customs are noted for the Chiricahua (Opler 1965, 472–478) and Western Apache (Goodwin 1969, 518–521).

The coexistence of different ideas about the fate of souls after death is not uncommon. All Hopis say that the dead travel to the spirit world. However, some maintain that the spirit world is underground, just as in myth the person who died first is seen underground from the place of emergence, whereas others say that souls go to the spirit world in the sky and become clouds to bring the rain and, ultimately, may become katsinas (Emory Secaquaptewa, personal communication). Differences of opinion among the Navajo are more marked: opinion is divided not just about whether the soul goes to an upperworld or an underworld but whether the soul (*nił'chi*) is the same as the ghost (*ch'įįdii*) and whether the soul retains or loses its personal identity.

In examining this difference of opinion, two items demand attention: first, the Navajo account of the first death combines an old and widespread account of how the culture hero or trickster brought death with the Hopi story of the first death caused by a witch; second, there are two ways to refer to the soul, the commonly found reference to "wind" or "breath," and words that also refer to the mind and thought. Navajos

14. See the discussion of myths of First Death Woman in John Farella (1984, 209–210).

are unconcerned by disagreement about the location or presence of the spirit world. But they take seriously the issue of the retention of personality after death: many brand as witchcraft the idea that the soul retains its individuality (Farella 1984, 127–128). During the years immediately prior to the World War II, Wyman, Hill, and Òsanai (1942) found that most of their informants believed that the *ch'įįdii* (ghost) would remain in this world to avenge insults or slights suffered during life. This belief would seem to indicate the retention of individual personality. There was considerable disagreement among Navajos over whether the soul and the *ch'įįdii* constituted a single entity representing the good and evil nature of an individual. An evil person's soul could become ghost *ch'įįdii* and endanger the living. If the individual was predominantly good, the soul never became *ch'įįdii*. Many, however, argued that there were two distinct entities involved. Both the soul and the ghost entered the body soon after birth and went to different places after death. I argue that an earlier set of soul beliefs that Navajos brought with them from the north came, in time, to conflict with Puebloan beliefs that became integral to the Blessingway tradition, and that this conflict was difficult to reconcile.

We recall that, as narrated by Sandoval to O'Bryan, the first death was caused by Coyote: he threw a stone into the water, saying that if it sank people would die. Because First Man had cast a stick into the water saying that if it floated people would not die, Sandoval added: "So it was decided that, although there would be death . . . , sometimes the very ill would recover because the log had floated" (O'Bryan 1956, 30–32) However, some four years earlier, when Sandoval told the myth to Goddard, Goddard translated the passage as: "The axe sank but the stick floated. Because it floated, a person's soul comes to life again. Because the axe sank, people die" (1933, 138). Farella assumes that Sandoval used *nilchi* for what Goddard translated as "soul" (Farella 1984, 127), but in the original transcription it says "because of this his *mind* (*'ání* or *bíni'*) will live again" (Goddard 1933, 36,37). It is unfortunate that we don't have the original Navajo of Sandoval's second narration. I suspect that, because he did not use *nilchi*, his intent was closer to O'Bryan's translation.

The use of *mind* for the soul echoes an earlier dual-soul concept. In all of North America except the Southwest, the dual-soul concept is found in one form or another. Humans are equipped with two souls: one that invests the body with life, and another, the dream or free soul, that may leave the body during dreams, trances, and states of altered consciousness. Death comes when a person's free soul is caught in the world of the dead; when the free soul is caught, the body soul, often conceived as breath, also slips its moorings (Hultkrantz 1980, 130–132). The reader will immediately recognize that the notion of soul loss as a cause of disease occurs when the free soul is stolen by witches or carried away by the dead. When it reaches the land of the dead, the patient, who has been delirious or more or less unconscious, dies. The shaman has the ability to attain a trance state during which his free soul follows to the spirit world and retrieves the patient's free soul. The belief in a life here-after in a spirit world was repeatedly strengthened by the evidence of dreams and visions during which individuals traveled to the land of the dead and returned.[15] The decline of shamanism among the civilizations of Middle America and among the Pueblos of the Southwest led to a weakening of the dualistic conception of the soul and the development of a pantheism according to which the soul was referred to as the breath or wind and represented the life force that animated the universe.

There can be no doubt that the Navajos once had a dual soul concept and shared it and related ideas with other northern Athabascans. The Kutchin, for example, believed that the "breath soul" went into the sky at death but the "shadow soul" left the body sometime before death took place and lingered after death before going underground. The shadow soul might linger about the place of death or former residence out of a desire to remain with friends or to obtain revenge for past injuries. In consequence, the time during which it lingered and might come into contact with the living was dangerous (Osgood 1937, 169). The Kaska believed that the wind soul did not die but continued in an afterworld and might be reincarnated. The shadow soul remained near the scene of death and manifested itself as a ghost (*tsune*). The afterworlds were in the sky—one afterworld was one for good souls, another was for evil souls, and a third was for suicides. Evil souls could be reincarnated be-cause they would be refused entry to the afterworld (Honigmann 1954, 136, 154–156). In contrast, the Fort Nelson Slave were vague about the afterlife (Honigmann 1946, 86, 87). Other Slave identified the shadow soul with "thought" residing in the head. After tiring of wandering about the earth, it could enter the body of a woman and be born again (Mason 1946, 33, 37). Dead people also lived in the sky, but there are no other kinds of spirits because animals were formerly human.

I believe that the soul that is referred to as the mind or "that by which I think" was once the free soul and that, once the Navajos abandoned

15. On travel to and return from the land of the dead, see also Åke Hultkrantz (1953).

the dual-soul concept, the *ch'įįdii* came to represent the temporary, dangerous phase experienced by the free soul before it departed finally for the spirit world. Because the Navajos have in general adopted the Pueblo concept of a single soul, the persistence of older beliefs causes not only disputes but also confusion. The old idea that evil souls may be reincarnated is consistent with a notion of the persistence of individual identity and thus also causes confusion because reincarnation is denied by virtually all Navajos. And yet those who argue against the continuation of individuality after death explain that witches steal the bodies of recently deceased relatives and then eat or have intercourse with them so that, in a sense, they continue to live in an attenuated and evil form (Farella 1984, 128).

Hopis refer to the witch as a "two heart," a belief that indicates no more than a lingering remnant of the dual-soul concept, because the heart is not thought of as the seat of the soul. To live, the witch must take the soul of a living relative, who then dies. As long as the witch is able to feed off the souls of relatives, he or she continues to live. Finally, however, the witch dies and turns to dust because he or she really has no soul. This lack of soul resolves the problem presented when the dual-soul concept is abandoned. Witches have no real souls and so cannot merge with the cosmic life force. They do, however, prolong their lives by stealing the souls of others. The Navajo notion that any continuity of individuality after death is witchery appears to approximate the Hopi view.

Neither Navajos nor other American Indian societies ever come close to the biblical conception of man created in God's image to have dominion over the earth and all life upon it. At one time, animals were in human form but could change their form at will. At death, animals return to their original form as souls identical to those of humans. The return of the wind or souls of animals, humans, and the "instanding ones" of natural phenomena to the cosmic life force obliterates any distinctions. There are, nevertheless, indications of a tendency to make humans the center of the universe.

When animals are hunted, the hunter must observe rituals to avoid offending the soul of the hunted. Yet not all animals are accorded the same degree of respect; some are hunted with elaborate ritual, others with none at all. Deer and elk are highly valued economically and therefore demand greater ritual care. The grizzly bear is powerful and dangerous and may only be killed for ceremonial purposes or if it has killed a human (Hill 1938a). Similarly, some natural phenomena appear more powerful than others; sacred mountains, whirlwinds, thunder, and lightning all appear to possess more powerful souls than hillocks and other minor physiographic features. And insects, despite their mythological importance, receive little ritual attention.

I have never been told, nor have I found any reference to Navajo belief that some animals have no souls. Among the Hopi, however, some of the smaller animals are believed to have no souls. Prayers sticks are not offered and no ritual is performed for the killing of rats, mice, or prairie dogs, because they do not have souls. There is nothing said about any birds except the eagle having souls (Beaglehole 1936, 18).

Psychologically, there would seem to be a tendency for the self to be perceived as the center of the universe: As the GI in one of Bill Mauldin's cartoons in *Stars and Stripes* maintained: "The hell this isn't the most important foxhole in the world. I'm in it." Thus there might be some question concerning the existence of souls among the smaller and less important species, especially insects. Nevertheless, one must conclude that the extreme species-centrism of Christianity and Judaism is not a part of Navajo, or indeed of other American Indian, cosmologies. Moreover, I suspect that theological reasoning leads to the idea of a single life source to which all souls return after death and the subsequent loss of individual identity, whereas the psychological tendency to be egocentric leads to the relative inattention paid to unimportant species and the occasional belief that they do not possess souls. That the belief that unimportant species lack souls has not been elaborated or become a part of recognized eschatological belief certainly makes Navajo belief very different from Christian notions.

Scientific knowledge of human evolution has expanded rapidly in recent years, accompanied by a steady erosion of our notions of human uniqueness. Insofar as we share over 90 percent of our DNA with chimpanzees, the difference is more one of degree than of kind. Chimpanzees learn, make tools, and have a social structure, individual personalities, and even rudimentary communication skills.

Advances in the neurosciences have led most sciences to abandon dualistic ideas that separate the mind or consciousness from the matter of our bodies. It is now generally accepted that inside our skulls there is a brain that is sometimes conscious, and that brain processes cause consciousness in all its forms. Consciousness, however, is the central mental phenomenon, and the one that has been the most difficult to explain and understand.[16]

16. For a recent critique of current theory concerning consciousness, see John Searle (1992).

In the present state of our knowledge, we have no clear idea of how brain processes cause consciousness. We all have inner subjective, qualitative states of consciousness, and we have intentional mental states such as beliefs and desires, intentions and perceptions, but we understand the notion of an unconscious intentional state only in terms of its accessibility to consciousness. We know there is an unconscious capable of producing seemingly intentional behavior from such conditions as the "absences" of the petit mal seizure, during which the brain functions and the individual is able to continue to play a piano or drive an automobile. Afterwards, however, the individual is unable to recall what was done or why. We are also inclined to attribute intentionality to these unconscious states, although they do not meet the conditions for having intentionality. Indeed, some have even argued that there is no such thing as the unconscious, at least in the sense that Freud conceived of it.

I suspect that the difficulty contemporary psychologists and philosophers have in understanding the relationships between the conscious and the unconscious is similar to the difficulty many Navajos have had in understanding the mind and the soul. Moreover, I suggest that this difficulty was caused in part by the transition from the dual to the monistic soul concept. During sleep or trance states, the body continues to live (breathe) while subjectively the consciousness is active and operating apart from the body. With only the breath soul, dreams about travel to the spirit world, which are accepted by Hopis and Navajos alike as being "real," make it difficult to explain why the body is still breathing when the soul is on its journey. In any case, however, given the lack of any knowledge of the workings of the brain, the concept of a soul is neither unreasonable nor irrational.[17]

In sum, it appears that Navajo ideas about the creation of the cosmos and life are at times similar to the ideas of modern science and at other times closer to biblical notions. In neither case, however, may they be thought of as unsophisticated and certainly not simple or primitive. Moreover, the lack of clarity regarding the nature of the soul and its fate is caused by the persistence of earlier ideas and by the difficulty inherent in any attempt to conceptualize the intangible. Even today, religious practitioners differ among themselves concerning the nature and the fate of the human soul.

17. Even in the modern world, many people are convinced they have traveled to the "other side" during near-death, out-of-body experiences, and many of the movements within what has been called the New Age seek to reconcile these beliefs with modern science.

8

Good and Evil,
Order and Chaos

Because life is sometimes pleasant and sometimes remarkably unpleasant, most societies consider the divine principle ambivalent; God is a coincidence of opposites. Where there are many gods,
individual deities may be either wholly good or evil, or they may embody both principles. In myth, deities are seldom seen as exclusively one
or the other. Sometimes these dualities are seen as both opposite and
united, as in the cosmic symbol of the yin and yang, or they may be conceived as opposing parts of the same deity seeking integration. In the
view of some contemporary scholars, this ambivalence of good and evil
is natural not only because nature is sometimes hostile but also because
the unconscious is ambivalent. According to this view, myth is very close
to the unconscious and often its direct expression; it is only the rational
intellectual conscious that separates the natural ambivalence into polar-
ized absolutes (J. Russell 1977, 56).

Evil, however, is never clearly defined. Is it possible that evil is nothing more than everything unpleasant as opposed to everything pleasant?
According to the *Random House Dictionary* (2d edition), evil is anything morally wrong or bad, anything harmful or injurious, and anything characterized or accompanied by misfortune or suffering. The *Oxford Dictionary of English Etymology* says that the primary sense is
"exceeding due limits." It might appear that natural events that cause
harm and suffering are as evil as events or actions that exceed due limits—limits that must refer to man made boundaries of morality. Yet in
fact, evil is conventionally divided into passive evil, that which occurs in
nature, and active evil, that which results from human malevolence.

The development of monotheism in ancient Israel presented problems not found in earlier religions—namely, how to justify God's omnipotence, his holiness and justice, when he also created or allowed the existence of physical and moral evil. God's creation is good, and man is a unique creature, the darling of God. By forbidding Adam the tree of knowledge of good and evil, God concealed evil from Adam without blocking his way to it. Adam was not entirely unaware of evil, however; he knew the difference between right and wrong but disobeyed God's command, knowing that a punishment would ensue. That is, he knew the difference between life and death and that death was something to be avoided. The Bible conceives of sin as a consequence of human freedom: "See, I have set before you this day life and good, death and evil . . . therefore choose life, that you and your descendants may live" (Deut. 30:15, 19). This conception has meaning only if good and evil were within the range of experience from the beginning.

After eating the forbidden fruit, "The eyes of both were opened, and they knew that they were naked" (Gen. 3:7). Eve had been created to be a helpmeet for Adam; they had intercourse and bore children only after their expulsion from the Garden of Eden. Thus, the archetypal sin according to the view expressed by the J tradition was sex and procreation, and procreation is not the blessing it is in the tradition of P in Genesis 1:28, where humankind is told to be fruitful and multiply. Man and woman did not become absolutely evil, but their evil tendencies raged more fiercely. With Cain, envy, murder, and the lie came into the world, and by the time of the flood, "The lord saw that the wickedness of man was great in the earth, and that every imagination of the thoughts of his heart was only evil continually" (Gen. 6:5). But even though humans chose evil, the one God was the source of both good and evil: "I form light and create darkness, I make weal and create woe, I am the Lord who do all these things" (Isa. 45:7).

In an attempt to explain the workings of God's justice, retribution for the sins of others could be visited upon an individual who had done nothing. Thus, the sins of the fathers were visited upon the sons; so also were the sins of relatives, countrymen, and the king. And God could afflict humans in order to test their loyalty, as was the case with Abraham, Job, and the people of Israel condemned to wander in the wilderness. God might be patient with sinners or change his mind and so withhold his punishment (Exod. 34:6; Jon. 4:2), or he might wait until the sins had reached a certain level before punishing them (Gen. 15:16).

But, because God was the only power in the universe, no human act could be performed unless God willed it. God caused Abraham to pretend Sarah was his sister and not his wife (Gen. 12:17). When Pharaoh innocently fell in love with Sarah and proposed marriage to her, God proceeded to punish him and his family with disease. And it was God who hardened Pharaoh's heart so that he refused Moses permission to lead the Hebrews out of Egypt, and God who punished the whole country with plagues and the deaths of all the Egyptian firstborn. This would seem to contradict the idea that humans could choose to sin. Perhaps because of this contradiction, another line of speculation was set in motion: that the devil was permitted by God to tempt humankind to do evil.

The book of Job introduces the *satan* (advocate, adversary), a member of the heavenly court who, with God's permission, tests Job's faith and loyalty.[1] Satan is an aspect of the one God, but a trend toward dualism has begun, a development that has produced a constant tension within Judaism and Christianity that continues to the present day.

In the time of Zechariah and in later Judaism and Christianity, *Satan* became a proper name.[2] In the first work of apocalyptic literature, the book of Daniel (167–164 B.C.), evil is not clearly personified as an adversary of God, but to man and woman's disobedience is added the revolt of the fallen angels. In later apocalyptic literature, the world and history are dominated by the forces of evil and the idea of two kingdoms takes form. Two ages are created by God (4 Esd. 7:50): In the first Satan will triumph and Satan is the "god of this world" (2 Cor. 4:4). Ultimately, however, God will conquer Satan and overcome all the demons. In God's kingdom there will be eternal life, joy, and peace. It is likely that this approach to complete dualism was influenced by Iranian Manichaeanism, which saw the opposites as two dissociated, independent forces.

The contrast between experienced reality and the religious ideal was so disturbing that the Bible continually questions the discrepancy, asking how faith in a just and good God can be maintained in the face of experience. Always God is justified. Koheleth (Ecclesiastes) was the most

---

1. In the Hebrew, the definite article is used (*hasatan*) and refers to someone like a prosecuting lawyer in a court, an advocate or adversary. In an earlier passage, an angel of the Lord who blocks the road in front of Balaam on his ass is referred to as a satan (Num. 22:22–35).

2. Zechariah began prophesying after the return from exile and the rebuilding of the temple circa 520 B.C. (Zech. 3:1–2).

pessimistic of questioners, concluding that there was no justice in life and that all the individual could do was to enjoy to the full the good things God had given and to be resigned to endure the evils, knowing that in the end all die and return to the dust. The six concluding verses of the book were written by an editor who, fascinated and troubled by its contents and recognizing the danger to faith posed by its skepticism, added the final statement: "In sum, having heard everything, fear God and keep His commandments, for that is man's whole duty. For God will bring to judgement, even everything hidden, whether it be good or evil" (Eccl. 12:13–14).[3]

By the time of Basil the Great (circa A.D. 330–379), Christian theologians attempted to solve the problem of dualism by denying the ontological reality of evil (Eliade 1982, 46–50). Earlier, Plato had made this same argument, and Augustine, Aquinas, and Maimonides were also to develop the theme. The world created by God is real, and therefore good. Evil contains no good and therefore has no substance or reality. But if evil has no being, it can have no principle. This approach does not deny the reality of moral evil, which exists as an absence of good; it does, however, remove the responsibility for evil from God.

The conflict between good and evil stands at the center of New Testament Christianity. Traditional monotheistic theodicy tries to dismiss the Devil, thus leaving the idea of God incomplete and unbalanced through the abolition of its antithesis.

In spite of the efforts of generations of theologians to reduce or abolish the role of Satan, the concept of the Devil has persisted. Christianity is in fact a semidualist religion. . . . The tension between monism and dualism has led to inconsistencies in Christian theodicy. The function of the Devil in the New Testament is as counter principle to Christ. The central message of the New Testament is salvation: Christ saves us [from] the power of the devil. If the power of the Devil is dismissed, then Christ's saving mission becomes meaningless (J. Russell 1977, 228).

The notion of original sin is never developed as a doctrine in the Old Testament and is not mentioned in the Gospels. Paul, however, explains that sin and death entered the world through the sin of Adam (Rom. 5:12–21), and neither New Testament nor later Christian tradition held that the Devil forced Adam's will. Not only does the later Christian emphasis on the importance of original sin deny to the Devil the role of the

---

3. This translation is from Robert Gordis (1951, 190). See also his chapter 14, "The World View of Koheleth."

originator of evil—his fall came after that of Adam—but it also detracts from the godlike nature of humans by making them a combination of opposites, both good and evil.

Before turning to Navajo conceptions, let us consider chaos as an aspect of evil. Chaos appears in almost every mythology as the formless, inchoate state that exists at or before the beginning of the world. Cosmogonically, blackness is chaos; ontogenically, it is the sign of death and has ambivalent associations with the Devil. "It is in one sense good: it is the creative potency, the unleashed power, without which nothing would be. But in another sense it is bad: it must be transcended for the gods or men to exist. So chaos may be perceived as a monster, a Leviathan or a Tiamat, that must be overcome" (J. Russell 1977, 66–67).[4] So, too, is the trickster, the spirit of disorder, the enemy of boundaries. But by upsetting order, the trickster may release creative energies as well as destroy established values.

Israel was impressed with the regularity of nature and saw it as an evidence of the grace of God who chose to order his world for the benefit of humankind. After the flood, God promised that

While the earth remains, seedtime and harvest, cold and heat, summer and winter, day and night, shall not cease. (Gen. 8:22)

In contrast, the most terrifying aspect of the land of the dead was that it had no order:

"Let me alone, that I may find a little comfort before I go whence I shall not return, to the land of gloom and deep darkness, the land of gloom and chaos, where light is as darkness." (Job 10:20–22)

Only the regularity and system of nature make planning and purpose in human life possible:

Let us fear the Lord our god, who gives the rain in its season, the autumn rain and the spring rain, and who keeps for us the weeks appointed for harvest. (Jer. 5:24)

After the biblical period, chaos loses importance for New Testament and later Christianity. It does, however, reappear much later in works such as Milton's *Paradise Lost,* Goethe's *Faust,* and Karl Barth's *Kirchliche Dogmatik.* In *Paradise Lost* God creates chaos along with the rest

---

4. Tiamet was the Babylonian goddess of the primeval water—in other words, the goddess of chaos.

of the cosmos. It becomes a nonplace separating Heaven from Hell but is not equated with evil. Goethe's Mephisto is the very spirit of chaos in nature who also promotes disorder in society by disrupting justice. The modern Protestant theologian, Karl Barth, included "nothingness" as one of the three elements of reality with God and God's creation. This echoes the Platonic conception of evil because, lacking true being, chaos is not a part of God and God has, therefore, no evil side. Unlike Plato, Augustine, Aquinas, and Maimonides, however, Barth believes that the Devil who is nothingness, chaos, and the opposition to real being has enormous power to distort and destroy. The Devil is the lie underlying all lies (J. Russell 1986, 9, 159, 265).[5]

Both evil and chaos are central concerns in Navajo myth. The Navajo word for evil is *'iiníziin*, meaning "malevolence, evil wishes, and witchery." Coyote is the symbol of chaos, which may also be expressed by *tsi' hahashłááh* (to cause disorder). And we recall that the *tsi* prefix connotes all forms of extreme and irrational behavior.

"Now in the first dark world there were First Man, Water Coyote who knew all about water, First Angry Coyote who knew all about land, and various insects—wasps and ants who killed with their witchery" (Goddard 1933, 127; O'Bryan 1956, 1–3). Chaos and witchcraft as well as the male and female principles were there from the beginning. Unlike Coyote of the Plateau, Great Basin, and Plains, here Coyote is twinned: Coyote of the primeval waters is still the creative principle, and First Man deferred to him in all things; First Angry Coyote, presumably the evil side of chaos, nevertheless claims priority of creation. Despite Coyote's primacy and the statement that First Man deferred to him, no instance of Coyote's leadership occurs in the narrative. Instead, First Man is the planner and prime mover, and Coyote serves only to disturb the plans occasionally. First Man is cast as a creator deity, and First Woman plays a subordinate role, serving primarily as the opposite twin of an essentially monistic deity.

According to Sandoval, there was no unity of opinion concerning the origin of evil: "Some medicine men claim that witchcraft came with First Man and First Woman, others insist that . . . witchcraft originated with the Coyote called First Angry" (O'Bryan 1956, 3). I would like to think that this diversity of opinion represents the opposition of the Blessingway to the Coyote-Begochidi tradition, although it may just as easily have arisen from the complexity of the problem as it was explicated in the myths.

---

5. Martin Buber also holds this view of the Devil in *Good and Evil* (1952).

According to the Evilway singer Gishin Biye', First Man drew all the witchery of the first underworld into himself and thus became imbued with witch power. But this was done in order to create the medicines of the *haneełnéehee* used to combat witchery. In this way, First Man as creator contained within himself both the evil and its antidote in preparation for the surface world yet to come. After the creation of genitals, Coyote announced there would be birth, and Gishin Biye' claims that Coyote was the source of an evil that did not exist before (Haile 1981, 38). As in the Bible, sex is labeled as evil, and the reason for that label is not given.

Torlino, the Blessingway singer, omits all mention of First Man and First Woman in the first underworld. Instead, it is in the fourth world, the last before the emergence, that the masked Gods appear and create First Man and First Woman from corn and instruct them to live together as husband and wife. They teach First Man and First Woman about the use of masks and witchcraft, and witchcraft is associated with the incest of the children born to First Man and First Woman (Matthews 1897, 70). Torlino also denies Coyote's primacy by having him born after First Man and First Woman and only play a key role during the separation of the sexes. In this extreme expression of the Blessingway tradition, although witchcraft still appears in the underworld, it is not associated with the demonized Coyote but with the Pueblo Masked Gods, who give it to First Man in order that it may be controlled. Coyote may symbolize all evil, but he is not the originator of evil—except for sexual excess. His association with this single evil is consistent with the Navajo concern about uncontrolled sexuality that developed during and after the period of intense contact with the Pueblos. It also reveals the internal contradictions that emerge in the struggle to give Changing Woman and the masked gods domination over the earlier deities: Coyote is evil and First Man practices witchcraft, but the masked gods must be omnipotent, and thus they must have created First Man and given him witchcraft. In the process that dualizes good and evil, the Navajo ceremonialist faced the same problems as did the Christian theologian.

Witchcraft is clearly an active evil practiced by humans in the present world. Like biblical sin, in doing evil, the individual chooses to act malevolently. In order to become a witch, one must be initiated into a fraternity of witches as well as kill a near relative, usually a sibling. Witchcraft is also associated with sibling incest, although it is unclear whether incest is a prerequisite for learning witchcraft. Witches also practice necrophilia and cannibalism. In short, they are the negation of all that is good. "Persons become Witches in order to wreak vengeance, in order to gain wealth or simply to injure wantonly—most often motivated by envy" (Kluckhohn 1962b, 25–26). All of these acts are breaches of the moral code, but unlike in Christianity and Judaism, there is in Navajo religion no equivalent of the Ten Commandments and no divine sanctions.[6] Navajo culture has been described as shame-based rather than guilt-based (Leighton and Kluckhohn 1947; Piers and Singer 1953): "The Navaho never appeals to abstract morality or to adherence to a divine principle. He stresses mainly practical considerations: 'If you don't tell the truth, your fellows won't trust you and you'll shame your relatives'" (Kluckhohn and Leighton 1974, 297).

It is the malevolent intent that is evil, not the act itself. An individual may be the victim of witchcraft that makes him or her commit a bad act. A person might kill another by accident or out of uncontrollable passion. This latter comes close to the notion of possession: "He was not himself," or "I don't know what came over me." In fact, even a murderer is often not condemned for the act (Levy, Kunitz, and Everett 1969).

Passive evil—the catastrophes that modern humans attribute to natural causes—are, in most instances, not considered evil by the Navajo despite the fact that evil originated in the first underworld. Often such events are attributed to witchcraft: a riding accident may be considered the result of a witch's evil intent. Famines and epidemics may also be considered the result of witchcraft. The general class of passive evils, however, has been handled in a very different manner.

As a consequence of the abnormal sexual acts engaged in by women during the separation of the sexes, numerous monsters were created that inhabited the present surface world at the time of the emergence. These monsters preyed on the people, who were technically Holy People but are portrayed as mortal humans insofar as they were killed by the monsters. The Hero Twins born to Changing Woman killed most but not all of these monsters. We may think of the monsters as aspects of chaos in much the same way as Leviathan is the primordial dragon of chaos fought by the king of the gods in Canaanite myth. In Isaiah (27:1) it is God who will defeat Leviathan, the fleeing serpent. Job (3:8) refers to magicians who have the power to "rouse up Leviathan," and God himself describes the terror of the monster in graphic terms (Job 41).

---

6. The possible exception to lack of divine sanctions is the belief that sibling incest will result in generalized seizures.

Monster Slayer and Born for Water rid the world of these monsters, including those that Leland Wyman labels "obstacles treated as monsters": Crushing Rocks, Slashing Reeds, Cane Cactus, and the Sliding Sand Dune (1970, 52–59). Others monsters are attacked but spared— Sleep, Hunger, Poverty, Lice, Old Age, and, according to some, Death.[7] Thus, the evils of the world that plague humankind continue because, in some way, they also serve useful purposes.

Although the monsters were the result of the women's deviant sexual acts, it was Sun who mated with a woman and so sired Big Ye'i (Fishler 1953, 54; Haile 1938, 79; Wyman 1970, 507; Zolbrod 1984, 216). And Gladys Reichard (1963, 76) notes that the elk antler, cactus, stone, and other items used as dildos "were manifestations of Sun, to whom generation is ultimately ascribed," which suggests that all the monsters were children of Sun rather than Coyote's creations. In this manner, the Blessingway tradition is able to account for the origin of evil, passive as well as active, without having recourse to a primal Coyote. This, of course, tends to contradict the coeval notion that Coyote is the prime symbol of evil.

Coyote, First Man, and, indeed all of the First Man Group are evil despite the fact that Sun is here conceived as the prime source of creation and its evils. It is not until the appearance of Changing Woman that we are provided with a deity who is wholly good—who embodies all that is valued by the Blessingway tradition and who totally divorces herself from the Holy People who emerged from the underworlds.

The Navajo response to passive evil is closer to the solution presented in Ecclesiastes: one must do good and be resigned to suffering the inevitable miseries of this life. Christianity and Judaism have not been able to accept this resignation that makes it difficult to have faith in an omnipotent God. Instead, there is the promise of an afterlife, either in Heaven or Hell, or a final judgment heralded by a Messiah and followed by God's kingdom. Ultimate justice may be expected only after death.

Christians have never been entirely satisfied with these answers. Pelagius, an elderly British monk who arrived in Rome in A.D. 400, had an unlimited confidence in the possibilities of human intelligence and will. He believed that by practicing virtue and asceticism, every Christian was capable of attaining perfection and thus sainthood. The individual alone

---

7. In several versions of the Monsterway myth, death is not even mentioned as a monster.

was responsible for his or her sins, but since a person has the capacity to do good and avoid evil, Pelagius rejected the idea of an automatic and universal original sin. If sin is innate, it is not voluntary; if it is voluntary, it is not innate. The goal of infant baptism is not to wash away original sin but to sanctify the new life in Christ. This view was considered heresy and was attacked by Augustine but not definitely condemned until A.D. 579. In contrast, Martin Luther affirmed that free will is a fiction, that no one has it in his or her own power to think a good or bad thought, and everything happens by necessity (Eliade 1982, 244).

In the modern world, several secular explanations of active evil have been proffered. Some believe that the source of human evil is biochemical, an aggression response to perceived threats. According to this view, aggression is universal and may even be powerful enough to destroy us completely when coupled with advanced technology. But this can hardly explain violence and evil that go well beyond the bounds of defense of life or territory. The second popular view is that environment determines behavior—that society, not the individual, produces evil. Behaviorism undermines notions of responsibility and choice so that there is no longer any basis for values that are not arbitrary (J. Russell 1977, 26–28). Societies develop moral codes, but these are specific to the needs of each society. Situation-based ethics—ethical and cultural relativism—make all values arbitrary.

In *Anatomy of Human Destructiveness*, Erich Fromm argues that genetic traits and the environment may predispose one to destructive and cruel acts but that they are not the sufficient cause. Destructiveness—that is, evil—is rooted in the individual's character, a character that chooses to do evil. But Fromm's view is almost a nonanswer: free will is asserted but not demonstrated and, other than the predisposing factors of genetic makeup and social environment, no other source of destructiveness is identified. One wants to know what makes one individual choose to do evil whereas another with the same predispositions does not.

Freudian theory posits a chaotic libido that is controlled by the ego and superego. The libido is amoral, the ego is reality oriented, and the superego represents the society's morality. Presumably, evil human actions are the products of unresolved tensions generated as the superego seeks to control the libido and, at times, the ego. Society, representing the parents, is cast in the role of the controlling, judging god. The libido is chaotic human nature that can know neither good nor evil until it is socialized.

None of the psychological explanations can really deal with evil in the sense that religions do because such explanations never go beyond the limitations of ethical relativism. A contemporary attempt by a psychiatrist to transcend these limitations has no better success. In *People of the Lie*, M. Scott Peck admits the inability of modern psychology to deal with the question of evil: "We do not yet have a body of scientific knowledge about evil sufficient to be dignified by calling it a psychology" (1983, 10). Like Fromm, Peck does not find a single source of evil but finally concludes that a major factor is "the mysterious freedom of the human will" (Peck 1983, 84). Peck is, today, a believing Christian: "After many years of vague identification with Buddhist and Islamic mysticism, I ultimately made a firm Christian commitment" (Peck 1983, 11). His modern desire to find a scientific explanation of evil and, I suspect, his reluctance to accept behaviorist ethical relativism have led him to accept an objective system of values.

Cultural and ethical relativism have also engendered controversy in modern anthropology. Reacting against evolutionists' acceptance of cultural and, hence, religious superiority (albeit a superiority tempered by tolerance), anthropologists first developed the concept of cultural relativism as a tool for cross-cultural research. In order to understand another culture, the observer must hold all judgment in abeyance and seek to understand each society in its own terms. Inevitably, this led some to accept a relativist philosophical position. Others have been unable to accept such a position. In a critique of Ruth Benedict, George Peter Murdock says:

> Benedict held, not only that cultures must be viewed in the context of the situations faced by the societies that bear them—a position with which few modern social scientists would quarrel—but also that they must be viewed as wholes. To her, every culture is a unique configuration and can be understood only in its totality. She strongly implied that the abstraction of elements for comparison with those of other cultures is illegitimate. An element has no meaning except in its context; in isolation it is meaningless. I submit that this is nonsense. Specific functions, of course, are discoverable only in context. Scientific laws or propositions, however, can be arrived at, in anthropology, as in any other science, only by abstracting and comparing features observable in many phenomena as they occur in nature. (1965, 146)

Clyde Kluckhohn has summarized psychologists', sociologists', and anthropologists' arguments against ethical relativism and argued that "ethical universals are the product of universal human nature, which is based, in turn upon a common biology, psychology, and generalized situation. . . . One cannot derive values from scientifically established facts, but these facts can be meaningful in validating ethical norms" (Kluckhohn 1962a, 285). All cultures have moral systems that go beyond temporary circumstances or special situations. Every culture, for example, has a concept of murder distinguished from various forms of "justifiable homicide." Regulations of sexual behavior are also universals of human society.[8]

Contemporary social science places good and evil firmly in the realm of the human condition and places the nature of a moral code within the historical situation of each society and culture. The affirmation of the universality of human nature may make possible a vision of a uniform worldwide society in which all inhabitants agree upon what is right and wrong and what is good and evil, but even this utopian vision cannot disallow the view that good and evil are human and not objective constructs.

Other than the chaotic nature of the inferred unconscious, the social sciences tell us little about chaos. However, the current interest in chaos theory may help us gain insight into how cultural factors affect the scientific project.

Most nonscientists who have read about it know chaos theory through the "Butterfly Effect" or by its technical name as "sensitive dependence on initial conditions." This dependence makes chaotic systems unpredictable, because even the smallest degree of vagueness in specifying the initial state of the system will produce enormous errors in calculations of the system's future state (Gleick 1987, 20–23). The discussion that follows is based on Stephen Kellert's book *In the Wake of Chaos* (1993), unless otherwise noted. Kellert's elegant exposition of the implications chaos theory holds for our notions of predictability and determinism applies not only to modern science but also to more popular conceptions of the universe and the world around us.

The chaos with which the theory is concerned is not the chaos of incomprehensible tumult but rather of the intrinsically unpredictable nature of unstable aperiodic behavior. Chaos theory strives to apply mathematical techniques to phenomena like turbulence and thus may provide a new understanding and conception of nature that accepts randomness and contingency. Moreover, chaos theory insists that we rethink all our notions about the applicability of classical models.

---

8. A cross-cultural study of sexual morality found that incest and the abduction of a married woman were punished in 100 percent of societies studied; rape and bestiality by an adult were punished in over 90 percent (Cohen 1966, 13).

The deterministic worldview of classical physics holds that the next moment in the evolution of the universe flows out of the present one according to intelligible rules—that is, the entire universe is a deterministic system. In fact, the ideal goal of total predictability has been called the "classical myth of science."[9] For the purpose of this book, the important questions to be asked are: What accounts for the current explosion of interest in chaos theory? Why did it take so long for scientists to focus attention on these phenomena?

The problem of the ultimate stability of the solar system was of concern at least as early as Gottfried Wilhelm Leibniz. In 1892, Jules-Henri Poincaré provided a proof of the very weakness that Leibniz suspected in Newton's system of mechanics; in fact, Poincaré discovered the tangled homoclinic trajectories that yield sensitive dependence on initial conditions in conservative systems. But, for some reason, almost all scientists ignored these results for some fifty years.

Much of the mathematics relevant for the study of chaos was available but not utilized, and many of the relevant experiments were feasible but not carried out. Moreover, when one of these experiments was in fact conducted, the chaotic behavior was dismissed and subsequently ignored. Yet engineers have always known about chaos. They called it "noise" or "turbulence," and used fudge factors to design around these apparently random unknowns that seem to crop up in every technical device. The mathematical models, analytic tools, and experimental devices to study nonlinear behavior were all present and available in 1920. But chaos theory did not emerge until after 1970.

Before 1970, solutions to a physics problem that contained probabilistic terms were not considered adequate. Scientific training skewed intuition, and students were turned away from nonlinear systems by placing an overwhelming emphasis on the study of linear systems. Scientists trained themselves not to see nonlinearity in nature. One factor contributing to this view was the pervasive social interest in the exploitation of nature, an interest that contributed to the institutionalized disregard of physical systems not readily amenable to analysis and manipulation. Nonlinear systems were simply seen as not being useful. The overriding interest in the domination of nature and the vision of the world as a clockwork mechanism implies that physical matter is inert and dead, and this attitude may be traced back to the biblical account of creation. God, after all, created the earth and gave dominion over it to humankind.

9. I. Prigogine (1980, 214), quoted in Stephen Kellert (1993, 52).

There is no sharp division between the scientific endeavor and cultural ideology. Nor is there such a thing as an intrinsically interesting problem. Science is influenced by ideology in the choice of phenomena considered important, the preference for certain methods to study them, and the judgment of which results are successful. The image of the universe as a machine arose during the scientific revolution: It "answered pressing needs for social order, and it bequeathed to science a concern for certainty, law, and predictability" (Kellert 1993, 156). The metaphor of the world as machine also functioned as a justification for power and dominion over nature. In the context of the social upheaval of the seventeenth century, the vitalist idea that matter is alive "could be seen as aiding and abetting disorder and chaos."[10]

At the time of the rise of modern science, women became strongly linked to the wild, disorderly features of the natural world, which supposedly had to be subdued.[11] American Indians were likewise linked to disorderly nature:

American practice in dealing with [the Indian] was largely rationalized by the theories of the Scottish Moralist philosophers. Wild nature for most Americans was not valued in itself but for what could be made of it—"A terrain or rural peace and happiness." Indians were a part of savage nature and, like the wilderness, had to be conquered so that nature could be domesticated. In its wild state, nature is not nearly as bountiful as we sometimes like to think. It is civilized man who domesticates nature and makes it over into productive gardens. Because Indians were a part of untamed nature, they too had to be domesticated. (Levy and Kunitz 1974, 9)

Attitudes toward nature have changed, and so have our metaphors about the world. The current explosion of interest in chaos may be accounted for by changes in the larger society and not just by the advent of digital computers that make it possible to see chaos almost everywhere one looks. Perhaps the emergence of the Gaia hypothesis and the increased concern over the preservation of the environment have played a role in this explosion of interest in chaos. And perhaps our perception of the orderliness of the world has changed because of the growing unease as the economy of the western world changes in ways that we do not yet fully understand.

The need for predictability seems deeply imbedded in the human animal. The mother's response to the infant, if consistent and predictable,

10. C. Merchant (1980, 195), quoted in Kellert (1993, 156).
11. Merchant (1980, 132), referenced in Kellert (1993, 156).

gives the baby a sense of security that prepare it for the changes to come. Human society is also dependent upon the predictable behaviors of its members—hence the development of rules, norms, and punishment for deviance. And as modern Westerners are being advised not to aspire to stable careers but to adapt themselves to a more mercurial and unpredictable work environment, so, I believe, Navajos once had to radically rearrange their notions of chaos and the predictability of the world around them.

From the time when the Navajos entered the Southwest, established contacts with the Pueblos, and began to learn the arts of agriculture, two centuries passed before the period of intense Puebloization demanded considerable adjustments in their way of life. Knowledge of Pueblo "maize lore" and hence the relevant myths accompanied the technological adaptations but did not necessarily lead to radical shifts in values or social organization. Between 1690 and 1770, however, when Pueblo refugees lived among the Navajo, intermarried with them, and formed small sedentary settlements, the pace of change must have quickened and the agriculturalist's ideal of a predictable world must have become dominant.

Hunters and gatherers lived in a world constantly threatened by capricious nature. There was order, of course, but it could give way to disorder at a moment's notice. The habits of game animals were closely observed and known to all, yet game could disappear without warning. In harsh climates, a sudden storm could not only disperse the game but also cause accidents that injured hunters and endangered their lives. Shamans attempted to gain a degree of control over nature by using sympathetic magic. Together, keen observation of nature and shamanistic magic provided hope for success and a good life. Under such conditions, imbuing the trickster Coyote with creative as well as destructive and capricious qualities was eminently sensible. One could adapt and live with chaos but never subdue it. Conversely, the regularity of the agricultural cycle fostered the perception of a predictable world disturbed only by "unnatural" factors such as witchcraft.

We cannot see the adjustments made by the Pueblos as they adopted the agricultural way of life, but these adjustments must have been far more gradual than the changes experienced by the Navajos. For this reason, we do not find contradictions in Puebloan myths about Coyote. He may still retain his association with hunting—an activity less important to the agricultural society—but he is never seen as a creator or the ultimate source of evil. In contrast, among the Navajo, Coyote oscillates between being the representative of total evil and a bringer of all-essential rain. His chaotic nature is mentioned but hardly elaborated upon. Nevertheless, as the shift away from a reliance on agriculture to pastoralism took place less than a century after the period of intense Puebloization, older perceptions did not die entirely. The life of pastoralists living in dispersed family settlements, preyed upon by Ute raiders, and intermittently at war with Spaniards and, later, Mexicans reintroduced elements of chance and unpredictability even as the perception of a predictable world was firmly in place. We recall that Frank Mitchell, one of the Blessingway singers mentioned in chapter 6, details Coyote's actions more than the other singers of Blessingway. Of special interest here is his argument for preserving some disorder in agricultural practices. Coyote argues against planting vegetation in orderly rows: "Make it so that [the rows of plants] exist everywhere on its [earth's] surface without any special order!" Mitchell also has Coyote argue that the inner being of humans should be allowed some unpredictability: "In like manner let it be so regarding those things which exist within him" (Wyman 1970, 346). This is an argument for the preservation of randomness or chaos.

As Berard Haile and Leland Wyman observe, this is a means by which the creative, good side of chaos is retained as part of Blessingway. But, because other Blessingway singers of that time did not show any tendency to argue for chaos, it is likely that Mitchell was more aware of the need to deal with chaos than were other exponents of Blessingway. Unlike many of the older religious practitioners, Mitchell had much experience in the world of wage-work and, as a tribal councilman, was familiar with the problems attendant on the implementation of the stock reduction programs (Frisbie and McAllester 1978). By the time he gave his version of the Blessingway myth to Haile in 1930, at age forty-nine, he had lived off the reservation while doing railroad work in California, worked for the federal government, a trading post, and a sawmill, and done construction work and freighting. He had also assumed the role of local headman and was conversant with government programs. He began to learn Blessingway seriously in 1918, when he was thirty-seven years old. He became a ceremonialist during some of the most turbulent years of the reservation period and, by the time he recorded his version of Blessingway for Haile, there were already large areas of the reservation that were noticeably depleted, which had led to discussions of possible stock reduction (Aberle 1966, 53).

Returning now to Navajo notions of good and evil, we can see that, by placing morality firmly in the realm of society, the Navajo appear more like modern psychologists and anthropologists. But attributing active evil to the malevolence of individuals who chose to become witches is similar to the biblical notion of free will. The belief that individuals are neither wholly good nor wholly bad is not only consistent with modern psychology but also permits judging the act without condemning the actor. It parallels modern discriminations among acts performed while insane, without premeditation, or by accident. And the willingness to insist on the desirability of living a "good" life according to *sạ'a naghái bik'e hozhǫ* without the promise of rewards in this or another life comes close to the view of Koheleth. Entirely lacking, however, is the notion of institutional, impersonal, or abstract evil that is found in many modern discussions. This may, perhaps, be because the Navajo have never experienced horrors such as the holocaust or, until recently, exploitation by large anonymous bureaucracies of the nation state.

According to the hunter tradition, chaos and evil were integral parts of the original creation, which also included order and good, and humans contained all these elements. People accepted the existence of chaos but tried to exert control over it whenever possible. Thus Coyote represented the primal life force that animated the cosmos. First Man was not only the original human but also the shaman who possessed supernatural power that enabled him to perform witchcraft as well as to protect against it. He was also a planner and transformer who worked to make the world habitable.

The Blessingway tradition seeks in every way to divorce chaos from the present world. Changing Woman supersedes those beings who emerged from the underworlds. The Twins destroy passive evil, the chaos represented by the monsters, and thus make the world safe for humanity. The monsters spared by the Twins must be endured because they perform positive functions. Hunger persists so that people will not constantly overeat. Poverty stimulates people to strive for better things and to replace their old, worn-out clothing. Even lice serve to combat loneliness and promote affection. And, although humans are not godlike, neither are they evil. Moreover, they may strive to approach a state of blessedness by living according to *sạ'a naghái bik'e hozhǫ*. Active evil remains, except that now it is brought by the masked gods themselves and is not an uncontrolled aspect of the cosmos.

In its notions of good and evil, Navajo philosophy is more akin to modern secular ideas than to Christianity. Moreover, the opposition between the two Navajo religious traditions appears not to have fostered any division of opinion among the people themselves. Evil is almost entirely a matter of free will and morality, and although a relativistic conception of morality and values is not salient, there is considerable leeway allowed when judging the actions of individuals. However, opposing ideas about the nature of order and chaos continue to exist, and some ceremonialists are more willing than others to assume a monistic position.

9

Men, Women,
and Men-Women

The division of humankind into two sexes has been a major concern of religions over the centuries. The reasons for this are numerous but probably derive in part from the perception that the task of uniting the sexes in a stable society is difficult. If procreation is the sole provenance of the female, does this imply that only the female possesses the power required for life? In the daily struggle for subsistence, the division of labor requires mutual cooperation if succeeding generations are to survive, yet the task of controlling and channeling disruptive sexual drives in the service of social stability leads to all sorts of conflicts. The persistence of social division in the face of an overriding need for unity and harmony has demanded explanation as well as justification.

In myth, the androgyne combines the attributes of the male and female and symbolizes perfection. When, however, the opposites split and are in opposition, the female most often appears inferior or evil. Alone she may have a positive character, as do Changing Woman and Spider Woman of Pueblo myth, or she can be a monster or a witch. Perhaps because religious specialists are most often male and males are most often the narrators of myth, dangerous and evil females figure prominently in the myths of most societies, and evidence for conflict between the sexes is found virtually everywhere. However, despite the ubiquity of female demons and witches, the source of all evil is rarely a female—perhaps because men are reticent to elevate the "inferior" female to such preeminence.[1]

1. In the classical world, high, intellectual magic was ascribed mainly to men, and low, practical magic was considered the province of women (J. Russell 1977, 172–173).

Myths accounting for the creation of the sexes are common world-wide. The creation of men and women is usually said to occur after the creation of the cosmos, the earth, and life in general. Often, men are created before women, as in the Bible. The Netsilik and Iglulik Eskimo tell of a terrible deluge that killed all the men and animals, after which two shamans emerged from the earth and lived together as husband and wife. One became pregnant: His penis split with a loud noise and he became a woman and gave birth to male and female children (Balikci 1989, 210; Rasmussen 1929, 252). Throughout South America, men and women are said to have been created separately and almost always from separate causes (Bierhorst 1988, 16).

Navajo myths are replete with the conventional figures of dangerous females: beautiful seductresses who appear as ugly hags the morning after or witches like Changing Bear Maiden, who murders her own kin. And we have seen that, in the creation, First Man is associated with white and the light, and First Woman is associated with darkness and death. Yet in several respects, Navajo myths refer to the sexes in a manner quite unlike the myths of other North American Indian societies.

The Navajo myth is unusual in that male and female are present at the beginning of creation, before the creation of the earth and the emergence of life from the underworlds. Pairs of male and female deities are not uncommon, but the Navajo first pair are presented more as progenitors of humans than as great creator deities like the male Sun and female Earth. This early division is not found in Pueblo creation myths. As we have seen, the Zuni have a preexisting "He-She" creator, and the original goddess of the Keresans is Thinking Woman, whose thoughts became reality.[2] There were already people in the underworld when the Tewa Corn Mothers were born, but in all other respects they are the supreme deities (Parsons 1926, 9). In any event, none of these deities presage the humans who come later.

The male-female division is, in fact, ubiquitous in Navajo cosmology and ritual. There is male and female rain, and ceremonies are performed according to their male or female sides. Stories, fabrics, and jewels may also be described as being either male or female: "Of two things that are nearly alike, or otherwise comparable; it is common among Navajos to speak of or symbolize the one which is the coarser, rougher, or more

2. See Franz Boas (1928, 7, 221, 222, 228), John Gunn (1917, 89), Matilda Cox Stevenson (1894, 26–27), and Matthew Stirling (1942, 1). The creative power of thought and the spoken word is comparable to the New Testament *logos* (John 1:1).

violent as the male, and that which is the finer, weaker or more gentle as the female" (Matthews 1902, 6).

The Navajo creation is also unusual in that the separation of the sexes is the most dramatic and detailed event in the long account of the journey through the underworlds. The event is not only a powerful argument for harmony between men and women but also for limits to be placed on unbridled sexuality, which gave birth to the monsters. Subsequent events like the creation of genitals and the origin of procreation also emphasize the dangers of sex and tensions between the sexes.

Countering these divisive forces is the beneficent deity, Changing Woman, and the hermaphrodite who serves as a mediator. The Navajos modeled the benevolent Changing Woman after the Hopi Huru'ingwuuti. But the first appearance of Changing Woman did not take place in the underworlds, and Changing Woman is not an original creator but the creator of mortal humans who were already prefigured by First Man and First Woman. The late appearance of Changing Woman in the myth is a reflection of the late adoption of agriculture, coming as it did after the Navajos' arrival in the Southwest, and it is likely that assigning the role of prime mover and creator to a female deity would have conflicted with the already well-entrenched Coyote or First Man.

In this chapter, I explore the notion that the division of phenomena into male and female and the pervasive theme of conflict between male and female are not the usual expression of conflict found in the myths of other religions but reflect an ongoing problem in Navajo society that resulted from the two major transformations of the subsistence economy, which, in turn, led to changes in the status of women.

The transition from hunting and gathering to agriculture, from a bilateral to a matrilineal descent system, and, later, from agriculture to pastoralism has made the relations between men and women in Navajo society more problematic and conflict-ridden than they are among other societies of the Southwest. During the approximately two hundred years it took for the Navajos to adopt agriculture and a matrilineal social organization, the position of women became secure: they inherited agricultural resources, became the owners of their homes and children, and formed the center of the extended family. After 1770, the population became increasingly dispersed until, circa 1830, pastoralism had become the dominant subsistence pursuit. Pastoralism is a male-dominated activity, especially where large herds of livestock are involved. Yet the position of women was well established, and the matrifocal family and matrilineal descent has persisted to the present. With the exception of marriage regulation, the matrilineal clans lost their functions, and, as agriculture declined, matrilineal inheritance of fields gave way to the bilateral inheritance of livestock.[3] In much the same way that the shamanism of the hunting past conflicted with the newly adopted Pueblo forms of religion, so the competition between men and women first emerged during the period of intense Puebloization. This competition later reemerged during the transition to pastoralism and became even more acute.

As warfare and transhumance developed and required that grazing land be protected from encroaching neighbors, men who were subservient to their in-laws found it difficult to exert the influence they felt was their due. The question arises whether references to the sexes in myth reflect these conflicts. If the references to conflict and changes in status that are found in myth are to be interpreted as something more than what is found among the myths of other North American societies, evidence for tension between men and women of a more intense nature must also be found in Navajo daily life.

There are several mythic events that seem to reflect changes in the status of women that took place as agriculture replaced foraging. Although the postnuptial residence rule among all the southern Apacheans is matrilocal, First Man asks First Woman to live with him. This event suggests that at one time it may have been patrilocal, and Sandoval comments, "So instead of the man going to the woman, as is the custom now, the woman went to the man" (O'Bryan 1956, 3). At one point after the emergence, a cuckolded chief mutilates one of his wives so severely that she dies. He cuts the ears off another and amputates the breasts of a third. After the third wife dies, he cuts off the nose of the fourth and, when she does not die, decrees that the greatest punishment for an adulterous wife is to have her nose cut off because the disfigurement will not kill (Haile 1938, 79, 81; Matthews 1897, 143–144). Mutilation for adultery was practiced by the Apaches but was known to Navajos only by tradition. The practice is unknown among the Pueblos. Thus the myth seems to refer to a custom abandoned after the period of intense contact with the Pueblos.

Changes in the girls' puberty rite also suggest a significant change in the status of women during this period. Unfortunately, the meaning of menstrual taboos are not clearly understood. In western North Amer-

---

3. For a discussion of these transitions, see Jerrold Levy, Eric Henderson, and Tracy Andrews (1989).

ica, it was universally believed that the menstrual discharge was dangerous and that it polluted the sacred as well as the profane. Moreover, the
menstruant was not thought to be in control of the discharge and so
was herself susceptible to harm. Robert Lowie notes that the horror of
menstruation is widespread and that the segregation of menstruants is
commonly accepted by anthropologists as a proof of women's degrada-
tion (1961, 203). However, he believes it far more likely that the causal
sequence was reversed and that the menstruant's exclusion from certain
spheres of activity resulted from the awe inspired by the phenomenon
of periodic bleeding.

In respect of the former interpretation, Mary Douglas suggests that
to express female uncleanness may not only express female inferiority
but may also serve to set clear limits to female intrusion in male affairs
(1975, 62). Biblical restrictions placed on the menstruant as well as the
woman giving birth define the woman as unclean and require purification and sacrifice before she returns to normal life. Moreover, the period of uncleanness is twice as long after the birth of a girl as it is for that
of a boy (Lev. 12).

Supporting Lowie's latter interpretation, Bruno Bettelheim states
that "the ability to demonstrate sexual maturity and childbearing probably aroused . . . admiration and envy in the male" and that men's attitude toward menstruation has a greater effect on the puberty rites of
girls than the physiological event itself (1954, 244, 245). George Devereaux goes even further, claiming that the taboos on menstruation reflect women's exalted state and their powers of creation (1950). Moreover, how the men in a given culture interpret the beliefs about
menstruation may diverge radically from the interpretations of women,
the former viewing the menstruant as unclean and dangerous, the latter
emphasizing their creative powers. For example, the restrictions placed
upon Papago Indian women would lead many observers to believe that
women in that society were subservient to men. Nevertheless, some Papago women viewed these and other restrictions as evidence of their
power (Underhill 1979, 17, 33, 41, 55, 57–61).

Seclusion of the menstruant is one of the key features of girl's puberty
ceremonies in North America. Among the northern Athabascans, seclusion was lengthy and at considerable distance from the family's camp.
Girls built rude willow breaks for themselves in the bush, where they sat
for ten days during their first menstrual period. Only six or seven days
were spent in seclusion at the time of each subsequent menstruation
(Honigmann 1946, 85). Among the Kaska, sequestration at menarche

was in an open camp located about a quarter of a mile from the dwelling and lasted for a month (Honigmann 1954, 122–123). Kutchin girls were sequestered at menarche for a period of up to a year in a special shelter sometimes a mile away from the regular camp (Osgood 1936, 141, 147).

John Honigmann's observation that "although any connection between menstruation and hymeneal bleeding was denied, people asserted that the initiation of sexual relations brought on menarche some five months later" may be interpreted as an attempt by men to claim responsibility for menstruation, thus denying women an independent source of power (1954, 122–123).

When the Apacheans entered the Southwest, they came into contact with Pueblo societies that placed little emphasis on girls' puberty rites. Indeed, the matrilineal societies of the continent usually did not have public ceremonies to mark the transition (Jorgensen 1980, 281). Moreover, the Pueblos tended not to seclude the menstruant or observe the restrictions found elsewhere (Jorgensen 1980, 536–546).[4] Over time, the Navajos made two major changes that moved them closer to Pueblo practice: the menstruant was no longer segregated, and the ceremony itself became a celebration of the attainment of reproductive power (Reichard 1963, 173).

At one time, according to Haile's informants, a girl was secluded in a separate dwelling during her first menstruation, and during this time she was feared and considered taboo. We recall also that in Gishin Biye's Blessing Rite version of events, it was First Man, First Woman, and Coyote who find the baby, name her Changing Woman, and perform the puberty rite over her after she experiences her first menstruation (Haile 1981, 154–161). In the Blessingway myth, however, the second menstrual period of Changing Woman is the occasion for a second puberty ceremonial. Berard Haile thought "this second ceremonial was introduced to wean Blessingway from every influence of the First Man group and place it under the direction of Talking God so that he and Changing Woman would control the entire rite in the future" (Wyman 1970, 9). In this way, an important older custom brought south by the Apacheans was incorporated into the newer tradition. Moreover, the

---

4. Among the Pueblos, first menstruation did not indicate the need to recognize the transition. At Hopi, changes in the status of girls were traditionally marked at around ten years of age by a change of hair style after the girls had spent four days grinding corn in their father's sister's house. On First Mesa, this ritual began on the evening of the day of first menstruation, a timing that Fred Eggan believed was the result of Navajo influence (Eggan 1950, 50–51).

puberty rituals of almost all the Apaches, like that of the Navajos, became in time large public occasions celebrating the attainment of reproductive power (Reichard 1963, 173).

The Navajos also adopted a tribal initiation ceremony for boys and girls similar to that of the Pueblos. Between the ages of eight and ten, Hopi boys and girls are initiated into the katsina cult during the Powamu ceremony in February. The ritual is marked by fasting and being whipped by the katsinas, after which they are shown the katsinas dancing without masks. "The Katcina initiations mark the introduction of the child to status in the tribe as a whole" (Eggan 1950, 49). A similar initiation for Navajo children was held on the next to last night of the Nightway. Instead of being whipped, the girls were touched with ears of corn wrapped in spruce twigs (Franciscan Fathers 1910, 498–500; Kluckhohn and Leighton 1974, 207–209). There is no mention of this initiation ritual in any of the Navajo myths.

These changes reflect the improving status of women coincident with the development of matrilineal descent and a subsistence economy based more on agriculture. There is evidence that this transition generated considerable tension. Throughout the myths, there are many references to marital discord and conflict, with adultery and sexual jealousy being mentioned most frequently. Either women are in rebellion against men or men appear to resent women's status and try to reassert their dominance. The most vivid account of the conflict between men and women is the story of the separation of the sexes in the lower world, which occurs in all versions of the origin myth. It is one of the pivotal episodes in the emergence, although the incident leading to the separation varies.[5] Some singers like Torlino and Gishin Biye' say that the incident was precipitated by a chief's wife who claimed that she had no need of men and could live without them (Matthews 1897, 71, 218, n32; Stephen 1930, 97). Klah and Goldtooth attribute the separation to the wife's adultery (Wheelwright 1942, 45–46; Fishler 1953, 24–25). Goldtooth, however, adds that when scolded by her relatives, the wife argued that she did not need a husband. He also states that Yellow Fox, Blue Fox, and Badger were gambling and causing divorces, which was another reason

5. The First Mesa Hopi and Tewa also have an account of the separation of the sexes that closely parallels that of the Navajo (Parsons 1926, 169–72; Stephen 1929, 3–6, 10–13). Elsie Parson's informant was aware of the Hopi origin of the tale but knew of no corresponding Tewa account. Because episodes leading to the emergence do not include a separation of the sexes in accounts recorded on either Second or Third Mesa, these First Mesa myths are most likely borrowed from the Navajos.

for the separation. Sandoval told Pliny Goddard that adultery was the cause of the separation but later told Aileen O'Bryan that it was because the wife thought she could live without men (Goddard 1933, 13, 128; O'Bryan 1956, 6).

The inability of the women, but not the men, to live alone becomes apparent when the women's crops fail year after year. After the women admit they cannot live without men and beg forgiveness, they are allowed to rejoin the men, but only after a purification ritual is performed and they are kept apart in a corral for a night (Matthews 1897, 73; Franciscan Fathers 1910, 350). Later, First Woman is still resentful about the separation and, out of pique, asks Coyote to steal the water monster's children, which causes the world to be destroyed by a flood (O'Bryan 1956, 8).

Accounts of adultery most often blame the woman. It is First Woman who decides "that she would not be the only one to commit adultery, but that woman in general would do that" (Goddard 1933, 138). Male resentment is also in evidence when, after the reunion, Begochidi decrees that "the male shall rule, and whatever your chiefs say, that must be done" (Wheelwright 1942, 48). The women then say, "Very well, we will keep the home clean, cook the food, and care for the children." In this way, the division of labor is made clear and permanent.[6] According to the plan of creation, woman is to be weaker than man: "They could not attend to the planting and harvesting as the men could, therefore men would be worth more than women" (O'Bryan 1956, 32–33).

Despite these conflicts, the ideal was for husband and wife to live together in harmony. In the myth, reproduction is originally intended to be asexual, but women begin to menstruate and babies are born as a result of copulation. This development, caused by Coyote fathering a child, makes it necessary to plan how husbands and wives should feel toward each other (O'Bryan 1956, 33). Unfortunately, with mutual love and sexual attraction comes jealousy. Wishing to lessen the disruptive power of sexual attraction, First Woman decrees that people should wear clothing. Yet sexual jealousy and adultery continue to plague marriages.

6. After the reunion, the women set to work making new clothing of cotton and deer skins, which points to an earlier period before wool clothing and a time when women worked the hides. Preparing hides continued to be woman's work among the Apaches, but among the Navajo, men came to work the hides, as is the custom among the Pueblos.

Patterns of suicide and homicide often reveal the "fault lines" of a society.[7] In Navajo patterns of suicide and homicide, we find dramatic evidence of the tensions between men and women. In the industrial West, suicide is predominantly an act of withdrawal committed by those individuals who are the least integrated into the social fabric—the widowed, divorced, and the single. The rate of suicide increases with age, reaching its peak with the elderly, especially the sick and isolated. Women appear to be less at risk than men: the proportion of male suicides is higher than that of female suicides (Durkheim 1951).

In Asian countries, most suicides are female, a fact that is thought to be related to the status of women; most Asian women have less freedom—legally, socially, and culturally—than do men (Headley 1983, 352–356). In his classic study of suicide in Europe, Émile Durkheim observes that female suicides lessen as divorces increase, and vice versa (1951, 188–189, 269, 274–275).

During the 1960s, when I studied Navajo homicide and suicide, their rates were comparable to those of the United States as a whole (Levy 1965; Levy, Kunitz, and Everett 1969). However, age-specific rates, the sex ratio, and motive were quite different. As in Asia and the Near East, age-specific rates for suicide are highest between the ages of twenty and forty years old. But, unlike these societies, Navajo men committed suicide fourteen times more often than women, and married men were more likely to commit suicide than the single, the sick, the divorced, or the widowed. The motive was most often sexual jealousy, and the act was an aggressive rather than a retreatist one. The suicides were aggressive because Navajos believe that the ghost of the deceased is dangerous and may cause illness or death among the living, and most male suicides took place in the homes of their wives, where they would be sure to be seen. There was also a high proportion of wife killing followed immediately by the suicide of the husband.[8] Women's suicides were more often retreatist in nature and took place away from the home.

More Navajo women were victims of homicide than were men, and women were killed at six times the rate of women nationally. The Navajo homicide victim was also most often the wife or lover of the offender.

---

7. Except where otherwise noted, data are from Levy (1965), Levy, Stephen Kunitz, and Michael Everett (1969), and Levy, Kunitz, and Henderson (1987).

8. During the 1940s, 32 percent of suicides were preceded by a murder, and in 78 percent of these, the wife was the victim. After 1954, however, only 7 percent of suicides were preceded by a murder.

Domestic quarrels and sexual jealousy accounted for 41 percent of all homicides from 1956 through 1965. By contrast, only 11 percent of homicides in the national population involved spouses or lovers, and husbands and boyfriends were victims almost as often as wives and girl friends (0.75 males to 1 female, Hacker 1983, 216–217). Moreover, these patterns in Navajo suicide and homicide had not changed appreciably since the nineteenth century (Levy and Kunitz 1974, 98–103).

Although the pattern of Hopi suicide is, in many respects, similar to that of the Navajo, it differs in its motives and causes. Like those of the Navajo, Hopi suicide rates are comparable to those found among neighboring non-Indian populations. And in both matrilineal societies, males are far more prone to commit suicide than females, a tendency that reflects the secure position of women in these societies, in which, incidentally, the divorce rates are high. Unlike the Navajos, however, Hopi suicides involve intergenerational rather than marital conflicts. The sons of parents who made disapproved marriages and sons rebelling against their fathers commit suicide far more than was found among the Navajos. In this respect, Hopi suicides are more like those found in Asia, where the older generation exerts considerable control over the lives of its children.[9]

Despite the many strains attendant upon contemporary Navajo adjustment to a wage-work economy that make the life of males particularly difficult, murder-suicide is not a new phenomenon among the Navajo. There are specific references to murder-suicide in the past. Leland Wyman and B. Thorne (1945) noted it in the 1930s, and A. H. Kneal (1950), writing of the 1920s, called a murder followed by a suicide the "Navajo custom." In a Navajo autobiography recorded by Walter Dyk, Son of Old Man Hat tells of a discussion he had with his mother when he was a boy sometime in the 1870s. Her response seems to refer clearly to a period before the removal to the reservation in 1868.

When a man talks as you're talking now, he gets that way. As soon as he gets a woman, as soon as they get acquainted he may start beating his wife, and they'll begin to have a quarrel every once in a while. . . . It's pretty dangerous to have a wife or a husband. Some men, when they have wives, may kill their wives or may get killed by them, and some commit suicide. (Dyk 1966, 47–49)

The descriptions of family conflicts in *Son of Old Man Hat* and those described in a more recent autobiography by Emerson Blackhorse

---

9. See Levy and Kunitz (1987) and Levy, Kunitz, and Henderson (1987).

Mitchell are strikingly similar (E. Mitchell and Allen 1967). The emotional lability of Navajo males and the traditional instability of Navajo marriage have been described by Dorothea Leighton and Clyde Kluckhohn, who also say that physical conflict between husbands and wives was frequent and common (1947, 109–111). It appears that the difficulties of Navajo marriage have not changed appreciably over the years.[10]

The position of the Navajo male was made difficult by the practice of matrilocal residence after marriage that demanded he take up residence with his wife's family. In many respects, the young husband was a servant in his wife's camp. He took orders from his father-in-law, who directed herding operations, and women dominated the domestic sphere. Unlike Hopi couples, whose families lived in the same village, a Navajo man lived too far away from his kin to draw emotional support from them or to have them take his part in marital quarrels. And whereas Hopi men found relaxation together in the all-male kiva, Navajo men very often found release from domestic tensions only when away on trading, hunting, or raiding expeditions or attending ceremonials.

This situation is dramatically illustrated by the different risk factors for hypertension found among Navajo men and women (Kunitz and Levy 1991). Among the last Navajo age cohort raised before the stock reduction programs of the 1930s and 1940s, there is no significant difference between men and women in the proportion of diagnosed hypertensives (about 17 percent), nor was there a significant difference among age groups. The prevalence was substantially lower than in the general U. S. population of the same age, in which it is 31.5 percent among men and 43.4 percent among women. Social isolation (namely, not living in extended families) and acculturation as measured by level of education, skill in English, and time spent living off the reservation put women but not men at risk for hypertension. For men, those who spent a year or more off the reservation tended to have a lower prevalence of diagnosed hypertension than those who remained on the reservation.

The most likely explanation is that Navajo men are exposed to as much stress in the "traditional" matrilineal society as in the more acculturated world of wage-work and off-reservation living. It might even

10.   In recent research among Navajo drinkers and nondrinkers conducted by Stephen Kunitz and me, 50 percent of a control group of women between twenty-one and sixty-five years of age in two areas of the reservation reported having been beaten by their husbands or partners. This is considerably higher than a lifetime prevalence of between 20 and 30 percent reported by studies in the general population.

be argued that, for many men, living in neolocal families and gaining experience in the Anglo world lessens the tensions generated by life among their wives' kin. The converse also fits the data: that women were more secure in the traditional matrilocal extended family and were exposed to more stress when forced to leave this protected environment.

Despite these conflicts and tensions, sex and fecundity are held to be desirable; the urge is not to be repressed, and no value is placed upon chastity or self-denial. Nor is there any idea that sexual indulgence depletes the male's strength. Nevertheless, sex itself may elicit fear and mistrust. Navajos do not expose their genitals to the view of members of either sex because it is widely believed that whoever looks at a woman's vagina will be struck by lightning and that viewing the male's glans penis will cause sickness. Moreover, the similarity between the words for the glans penis ('iich'ah) and the generalized seizure thought to be caused by incest ('iich'ạh) is striking, suggesting that, at some deep level, the sexual act itself is dangerous and may be associated with incest.[11]

Given these tensions between men and women, it would be reasonable to expect that the symbol of a bisexual principle might serve to mediate between the polarities in myth if not in real life, and it is to this possibility that attention is now drawn.

Nádleeh, The Man-Woman

In the first underworld, the male principle represents light and life, and the female principle represents darkness and death. "First Man burned a crystal for a fire. The crystal belonged to the male and was the symbol of the mind and of clear seeing" (O'Bryan 1956, 2). In Sandoval's account, the sexual polarity is mediated by male and female hermaphrodites who appear in the third world before the separation of the sexes. Beyond this rather formal presentation, however, the position of the nádleeh in the myths is ambiguous and not easily understood.[12]

11. The word for seizure is taken from that for the moth ('iich'ạhí), which flies crazily into the fire and serves as the prototypical symbol of incest in the myth of Mothway.

12. In one version, the hermaphrodites, when consulted at the separation of the sexes, object to the separation strongly but are forced to join the men (Curtis 1907, 85). The word nádleeh (hermaphrodite, transvestite), combines with dleeh (to become, to revert), with the prefix na again (he repeatedly becomes or changes).

Torlino averred that First Man and First Woman gave birth to barren hermaphrodite twins and, soon after, to another twin pair, this time a boy and girl who later committed incest (Matthews 1897, 70). Klah said that it was Begochidi who created the first hermaphrodite (Wheelwright 1942, 40). According to Sandoval, both hermaphrodites were originally female but when they later became the original sun and moon carriers, Turquoise Hermaphrodite became male (O'Bryan 1956, 5 n.18, 15). Because Sun and Moon demand a human life for each time they rise and set, their function is not entirely beneficial. Gishin Biye' said that the hermaphrodite, Begochidi, was the moon carrier and also possessed datura and other poisonous weeds (Haile 1981, 34). By naming Begochidi rather than Turquoise Boy as the *nádleeh*, Gishin Biye' associates the *nádleeh* with Frenzy Witchcraft and incest as well as with death.

According to the Blessingway singer Frank Mitchell, the sun and moon carriers are Rock Crystal Young Man and Sunlight Young Man (Wyman 1970, 378). The association of Sun and Moon with Begochidi is not denied entirely, however, as the two youths are married to White and Yellow Begochidi Maidens. According to Torlino, one of the twin hermaphrodites born to First Man and First Woman was the first to die in the present world (Matthews 1897, 77). In nearly all other versions, the first to die was a woman, sometimes a chief's wife. She goes to the underworld and is thought of as an evil spirit of the dead.

According to Klah, the Follower Pairs ("Two-Who-Follow-One-Another"), who figure so prominently in the Blessingway, were created as hermaphrodite twins by Begochidi in the second underworld, but because Black God did not like them, he remade them as a male and female (Wheelwright 1942, 41–42, 45).[13] This transformation allows Blessingway singers to omit all reference to Begochidi and to say that the Follower Pairs were the children of Dawn Woman and the Sun who were assigned to be the inner forms of the six sacred mountains (Wyman 1970, 10, 26). Moreover, the first pair of inner forms who were to become the inner form of the Earth were known as Long Life Boy and Happiness Girl (Wyman 1970, 28).[14]

Whether because of a preexisting ambivalent attitude toward hermaphrodite Follower Pairs, or because witchcraft involves inverting all

13. Berard Haile believed that the myth of the separation of the sexes referred to the hermaphrodite *nadleeh* as a man who appeared to be a woman but who was not (1978, 162).

14. Their names echo *Sǫ'a naghái bik'e hózhǫ́*, the key concept of Blessingway philosophy, discussed in chapter 7.

that is positive, we find the Pairs utilized by witches. Wheelwright tells of special ceremonies during which the Pairs are represented by masked impersonators (Wyman and Bailey 1943, 9), and Haile has also described such masks (Haile 1947a, 95–109). The short myth of the Follower Pair obtained by Haile proved to be that of the Return of the Two [Skulls] Outside, a major motif in the myth of Upward Reachingway. And, echoing Klah, the Pair, originally two girls, was later restored as a boy and girl. Moreover, during a witches' Sabbath, masks representing the Follower Pairs are worn (Kluckhohn 1962b, 228 n6).

In sum, we find that the hermaphrodite is not the unequivocal symbol of perfection that combines the attributes of the male and female and serves as mediator between polarities. Instead, the associations with death, incest, barrenness, and witchcraft suggest a highly ambivalent attitude. It is possible to see this as an expression of the antagonism between the Blessingway philosophy and the tradition represented by Begochidi, which continued to assert the creative powers of the tricksters, Coyote and Paiyatemu. Paiyatemu, we recall, was the model for Begochidi and, although himself not an hermaphrodite, was the tutelary of the Newekwe and Koyemsi clown societies. The Koyemsi were the barren children of the first incestuous pair and the siblings of the first hermaphrodite.

Proponents of Begochidi claimed that he created hermaphrodite twins who became the Follower Pairs. But these were transformed into male and female pairs by Blessingway singers and became central to Blessingway as the inner forms of the sacred mountains as well as representing the central concept of Long Life—Happiness (Sạ 'a naghái bik'e hózhǫ́) in their role as the inner form of the earth. It is the Blessingway singers who associate the hermaphrodite with death, incest, and witchcraft, demonizing Begochidi in the same manner as they do Coyote, even denying his role as creator and keeper of game animals and claiming that he was only the God of the Mexicans. It appears that the hermaphrodite mediated between the sexes only before and during the separation of the sexes.

Hermaphrodite katsinas are found at Zuni and Acoma. Although little is known of their function, at Hopi the hermaphrodite katsina, Korosto, was referred to as a *kwasaitaka* (male transvestite). "Like a farmer, Korosta [sic] carries a bag of seeds, which he hands out to spectators. Recipients are supposed to plant them at appropriate times. The obvious link of bisexualism and fertility is impressive" (Titiev 1972, 153, 214–215). This katsina was supposed to have come from Zuni and had not been impersonated at Oraibi since circa 1910.

The position of the Zuni hermaphrodite is ambiguous because, whereas the original creator Awonawilona was a He-She, the firstborn hermaphrodite was the child of the original incestuous union. In contrast, Tewa references to the concept of a man-woman are decidedly positive. In the Tewa creation myth, when the Corn Mothers send a man to the upper world to investigate, they tell him that he must think like a man and a woman (Parsons 1926, 9–10), and to be a "woman-man" is to have unusual power (Parsons 1929b, 262). The qualities of both the male and female are thought to be present in men but not in women, which suggests that the female is not valued as highly as the male: "There is a clear relationship of asymmetry between the sexes" that is expressed through the Winter and Summer moieties (Ortiz 1969, 35,36). The chief of the Winter (male) moiety is called "father" during the period when he leads the village and "mother" during the other half of the year when the chief of the Summer (female) moiety is in charge. The Summer chief, however, is referred to as "mother" throughout the year and is never called "father."

This asymmetry between the sexes is found also in the Tewa moiety initiation and in naming ceremonies. The sponsor of a child being initiated into the Winter moiety must be selected from among the moiety chief and his several assistants, and both the child and the sponsor may be either male or female. In contrast, the sponsor of a child being initiated into the Summer moiety may be selected from among any of the moiety adults who are of the same sex as the child. And when the spirits are addressed during the naming ceremony, they are asked for help in bringing a male infant to "womanhood and manhood," whereas the request for a female infant is for assistance to bring her to womanhood only. So, although the symbolism of bisexuality is valued, it is reserved for the male.

The fact that Pueblos have varied and ambiguous views of the hermaphrodite raises a number of questions. If the Hopis conceive of Korosto as a symbol of fertility, why do the Zunis associate the hermaphrodite with infertility and witchcraft and not with Awonawilona, the bisexual supreme deity? Why do the Tewas, who do not have a ceremonial image of the hermaphrodite, only use the bisexual image as the ideal for the religious practitioners and even then give the male a superior position? And is institutionalized transvestism also viewed with ambivalence in daily life?

Despite the fact that much has been written about institutionalized transvestism in North America, there is little agreement concerning its ontology or function.[15] American investigators have been interested in the possible demographic and psychosexual reasons for its origin, whereas Europeans have concentrated on religious aspects. In regard to the latter, it seems likely that Old World examples have shaped their general tendency to view the transvestite as a personification of the androgyne, the symbolic resolution of sexual opposites.

Some of the Old World examples are clearly to be interpreted in this manner. The shamans of the Ngadju Dyak of southern Borneo were believed to be intermediates between men and gods. They were known as *balian* and *basir,* the latter being true hermaphrodites ("incapable of procreation"). They dressed and acted like women and served the sacred function of joining feminine earth and masculine sky (Eliade 1964, 352). But such explicit sacred functions of the transvestite are not to be found in North America.

Among the Chuckchee and Koryak of Siberia, both male and female shamans change their sex ritually, psychologically, and to some extent even physically, and these "transformed shamans were believed to be the most powerful of all" (Bogoras 1907, 450; Jochelson 1905, 750).[16] Although it was not mandatory, North American transvestites were often shamans and were assigned a variety of ceremonial tasks. Crow transvestites chopped down the sacred tree of the Sun Dance (Lowie 1956, 48). Hidatsa transvestites performed many ceremonial roles, and in addition to locating the central log for the Sun Dance pole, they dressed like other members of the Holy Woman Society whenever a major ceremony was given (Bowers 1965, 166–168). They were the most active ceremonial class in the village, and their ceremonial roles exceeded those of the most distinguished tribal ceremonial leaders. Not just anyone could become a transvestite; without exception the individual who assumed the role subsequent to a vision experience was a brother or the son of a man having rights in the Woman Above and Holy Woman bundles of ceremonial paraphernalia. The Mandan, closely associated with the Hidatsa, assigned similar roles to the transvestite. However, despite the transvestite's ceremonial importance, parents did not want their children to become transvestites and believed that men began to wear women's clothes and follow female avocations because of the evil disposition and power of a supernatural spirit who was also believed to be

15. The reader is referred to the comprehensive review of the topic by Charles Callender and Lee Kochems (1983).

16. For a discussion of the worldwide distribution of the religious aspects of bisexuality, see Hermann Baumann (1955).

the cause of insanity, feeblemindedness, malformations, twisted jaws, and premature births (Bowers 1950, 77, 270–272).

Timocua transvestites were in charge of the preparation of the dead and care of the sick, as were the transvestites in a number of California tribes (Swanton 1922, 373). Zuni women approved of the presence of male transvestites because they were strong and helped women with their work. The men, however, objected strongly when their sons wished to become transvestites and did everything in their power to dissuade them (Parsons 1916; Stevenson 1904, 37–38).[17] Despite this difference of opinion, the transvestites, who were most often male, were thought to bring material benefits to their households.

Unlike the Europeans, American scholars have sought the reasons that the institution originated and have assumed that religious functions and beliefs developed after the institution itself. Two general hypotheses have been proposed. The first may be called demographic, the second psychological. According to the former hypothesis, small populations in harsh environments would need to rectify any imbalance in the sex ratio either by selective infanticide or by raising girls as boys in the event a family had no sons to help provide for them. Such cases are reported for several Eskimo groups, and John Honigmann reports similar cases for the Athabascan Kaska (1954, 130).[18] If the institution predates the coming of agriculture, families in hunting and gathering societies would have been more concerned by a lack of sons than of daughters, yet female transvestites are few, and the northern Athabascans appear never to have institutionalized the role. Equally unlikely is Alice Schlegel's suggestion that male transvestites would be tolerated or encouraged by societies in which female labor was highly valued and where there is an actual or potential shortage of female labor (1983, 462). The examples Schlegel provides are unconvincing, especially those of the matrilineal Pueblos, where the males did the farming, hunting, weaving, house building, and hide tanning, and the women prepared the food, tended gardens, and made pottery. Nor is it easy to see how a male transvestite can alleviate anxiety consequent upon the "loss of a fertile woman from the reproductive pool." In any event, male

17. Nor were Zuni transvestites allowed to cross the gender division completely after death: "Despite being buried in women's clothes, trousers are put on underneath and they are placed among the men not the women" (Parsons 1916, 528).

18. See Bernard Saladin d'Anglure for the Inuit of Quebec (1984, 492), Donald Clark for the Pacific Eskimo (1984, 192); and Margaret Lantis for the Aleut (1984, 179).

transvestites predominate in North American societies regardless of women's contributions to subsistence.

The psychological hypothesis has been offered more often and holds that, in addition to the natural incidence of hermaphrodites, there would be children born with normal anatomy but with a propensity for the activities of the opposite sex. This view is elaborated by Ruth Benedict, who conjectures that homosexuals and sexual deviants in general could escape from the strains of performing an uncongenial role by becoming transvestites or shamans (1932, 4). Ralph Linton also believes that the status of the transvestite was a desirable alternate in Plains Indian societies that stressed the male warrior role (1936, 480). However, in a cross-cultural comparison using a world sample of societies, Robert Monroe, John Whiting, and David Halley found that societies that do not emphasize sex differences were more likely to have institutionalized male transvestism (1969). In balance, the sacredness of the role appears to be more salient.

Navajo *nádleeh* were respected and thought to be sacred. And, as among many other tribes, the transvestite was thought to ensure wealth. Hermaphrodite livestock were valued and not slaughtered. The genitals of hermaphrodite deer, antelope, mountain sheep, and sheep were rubbed on the ends of the tails of female sheep and goats. This was thought to cause hermaphrodite sheep and goats to be born, and the owner would then have many sheep and would become rich (Hill 1935). Hermaphrodites were believed to have been in charge of all wealth since the beginning. Moreover, if there were no *nádleeh,* the country would change and it would be the end of the Navajo. This belief, especially in respect to flocks, was strong despite the fact that hermaphrodites are infertile.

The Navajos recognized the difference between the "true" *nádleeh* who were physiologically hermaphrodite and the pseudo-*nádleeh* who were anatomically normal.[19] Haile says that the older generation disapproved of the homosexual pseudo-*nádleeh* and that the acceptance of them during the twentieth century was a recent development. "If Navajo culture really approved of these imitations, we could reasonably expect a much larger number of *nádleeh* than the tribe has today" (Haile 1978, 167). He also notes that there was no ritual cure for the congenital hermaphrodite but that there was one for the pseudo-hermaphrodite and his partners.

---

19. The Navajo for *hermaphrodite* is *biziz hóló bijóózh hóló* (it has a bag [testicles], it has a vagina) (Haile 1978, 163).

W. W. Hill thought that there were as many female as male *nádleeh,* although he only identifies one. In addition to Klah and the woman named Kinipai who was a true hermaphrodite, Hill identifies four others and notes that, although there was nothing about *nádleeh* that made them better equipped to become singers, most seemed to excel in the performance of one or more ceremonials.[20] According to Hill, the *nádleeh* at White Cone was one of the few remaining Hailway singers, as was Klah, and Kinipai knew "the chants for insanity resulting from incest and for curing body sores and is noted as a midwife." In addition, she was thought to practice witchcraft. The ceremony for incest was surely Mothway, and because Hill mentions "chants" in the plural, one must wonder whether Kinipai also knew Coyoteway according to its evil side, which might well have been used for incest at that time and would account for the belief that she was a witch.[21]

The myths of both Mothway and Hailway featured Begochidi, which raises the question of why the *nádleeh* were drawn to these particular ceremonies, both of which were thought to be nearing extinction. Did *nádleeh* use Begochidi for personal reasons as a means to justify their status? Or were they the corporal representatives of the Coyote-Begochidi tradition? Considering that *nádleeh* were thought to be sacred and were held in high esteem, there would seem to be little need to justify the status.

Institutionalized transvestism is a remarkably old and widespread phenomenon in North America and may, at one time, have been universal. Although the positive aspects of the role have been documented for all the societies for which it was reported, it is also true that coexisting with the respect for the role was the widespread disfavor in which individual transvestites were held. Men did not want their sons to become transvestites, and transvestites were made fun of behind their backs. Some societies associated them with infertility, death, and witchcraft. One must wonder what gave rise to these radically divergent perceptions.

Although some Navajo attitudes may be explained by the tensions that existed between the Blessingway and Coyote-Begochidi traditions,

---

20. W. W. Hill described Klah as having a voice like a woman, doing women's work, but sometimes dressing as a man and sometimes as a woman. He did not mention that, as a baby on the way back from Fort Sumner, Klah was emasculated during a raid by Utes and later became a transvestite (Reichard 1963, 141). And several Navajos disputed Hill's assertion that Kinipai was a woman.

21. When Mothway was unavailable, a form of Coyoteway was used as a substitute as late as the 1960s (Levy, Neutra, and Parker 1987, 90, 91, 133).

it seems likely that the ambivalence about transvestism predated this development. Contradictory attitudes have been documented for many North American societies, as well as for the Navajos, as has the tendency for many societies to differentiate among the true and the pseudo-hermaphrodites, most of whom were homosexual. Not only was the hermaphrodite infertile and an anomaly, but homosexuality was non-productive. The survival of society—at least among small societies without advanced technology—depended upon fecundity and stable families. The intellectual desire to find a unifying principle for the opposition of the sexes was countered by the social imperative for reproduction and stability. Although resolving all the issues raised by the study of institutionalized transvestism is not within the purview of this discussion, it seems proper here to point to the need for continued investigation of this topic. Of special importance is the need to determine whether a religious symbol that unites the oppositions must necessarily give rise to ambivalent perceptions, or whether the ambivalence is the consequence of the social reality that involves actual individuals fulfilling the role.

Because shamans could send their souls to the land of the dead and not be affected, the association with death might well have coexisted with the idea that the hermaphrodite-transvestite brought success and wealth. And, insofar as supernatural power can harm as well as heal, the individual who assumed the role of the institutionalized transvestite might always have elicited some degree of fear, as did shamans. Moreover, it is conceivable that as the supporters of the Coyote tradition borrowed Paiyatemu as the new trickster symbol, they might have also had reason to emphasize the hermaphrodite element in Zuni tradition. In this way, Begochidi would be a trickster and a powerful shaman, and the symbol of the hermaphrodite could be perpetuated with positive associations.

In contrast, the Blessingway tradition—if only to counter Begochidi's influence—would emphasize the association of the hermaphrodite with incest and infertility and seek to deny the importance of the mediating function in their versions of the myths. There is no way to confirm this speculation; nevertheless, it is consistent with the positions taken by the different myth narrators as well as with the fact that Blessingway singers mention the infertility of hermaphrodites despite the persistence of popular belief concerning their positive affect on fertility.

The relationship between men and women as revealed by the myths and the function of the hermaphrodite as a mediating symbol highlight the problems involved when using myth to make inferences about the society in which they are found. Most societies experience conflict between the sexes. In order to demonstrate that this conflict has been more intense among the Navajos, it is necessary to provide supporting historical and contemporary social evidence. Similarly, to project the positive unifying symbol of the hermaphrodite onto the society and to infer that the Navajos viewed homosexuality with equanimity without social evidence would be a mistake. The differing positions adopted by the narrators of the myths appear to reflect theological debates deriving from the changing social and economic environment rather than from psychosexual propensities of segments of the population.

10

Envoy

The myths of the agricultural societies of North America are more structured than those of the hunting and gathering societies and tend to proceed logically from one episode to another. The myths of the western Pueblos are the best examples of this: Events proceed from the creation through the underworlds, then recount the events of and immediately following the emergence, which in turn lead into the myths of clan origins and migrations until a period close to the historical is reached. These myths stand in vivid contrast to those of smaller hunting and gathering societies, which may or may not have an account of the creation of the earth or the universe. The myths of the Great Basin have a "disjointed, kaleidoscopic quality," and those of the Eskimo Arctic, where myth "reaches its lowest ebb," consist of disjointed "miniature creation tales" (Bierhorst 1985, 59–60, 127). These are examples of the extremes. Eastern Pueblo myths are not as elaborately structured as those of the Hopi, Acoma, and Zuni, and the myths of the Eastern Woodland societies are somewhat less organized than those of the Southwest. Conversely, the myths of the Northwest and California coasts have more structure than those of other hunting and gathering groups. But what accounts for these differences, and do the fragmented incidents of hunters' myths convey messages of sophistication?

The Navajos have provided us with a unique opportunity to bridge the gap separating the two types of myth as well as to detect many similarities and continuities. Not only have Navajo myths been recorded in great numbers and their narrators been well identified, but we also know the general outline of the Navajos' history. The adoption of the structure of western Pueblo creation myths provided narrative coherence at the same time that motifs retained from the preagricultural past were integrated into the larger narrative, often with a change of emphasis.

Hunter-gatherers give prominence to trickster-transformer-creators, whereas in the New World, emergence myths are standard lore for most of the agriculturalists.[1] Corresponding to this contrast is the difference in the perception of chaos. The unpredictability of the natural world represented by tricksters is perceived by hunter-gatherers as only a part, albeit a large one, of a world that is governed by natural laws of causality. In contrast, Pueblos view chaos as the randomness, confusion, and incoherence that existed at the time of creation but has continually developed more order and coherence. As we have seen, the former perception is closer to that of contemporary chaos theory; that of the latter approximates the view of Christianity and Judaism. The hunter-gatherer societies retain a monistic perception that does not polarize good and evil, whereas the agriculturalist societies view unpredictability as evil to be fought at all costs.

In addition to the foregoing contrasts, there are also similarities between the myths of hunter-gatherer and agricultural societies. Just as hunting and the gathering of wild plants is not completely replaced by agriculture, so the older myths concerned with hunting are not completely erased in agricultural societies. And, because success in both subsistence economies is dependent on empirical knowledge about the growth cycle of domestic crops or the habits of the game, the methods of dealing with untoward events are the same: both societies attempt to control cause and effect by sympathetic magic. All of the societies of North America have hunt magic as well as witches and religious practitioners who have the skill and knowledge to control supernatural power. The agriculturalists put this power in the hands of priests organized into sodalities that also have healing functions. The hunters rely upon the individual shaman. The line between priest and shaman is not always clearly drawn. The individual Hopi healer is not a priest and does not have a sacred position, although he may have a vision of sorts. The priests of the Eastern Pueblos may also have visions but are organized into sodalities and cannot practice as individual prophets, shamans, or healers. And

---

1. For the distribution of emergence myths in the New World, see John Bierhorst (1985; 1988; 1990).

the Navajos have converted their shamans into priests who, although operating as individuals, do not rely on the vision as a source of power or as a method of curing. The Hopis and Navajos give prominence to breach of taboo as the major cause of disease, whereas the Keresan Pueblos believe that disease is caused by soul loss and possession. Their priests are most similar to the bear shamans of California, although they are organized into sodalities and may not function as individual prophets or innovators. What we see is not a radical, qualitative transformation but a shift of emphasis and a retention of older conceptions.

In much the same way, myths accumulate in any given society so that older myths coexist with newer ones or with different versions of the same myth. We have seen this process in the myth of the hoarding and release of game among the Navajos as well as the Pueblos. In Navajo myths, the identity of the game releaser has changed from the trickster to one of the masked gods. Among the Zuni, the myth no longer occupies an important position in the larger corpus of origin myths, and what it purports to explain is no longer the reason that game animals are difficult to hunt but rather the reason for the ritual directional locations of the game animals.

As we have seen, the myth of the *vagina dentata* accounts for the creation of humanity among the societies of the Great Basin. However, the Biting Vagina of Navajo myth may or may not even be mentioned as one of the beings created in the underworlds. And among the Hopi, it is a tale told to adolescents to caution them about casual sex. Certainly it would be premature to interpret all these myths as indicating that castration anxiety is a prominent feature of the average male personality or even that the myth conveys an important message about relationships between men and women.

Even in the Great Basin, where the *vagina dentata* myth is of central importance, one must exercise caution because there are two myths that account for the creation of humanity. The tribes of the western Basin tell of a secluded menstruant who escapes death when her people are killed by a giant. She flees, taking with her a small child who is caught and killed by the giant but is later revived and rescued by the woman. Together they come to the home of a hunter who marries the woman, and she subsequently bears many children, who then become the various tribes. Because the Mono and Panamint tell both these myths, it is difficult to determine which myth is the most important unless the two myths are integrated into a larger structured account of creation that allows us to infer which myth is salient (Gayton 1935, 593).

The Navajos have retained most Coyote tales found throughout western North America, but few of these tales are included in the Navajo creation myths. Instead, like the story of the Eye Juggler, they are told for entertainment or for the education of children. If the purpose of the myth and the context of its narration are not recorded, we cannot know whether the myth is considered sacred and therefore cannot confidently interpret its meaning for the society.

Because many of those who gathered these tales—anthropologists, folklorists, and interested amateurs—were not primarily interested in the tales' religious significance, we must be reconciled to the fact that information about that potential significance was never elicited. I was surprised to learn from John Bierhorst that Franz Boas, the great collector of myths who recognized their importance for reconstructing tribal histories, believed that they were "merely a kind of primitive fiction, depicting human situations" and that they were nothing more than "idiotic stories." And Julian Steward, whose interest was mostly in the adaptation of the people of the Great Basin to their environment, "used European literary standards to evaluate the various tales, concluding that many of the narrators had not perfected their art" and dismissing unrealistic elements as incoherent, entirely irrelevant, or lacking in motivation (Bierhorst 1985, 127).

If Boas's and Steward's estimations are correct, we must conclude that something mentally significant occurred with the development of agriculture and the creation of increasingly coherent myths. As Paul Radin surmised, the myths of hunter-gatherers must then be nothing more than projections of the subconscious that demand psychoanalytic rather than religious interpretation. According to Radin, the presentation of the trickster as a deity was a later development—that the original figure, "a Priapus-like protagonist . . . strutting across the scene, wandering restlessly from place to place, attempting successfully and unsuccessfully, to gratify his voracious hunger and his uninhibited sexuality. . . . represents not only the undifferentiated and distant past, but likewise the undifferentiated present within every individual" (Radin 1956, 168). In sum, Trickster is a projection of our libidinous selves, with a weak ego and certainly without superego. But if Christianity and Judaism are credited with religious sophistication despite having created God in our image as an authoritarian father figure, a projection of male-dominated Western society, why cannot a projection of a confused humanity attempting to control supernatural power also be the vehicle of religious truths?

Later scholars have accepted and elaborated on Radin's Jungian interpretation: "One cannot read many Coyote stories without being struck by the degree to which his creativity, his adaptability, his unreliability, and his buffoonery are reminiscent of the genus *Homo* (in this context, *sapiens* should perhaps only be added with a [*sic!*] after it)" (Bright 1993, 21–22). Or: "The trickster is man . . . the personification of all the traits of man raised to the highest degree" (Ricketts 1965, 336, 347, 349). And some have identified him with Levi-Strauss's *bricoleur* who "cannot stop himself from tampering with Original Creation and thus produces the world which we humans now know—imperfect, but ours."[2]

I do not doubt for a moment that Trickster is, to some degree, a projection of our libidinous selves. American Indians have seen him as such, as we have had occasion to note when discussing Frank Mitchell's views of Coyote.[3] I do not, however, see why we must assume that all theological aspects contained in these myths are later additions that have developed over time, because even if the psychological interpretation is true for some hypothetical "early human," it would not account for the fragmentary nature of the myths of North American hunter-gatherers as we know them, other than to suggest that these hunter-gatherers are mentally different from the humans who live in sedentary societies.

It is preferable to examine the role that demography and the absence of writing play in creating these differences. In this regard, Robert Lowie says, "Writing meant that any fruitful idea, instead of having to be transmitted by word of mouth, could be conveyed to future ages by a more precise and safer method and to a far larger circle of people in both present and future" (1940, 193). The invention of writing made possible the development of a sense of history that is only minimally expressed in myths. In *The Domestication of the Primitive Mind,* Jack Goody details the effects that writing has had on conceptions of time as well as its contribution to the development of scientific as opposed to magical logic. The lack of writing accounts for the timeless quality of myths—as when, for example, the death of supernaturals may be narrated before the account of the origin of death and the creation of mortals. Yet the

2. Thus William Bright (1993, 22) summarizes the views of Jarold Ramsey (1973).

3. Morris Opler notes that in order to account for a world with witchcraft, deceit, and misconduct, the Apaches say, "Coyote did it first. We follow in Coyote's footsteps" (1938, 215).

development does not occur as a quantum leap with writing suddenly creating new modes of thought. Rather, it is the technological advance that makes possible the completion of a process that had already started with the development of agriculture or sedentary villages.

Lacking writing, the teacher can only instruct his or her own pupils, and because the role of religious expert is confined to the few who possess the prerequisites for its performance, the philosophical speculations of a creative mind tend not to be spread widely. Unlike a Thomas or Augustine whose thoughts could be written and studied by contemporaries as well as by later generations, the speculations of a shaman do not result in the formulation of comprehensive and integrated philosophies beyond what may be retained in the minds of the more thoughtful and introspective religious practitioners.

The populations of small hunter-gatherer societies live for much of the year scattered over large areas. The numbers of contemporaries coming into contact with a creative thinker must be small at best. And when we consider that the majority of the audience is either ill equipped to understand or else disinterested in abstract religious speculations, the fragmentary nature of the myth corpus is almost guaranteed. The message must be in a form that is easily understood and remembered. And it must utilize actors and motifs that are already familiar and accepted as the truth. In consequence, it must be dramatic as well as entertaining. It may nevertheless also serve as the framework to which the philosopher may attach additions as well as commentaries and asides intended for apprentices and for other specialists. But these elaborations cannot be relied upon to transmit the traditions, because the presence and the survival of the requisite audience is never guaranteed.

As societies developed agriculture, settlements became sedentary and concentrated. The same individuals were in contact with each other continuously over the years. There were enough people in a Pueblo village for prospective priests to spend years learning myths and ritual details and, in consequence, to develop elaborate narrative structures. In the case of the Hopis, a priest's daily agricultural tasks could be performed by a substitute, which freed the priest to devote prolonged periods to learning the sodality's myths and rituals. Because the foraging societies of the Northwest and California also lived in sedentary villages for much of the year, their myths are also more structured than those of the Eskimo, northern Athabascan, or Great Basin people.

By allowing specific individuals to devote more of their time to learning, the concentration of permanent populations in villages also makes possible the development of a sense of history.[4] A part of the structured nature of Pueblo myths is the logical progression of events. There is not only a before and after—a myth time and a "now" time—but also stages of development. In the Navajo myth of creation, Blessingway singers recognize that the Navajos, vaguely represented as they are by the First Man Group before the emergence and the creation of humans, came into contact with and obtained corn and agriculture from the Pueblos who already inhabited the Third World. And a narrator was moved to comment on the contrast between what went before and contemporary custom concerning adultery, despite the fact that the story that prompted the comment was about beings that existed before the creation of humanity. This sense of a historical past is not found in the myths of the Great Basin, the subarctic, or the Arctic.

As we have seen, early scholars concluded that the "mind of primitive man" was less developed than that of modern, urbanized people— that this mind was, in fact, childlike, and that mental immaturity accounted for the seeming illogic and unreality of myths. Contemporary scholars have denied the qualitative difference but emphasized that, without writing, a classroom environment, or a number of abstract skills that must be learned for survival, the average preliterate has not been conditioned to live up to his or her biological potential.[5] But when we recall that, despite the scarcity and fragmentary nature of Eskimo myths, the Netsilik ideas of creation as described in chapter 7 appear sophisticated and complex, we are encouraged to assume that individuals in preliterate societies were capable of what has been called abstract, objective thought.

If preliterate individuals were capable of abstract thought, then interpretations of Navajo myths may help us find meaning in the more inscrutable myths of the hunter-gatherers. Let us concentrate on the trickster figure and the problem of chaos and unpredictability. As we have noted, people in all societies have been concerned with the problem of order and chaos and sought to know whether events may be controlled by humans.

The first question is whether the hunter-gatherer tribes of the continent perceive unpredictability and seek to control it in the same man-

4. In many village-dwelling African societies, specific individuals were assigned the task of memorizing genealogies. Keeping the sequence of generations straight served to expand the sense of history. Similarly, tribal calendars of groups like the Kiowa of the Great Plains kept events of the comparatively recent past in correct sequence.

5. See, for example Christopher Hallpike, *The Foundations of Primitive Thought* (1979).

ner as do the Navajos. Gambling and games of skill and chance help us answer this question. Social scientists have seen games as representations of interpersonal interaction and as "reflections of the dominant themes or patterns underlying other cultural institutions and activities" (Levinson and Malone 1980, 169). Games are generally classed as games of physical skill, games of chance, or games of strategy. These categories, however, are not mutually exclusive, and many games combine elements of two or all three. Games of physical skill are virtually universal, whereas games of strategy are found in societies with highly stratified social systems in which children are trained for obedience. Games of chance are found most often in societies where life is insecure and are "expressive models of an uncertain, unpredictable world" (Levinson and Malone 1980, 172). Nearly all North American societies have games of skill and chance, but in the Southwest, only the Pueblos are said to have games of strategy.[6]

Games have an important place in the Navajo myth of The Great Gambler (O'Bryan 1956, 48–70). As we have seen, the Gambler was a son of the Sun and a human woman and was trained to defeat the gamblers of an early pueblo, who possessed treasures coveted by the Sun. When, after winning these treasures, the Gambler refused to turn them over to his father, the Sun fathered another son by a woman and trained him to defeat the Gambler. In the contest between the Gambler and the young hero, nearly all the games of the Navajo were played.[7] In each contest, the hero won through the use of trickery, sympathetic magic, or the help of various deities. The Gambler—who is Turquoise Boy, the hermaphrodite also known as Begochidi, who is derived from the Pueblo Paiyatemu—cheated by weighting his rainbow stick, much as dice are loaded today, so that it fell on a predetermined side. Cheating became so common a practice in the kick stick race that it had to be guarded against (O'Bryan 1956, 36). The contest is repeated in the myth of Frenzy Witchcraftway, during which the hero defeats White Butterfly, also a personification of Paiyatemu. In Frenzy Witchcraftway, gambling magic, love magic, and hunt magic are one and the same and associated with Coyote as well as with the Paiyatemu figure, an

6. Cross-cultural studies that code the Pueblos as having games of strategy are by Robert Textor (1967) and John Roberts, Malcolm Arth, and Robert Bush (1959). However, Stewart Culin (1907) maintains that the board games found among the Pueblos were borrowed from the Spaniards or Anglo-Americans, as were card games.

7. These games were hoop and pole, seven sticks, kick ball, kick stick race, guessing, planted sticks, foot race, rainbow-shaped stick, and the moccasin game.

association that links this myth to the hunting past despite utilizing a Pueblo symbol.[8]

Turning now to the Pueblos, we find that games and gambling are also important but are kept under control in the same way as healers are organized in sodalities. Among the Pueblos, the "primal gamblers" are "those curious children, the divine Twins, the miraculous offspring of the Sun" (Culin 1907, 32). At Zuni, the Twins carry, among other things, shuttlecocks and race sticks: "All these things to divine men's chance, and play games of hazard, wagering the fate of whole nations in mere pastime, had they with them" (Cushing 1896, 423). Although gods of war, the Twins "resemble childish tricksters more than aggressive warriors"; they lead the people out of the underworlds, rid the world of monsters, and hunt "for large game, by the use of magic and trickery" (Tyler 1964, 209). At Acoma, the Twins are fathered by Paiyatemu, the trickster aspect of the Sun, whereas among the Keresans, their mother is Yellow Woman, huntress and sister of the spirit of game.

The Pueblos "control" games of skill and chance, first, by placing them in the charge of the Twins rather than the uncontrollable Coyote and, second, by incorporating them in ceremonies. At Hopi, shinny is played in the Powamu ceremony, and at Zuni, a guessing game is supervised by the Koyemsi at the last katsina dance of the season (Parsons 1974, 449, 801). Foot races were also part of rituals in all Pueblos. Aside from guessing, however, games of chance do not seem to have been included in ritual (Ortiz 1969, 108–111). And Pueblos appear to have been less addicted to gambling than other tribes.

Games invariably have myths of origin and are associated with one or more deities, but they are especially associated with the hunt as a means of controlling unpredictability. For example, consider the Great Basin myth of the Theft of Pine Nuts. Gathering was at least as important as hunting in the Great Basin, and the search for pine nuts corresponded most closely with hunting game. Piñon pines were the most important food plant, and an individual would gather between thirty and forty

---

8. "It was decided that San'hode'di and the White Butterfly should go through the same games that the Great Gambler used. And the young man won each of these games" (O'Bryan 1956, 162). There is a western Shoshone myth of a cannibal gambler who eats all whom he defeats until he is finally killed by hawk. His family is killed by Coyote. After this, his victims are found and resuscitated (Smith 1993, 142–145). The cannibal is defeated in much the same manner as the Navajo Great Gambler, but whether this similarity indicates that the same gambling myth has been elaborated over time by different societies is moot.

bushels of pine nuts in a single fall harvest (Steward 1933, 241–242). But good crops were irregular, coming every three to seven years. Among the more settled Owens Valley Paiutes, each "district" owned pine nut territory. Sometimes permission was granted to gather nuts, but trespass was resented and often led to conflict. This, notes Steward, was the most frequent cause of trouble between otherwise peaceful districts. Rights in a territory were respected because of tradition and because of fear of magic. In effect, the unpredictability of the location of a good harvest and the possibility that one would not be found in the area recognized as belonging to a specific local group paralleled the uncertainty faced by hunters. Presumably, among the other, less settled Paiutes, there were no definite territories, and people felt free to move over fairly large areas in search of a good harvest.

The pine nut harvest, which took place in the late fall, was one of the few opportunities for families occupying an area to come together to socialize, perform ritual, and arrange marriages. It was during this time that round dances were performed and prayers made to guarantee a good crop (Fowler 1986, 64). People gambled, playing stick, dice, and hand games. Opposing teams sang songs with ritual content to obtain the power to guess correctly as well as to distract their opponents. Such games could last through the night and sometimes even for more than a day and night.

The story of the Theft of Pine Nuts is about a group with no harvest of their own who steal the nuts of another group during the dancing and game playing. As such, it is one of Boas's "primitive" fictions that depict human situations. Coyote, Crow, or both together lead the raiding party while the owners of the pine nuts are performing round dances and playing the hand game. The nuts are tied in a bag in a high tree, and usually one or two woodpecker thieves magically stretch their tongues to reach the nuts.[9] In one tale, Crow arrives at the camp first and plays kickball with Crane, the leader of the resident camp. He cheats by substituting his own ball for Crane's, and Crane then refuses to let him take the pine nuts that he has won. In consequence, a raid is undertaken. In some versions, the visitors play the hand game in order to distract their hosts while one of their party searches for the nuts. The nuts are found and stolen, the thieves are pursued, and many are caught and killed. But Crow or Woodpecker has hidden the nuts in his rotten leg.

9. For different accounts, see Julian Steward (1943, 241–242) and Anne Smith (1993, 44, 84—86, 146–147, 152–153).

When he is caught and searched, his captors do not probe the rotten leg, and so the thieves are successful—or, magically, the leg runs off by itself, or the thief is let go and is suddenly no longer lame and thus escapes. Coyote may perform magic in order to delay the pursuers, or he may be the principal actor. In any event, cheating, magic, and distracting the opponents are all necessary to gain sustenance in the face of unforeseen events that could cause starvation.

But what is the meaning of "Coyote smelled pine nuts in the east, and blood gushed from his nose," which Bierhorst says is a "mysterious statement" (Bierhorst 1985, 124)? This is a fairly common opening for the story. In another account, a man is watching a hand game when he detects a smell of pine nuts so strong that it brings blood to his throat. In yet another version, Crow is watching a hand game, smells pine nuts, and faints; when people find him, blood is coming out of his mouth (Smith 1993, 84, 152). Given what we know of the importance of pine nuts and the prospect of starvation without them, the statement may be taken as an announcement that the story to follow is significant. Coyote, Crow, or whomever responds to the awareness of the presence of pine nuts with his whole being—with his life's blood.

Some tales warn against overestimating one's own power and are told to children or as an entertainment. In the popular and widely distributed story of the Eye Juggler, Coyote comes upon little birds who are throwing their eyes into the air and catching them again in their eye sockets. He asks them what they are doing and then tries to do it himself. He fails and loses his sight. "So Coyote had to make another sense, a sixth sense, which he put into his socket and it led him around" (Smith 1993, 94). The birds do not appear to be important or powerful, so their trick must also be relatively easy. Coyote is able to create a sixth sense, but even though he is the master of supernatural power, he is unable to perform the trick—and if he cannot do it, then nobody else should not presume to try. In sum: do not try this at home; do not reach beyond your abilities.

Not all tribes include such tales as part of their sacred lore, but some, especially in the Great Basin, narrate them as parts of more complex cycles of myth that may include such motifs as the Release of Game or the Origin of Death. Because narrators do not always include the same episodes or tell them in the same sequence, the tales are difficult to interpret.

We are, then, left with a choice: we may accept them at their face value as disjointed tales of little value except as entertainments and cautions for the young, or take on faith that, because they include the same elements out of which agricultural and more sedentary hunter-gatherers have constructed more coherent myths, they express equally sophisticated answers to the questions humankind has asked for as long as we have records.

The most recent chapter in the history of Navajo religion has yet to be written. This book does not address how the economic transition from pastoralism to wage-work, the incursion of foreign religions, and the incorporation of the Navajos into the national culture have affected core beliefs and attitudes or are reflected in the creation myth. Today, Navajos are literate, educated, and increasingly integrated into the national economy and culture. No longer may the student of religion consider them or indeed any North American Indian group in isolation. Has the process of incorporating foreign myths into the central myth of creation stopped ,or would a new study of the myth find that it has changed considerably during the past half century? Has literacy affected the creation myth? Will a Navajo canon emerge that "freezes" the myth in the same way that the Bible has kept the myths of Genesis unchanged for more than two thousand years? And if such a modern Navajo version is created, will it represent the tradition according to the Blessingway or will it attempt a synthesis of the two traditions?

I do not think that the process of mythologizing has come to an end, although I find no evidence that the creation myth or the myths of origin of the many ceremonies are changing. Karl Luckert has documented a myth narrated by a descendent of Hashkéniinii who avoided capture by Kit Carson's troops, which he believes to be a mythic account of the event. Although narrated as actions of the Holy People, the myth account was told as part of the creation myth itself (Luckert 1977, 48–49; 1982).

There is evidence that biblical myths have been borrowed for the purpose of glorifying past resistance to federal domination. A young convert to Christianity once told me the story of Bai-a-lil-le, a ceremonialist who resisted all the efforts of the Indian Agent in Shiprock to get Navajos to send their children to school and to introduce modern stockraising practices. According to the story, government troops pursued Bai-a-lil-le and his band to the San Juan River, which was swollen by recent rains. On reaching the river, Bai-a-lil-le used his supernatural powers to part the waters so that his followers could cross. The narrator was surprised when I interrupted him and told the end of the story: as the troops arrived, the waters came together and many of the soldiers died. The narrator agreed that this was, indeed, the end of the tale as he knew it. This borrowing from biblical myth is all the more evident from the fact that, in historical reality, the troops had no trouble crossing the San Juan and took Bai-a-lil-le and his followers by surprise (Correll 1970). Some years later, Bai-a-lil-le drowned trying to cross the river while it was at flood stage.

As suggested by the discussion of the decline of Navajo traditional religion in chapter 2, it is probable that there are now too few practicing ceremonialists to maintain a viable myth tradition. Instead, it seems more likely that a written version of the creation myth will be accepted as canon and become the contemporary Navajo "bible." Even as fewer Navajos practice the traditional religion, there is a growing interest in preserving tradition and fostering pride in Navajo culture. But this resurgent "nationalism" is taking place as the nation moves toward an ethos of what has come to be called multiculturalism. It appears that as we become more alike, we insist more on our separateness.

By 1970, the Rough Rock Demonstration School had established the Navajo Healing Arts Training Program in an effort to counter the decline in the number of practicing ceremonialists.[10] And the Navajo Community College at Tsaile, Arizona, has developed a curriculum in Navajo language and culture. The Navajo History and Culture course includes a section on the origin of the Navajos that is a version of the creation myth. It is not clear, however, just how the myth is taught—whether, for example, different versions are discussed in any detail.

According to Ruth Roessell, then the director of the Navajo Studies Program, one of the main purposes of the course is to relate the stories as they are told by Navajos *for* Navajos, and "only in a limited and secondary manner, does the work include the anthropological version of that origin" (Roessell 1971, 1). This Navajo "endorsed" myth was created from materials gathered from a number of elderly and knowledgeable men and women (Yazzie 1971). Recognizing that there are many different versions, the preparers of the book took the position that, because the tradition was transmitted orally, variation was random. The published version is, in effect, a committee effort that includes major events and sequences for which there was basic agreement.

---

10. It is important to note that the program was funded by the National Institute of Mental Health and thus did not run counter to federal policy (Bergman 1983, 677–678).

More than this, however, all points of conflict are omitted, despite the fact that these are usually included in some way in all complete narrations of the creation. Rather than being demonized, Coyote is merely demoted. Although he appears in the first underworld, it is only to explain how he received the names Child of Dawn, Child of Twilight, and so on. He is referred to as First Angry only after the emergence, and the reason for the name is not given (Yazzie 1971, 9, 32). Moreover, Coyote's actions are all for the benefit of the people. In the second world, for example, "he saw sorrow," and this motivated First Man to lead the escape to the third world. In the third world, Coyote steals Water Monster's baby at First Woman's bidding, but no reason for this is given (Yazzie 1971, 13).

The separation of the sexes does not occur until after the emergence and, although the reason for it is First Woman's adultery with Turquoise Boy, the flood is no longer caused by First Woman's continued resentment against the men. Turquoise Boy is not identified as an hermaphrodite, and Coyote does not indulge in sexual excesses during the separation. The women's sexual excesses do lead to the birth of the monsters later to be killed by Monster Slayer, but the monsters are also said to have already been in existence at the time of emergence. Finally, no conflict between Changing Woman and the First Man Group is mentioned. The final result is a myth that might be said to follow the Blessing tradition but without its dualism. Nor does it represent a return to monism, because all of Coyote's evil side is erased rather than incorporated and explained.

It is doubtful that this work will serve as the definitive Navajo view, if only because so many readily-available published works on the subject encourage a variety of other interpretations. Nevertheless it reflects an important trend in the interpretation of Navajo religion. We recall that, at the outset, a shamanistic monism was contrasted with a Pueblo-inspired dualism and that a tension between the two outlooks was an important aspect of the development of Navajo philosophy from the time of their settlement in the Southwest to the present. What the Navajo Community College rendition of the creation myth tends toward is a new, if still not well-elucidated, interpretation. This interpretation most closely approximates what John Farella has called the "synthetic premise," which he proffers in the place of earlier "dualistic" interpretations that focused on how Navajos conceived of good and evil: "The topic of good versus evil is just not very important in Navajo theoreticians' discussions of the nature of things. In short, the dualists divide things the wrong way" (Farella 1984, 34). According to Farella, the key to understanding is to recognize that there is no division between the Holy (*diyin*) and the earthly, so that, having attained knowledge, when humans die, they become Holy People. The relationship is symbiotic: The Holy People rely on the Earth Surface People in the same way that humans rely on the Holy People. Corn meal and corn pollen "are also the food of *diyinii*, and these are returned to *diyinii* in the form of offerings" (Farella 1984, 30). The corn provides sustenance to both: "With such sustenance the Navajo reproduce and grow in population, and there are more people to grow more corn. Similarly, the beings that are on the diyin side also increase, and thus there is more water, and the Sun becomes more powerful" (Farella 1984, 30).

It is not that good and bad things don't exist, but that they are inextricably entwined. "Things are bad on earth because the people have not maintained their half of the bargain. . . . Similarly, the people will say that diyinii are 'hurting' because they are receiving no offerings. The total system is decaying" (Farella 1984, 30). Thus, it is not good against evil or order against chaos but rather an equilibrium that can become unbalanced. The emphasis placed on harmony and balance by Navajo religion has been commented on by almost all observers, including those such as Leland Wyman and Berard Haile, whom Farella has called dualists. What appears new is Farella's preference, despite disagreement among Navajos themselves, for the idea that there is no continuation of an individual's identity after death but rather a return of the individual soul to the cosmic life force (Farella 1984, 127).

If I am correct in believing that the Navajo Community College version of the creation myth represents a step toward an acceptance of this version as an officially endorsed interpretation of Navajo philosophy, we must ask whether this step is a manifestation of internal developments or a borrowing from the outside world. In our recent book, Stephen Kunitz and I speculate that we are seeing a redefinition of traditional religion based in part on New Age interpretations of traditional American Indian religious values (Kunitz and Levy 1994, 210–221). We note younger Navajos' descriptions of Navajo religion and healing practices that indicate they accept the picture of their traditional religion painted by non-Indian New Age savants.

[One young Navajo] described the traditional Navajo view of each human being as being a circle divided into quarters, representing the physical body, the emotions, the mind, and the spirit, all surrounded by another circle representing the family and society. This is precisely one of the assumptions on which New Age thought is based and, we would argue, represents a diffusion into Navajo culture of formulations of personality organization that were not there previously. (Kunitz and Levy 1994, 218–219)

Equally important, however, is the fact that New Age philosophy has also borrowed from American Indian traditions. Consider, for example, the following quotes from recent New Age publications. These statements could equally well have been found in studies of North American Indian religion:

Each person is a microcosm of the macrocosm. To understand the individual one must understand the forces and elements of the cosmos. (English-Lueck 1990, 18)

All creation on this Earth contains a spirit, a life force. This includes rocks, plants, hills, trees, sky and animals. The Mother Earth is a living, sensitive, breathing organism. The forces of all creation are dynamically interwoven into a harmonious whole. Physical and mental illness occurs when this balance is upset. The purpose of all healing ceremonials is to preserve or restore personal and universal harmony. (Newhouse and Amodeo 1985, 48)

There is mutual influence of New Age and American Indian belief, and some Navajos are reinterpreting their traditions in light of the Euro-American understanding of those traditions. I would go further to venture that, just as earlier anthropologists were influenced by their Judeo-Christian upbringing to concentrate on the polarization of good and evil in Navajo philosophy, so contemporary scholars like Farella are shifting their attention to a more synthetic interpretation as they are influenced by New Age thought. It is important to recognize, however, that both monism and dualism coexist in Navajo thought and are not mutually exclusive. This is, of course, an expected characteristic of complex and sophisticated religions with long histories of development and change.

Classification of Navajo Sings According to Leland Wyman and Clyde Kluckhohn

1. Blessingway, *Hozhǫ́ǫ́jík'ehgo*
   1.1. Talking God Blessingway
   1.2. Enemy Monster Blessingway
   1.3. Chief Blessingway
   1.4. Mountain Peak Blessingway, a.k.a. Eagleway
   1.5. Gameway Blessingway
2. Holyway, *Diyink'ehgo*
   2.1. Shooting Chant Subgroup
       2.1.1. Hailway
       2.1.2. Waterway
       2.1.3. Shootingway Male Branch
       2.1.4. Shootingway Female Branch
       2.1.5. Red Antway
       2.1.6. Big Starway
   2.2. Mountain Chant Subgroup
       2.2.1. Mountain Topway Male Branch
       2.2.2. Mountain Topway Female Branch
       2.2.3. Mountain Topway Cub Branch
       2.2.4. Mountain Topway Male Shooting Branch
       2.2.5. Mountain Topway Female Shooting Branch
       2.2.6. Frenzy Witchcraftway Male Branch
       2.2.7. Frenzy Witchcraftway Female Branch
       2.2.8. Mothway
       2.2.9. Way to Remove Paralysis

2.2.10. Beautyway Male Branch
2.2.11. Beautyway Female Branch
2.3. Which Have God Impersonators Subgroup
   2.3.1.   Nightway
   2.3.2.   Big Tree Branch
   2.3.3.   Water Bottom Branch
   2.3.4.   Pollen Branch
   2.3.5.   Across the River Branch
   2.3.6.   White House Branch
   2.3.7.   Strings Acrossway
   2.3.8.   Big Godway
   2.3.9.   Plumeway
   2.3.10. Dogway
   2.3.11. Ravenway
   2.3.12. Coyoteway
2.4. Windway Subgroup
   2.4.1.   Navajo Windway
   2.4.2.   Chiricahua Windway
2.5. Hand Tremblingway Subgroup
   2.5.1.   Hand Tremblingway
2.6. Eagle Trapping Subgroup
   2.6.1.   Eagleway
   2.6.2.   Beadway
2.7. Uncertain Affiliation—Extinct
   2.7.1.   Awlway
   2.7.2.   Earthway
3. Lifeway, *'Ináájík'ehgo*
3.1. Flintway Male Branch
3.2. Flintway Female Branch
3.3. Lifeway Male Shooting Branch
3.4. Lifeway Female Shooting Branch
3.5. Lifeway Shaft Branch
3.6. Lifeway Hand Trembling Branch
4. Evilway, *Hóchxǫ'íjí*
4.1. Purification from Natives Subgroup
   4.1.1.   Moving Upway
   4.1.2.   Red Ant Evilway
   4.1.3.   Big Star Evilway
   4.1.4.   Evilway Male Shooting Branch
   4.1.5.   Evilway Female Shooting Branch
   4.1.6.   Hand Trembling Evilway
   4.1.7.   Reared in the Earthway
4.2. Purification from Aliens Subgroup
   4.2.1.   Enemyway
   4.2.2.   Two Went Back for Scalpway
   4.2.3.   Ghosts of Every Descriptionway
5. War Ceremonials

References

Aberle, David F. 1961. "Navaho." In *Matrilineal Kinship,* ed. David M. Schneider and Kathleen Gough. Berkeley: University of California Press. 96–201.

——. 1966. *The Peyote Religion among the Navaho.* Chicago: Aldine.

——. 1980. "Navajo Exogamic Rules and Preferred Marriages." In *The Versatility of Kinship: Essays Presented to Harry W. Basehart,* ed. Linda S. Cordell and Stephen Beckerman. New York: Academic Press. 105–143.

——. 1981. "Navajo Coresidential Kingroups and Lineages." *Journal of Anthropological Research* 37:1–7.

Abraham, Karl. 1949. *Selected Papers.* London: Hogarth Press.

Anderson, Bernhard W. 1975. *Understanding the Old Testament.* 3d ed. Englewood Cliffs, N.J.: Prentice-Hall.

Balikci, Asen. 1984. "Netsilik." In David Damas, ed., *Handbook of North American Indians.* Vol. 5, *Arctic.* Washington: Smithsonian Institution. 415–430.

——. 1989 [1970]. *The Netsilik Eskimo.* Prospect Heights, Ill.: Waveland Press.

Basso, Keith. 1969. *Western Apache Witchcraft.* University of Arizona, Anthropological Paper 1.

Baumann, Hermann. 1955. *Das doppelte Geschlecht: Studien zur Bisexualität in Ritus und Mythos.* Berlin: Dietrich Reimer.

Beaglehole, Ernest. 1936. *Hopi Hunting and Hunting Ritual.* Yale University Publications in Anthropology 4.

Bellah, Robert N. 1952. *Apache Kinship Systems.* Cambridge, Mass.: Harvard University Press.

239

————. 1964. "Religious Evolution." *American Sociological Review* 29:358–374.

Benedek, Therese F. 1959. "Sexual Functions in Women and Their Disturbance." In *American Handbook of Psychiatry,* ed. Silvano Arieti. New York: Basic Books. 1:727–748.

Benedict, Ruth F. 1932. "Configurations of Culture in North America." *American Anthropologist* 24:1–27.

Bergman, Robert L. 1983. "Navajo Health Services and Projects." In Alfonso Ortiz, ed., *Handbook of North American Indians.* Vol. 5, *Southwest.* Washington: Smithsonian Institution. 672–678.

Bettelheim, Bruno. 1954. *Symbolic Wounds: Puberty Rites and the Envious Male.* Glencoe, Ill.: The Free Press.

Bierhorst, John. 1985. *The Mythology of North America.* New York: William Morrow.

————. 1988. *The Mythology of South America.* New York: William Morrow.

————. 1990. *The Mythology of Mexico and Central America.* New York: William Morrow.

Boas, Franz. 1916. *Tsimshian Mythology.* Bureau of American Ethnology Annual Report 31:29–979.

————. 1917. *Folktales of Salishan and Sahaptin Tribes.* American Folklore Society Memoir 11.

————. 1918. *Kutenai Tales.* Bureau of American Ethnology Bulletin 59:1–387.

————. 1928. *Keresan Texts.* American Ethnological Society Publication 8, part 1.

Bogoras, Waldemar. 1907. *The Cuckchee. Reports of the Jesup North Pacific Expedition.* American Museum of Natural History Memoir 11, part 2.

Bowers, Alfred W. 1950. *Mandan Social and Ceremonial Organization.* Chicago: The University of Chicago Press.

————. 1965. *Hidatsa Social and Ceremonial Organization.* Bureau of American Ethnology Bulletin 194.

Brandt, Richard B. 1954. *Hopi Ethics: A Theoretical Analysis.* Chicago: University of Chicago Press.

Bright, William. 1993. *A Coyote Reader.* Berkeley: University of California Press.

Brugge, David M. 1963. *Navajo Pottery and Ethnohistory.* Window Rock, Ariz.: Navajoland Publications, Navajo Tribal Museum.

————. 1983. "Navajo Prehistory and History to 1850." In Alfonso Ortiz, ed., *Handbook of North American Indians.* Vol. 10, *Southwest.* Washington: Smithsonian Institution. 489–501.

Buber, Martin. 1949. *The Prophetic Faith.* Trans. Carlylle Witton-Davies. New York: Macmillan.

————. 1952. *Good and Evil: Two Interpretations.* New York: Charles Scribner's Sons.

————. 1958. *I and Thou.* New York: Charles Scribner's Sons.

Bunzel, Ruth. 1932. "Zuni Katcinas." *U. S. Bureau of American Ethnology Annual Report* 47:837–1086.

————. 1933. *Zuni Texts.* American Ethnological Society Publication 15.

Callender, Charles, and Lee M. Kochems. 1983. "The North American Berdache." *Current Anthropology* 24:443–470.

Clark, Donald W. 1984. "Pacific Eskimo: Historical Ethnography." In David Damas, *Handbook of North American Indians.* Vol. 5, *Arctic.* Washington: Smithsonian Institution. 185–197.

Cohen, Albert K. 1966. *Deviance and Control.* Englewood Cliffs, N.J.: Prentice-Hall.

Correll, J. Lee. 1970. *Bai-a-lil-le: Medicine Man or Witch?* Window Rock, Ariz.: The Navajo Tribe, Navajo Parks and Recreation Research Section.

Courlander, Harold. 1971. *The Fourth World of the Hopis.* Albuquerque: University of New Mexico Press.

Culin, Stewart. 1907. *Games of the North American Indians.* Bureau of American Ethnology Annual Report 24.

Curtin, Jeremiah, and J. N. B. Hewitt. 1911. *Seneca Fiction, Legends, and Myths.* Bureau of American Ethnology Annual Report 32:37–819.

Curtis, Edward S. 1907. *The North American Indian.* Vol. 1. Cambridge: Cambridge University Press.

Cushing, Frank Hamilton. 1883. "Zuni Fetishes." *Bureau of American Ethnology Annual Report* 2:9–45.

————. 1896. "Outlines of Zuni Creation Myths." *Bureau of American Ethnology Annual Report* 13:325–447.

————. 1901. *Zuni Folk Tales.* New York: G. P. Putnam's Sons.

————. 1923. "Origin Myth from Oraibi." *Journal of American Folklore* 36:163–170.

Davis, William D. 1971. "Social Complexity and the Nature of Primitive Man's Conception of the Supernatural." Ph.D. diss., University of North Carolina, Chapel Hill. Ann Arbor: University Microfilms, 72–10, 707.

Devereaux, George. 1950. "The Psychology of Feminine Genital Bleeding: Analysis of Mohave Indian Puberty and Menstrual Rites" *International Journal of Psychoanalysis* 31:237–257.

Dorsey, George A.. 1904. *The Mythology of the Wichita.* Washington, D. C.: Carnegie Institution.

Dorsey, J. O., and John R. Swanton. 1912. "A Dictionary of the Biloxi and Ofo Languages." *Bureau of American Ethnology Bulletin* 47:1–340.

Douglas, Mary. 1975. *Implicit Meanings: Essays in Anthropology.* London: Routledge and Kegan Paul.

Driver, Harold E. 1941. "Culture Element Distributions: XVI Girls' Puberty Rites in Western North America." *University of California Anthropological Records* 6:21–90.

Driver, Harold E., and William C. Massey. 1957. "Comparative Studies of North American Indians." *American Philosophical Society Transactions* 47, no. 2:165–456.

Durkheim, Emile. 1951 [1897]. *Suicide.* Glencoe: The Free Press.

————. 1965 [1915]. *The Elementary Forms of the Religious Life.* Trans. Joseph Ward Swain. New York: The Free Press.

Dyen, Isadore, and David F. Aberle. 1974. *Lexical Reconstruction: The Case of the Proto-Athabascan Kinship System.* London: Cambridge University Press.

Dyk, Walter. 1966 [1938]. *Son of Old Man Hat: A Navaho Autobiography.* Lincoln: University of Nebraska Press.

Eggan, Fred. 1950. *Social Organization of the Western Pueblos.* Chicago: University of Chicago Press.

Eliade, Mircea. 1964. *Shamanism: Archaic Techniques of Ecstasy.* Trans. Willard R. Trask. New York: Bollingen Foundation.

————. 1982. *A History of Religious Ideas.* Vol. 3., *From Muhammad to the Age of Reforms.* Trans. W. R. Trask. Chicago: University of Chicago Press.

English-Lueck, J. A. 1990. *Health in the New Age: A Study in California Holistic Practices.* Albuquerque: University of New Mexico Press.

Farella, John R. 1984. *The Main Stalk: A Synthesis of Navajo Philosophy.* Tucson: University of Arizona Press.

Faris, James C. 1990. *The Nightway: A History and a History of Documentation of a Navajo Ceremonial.* Albuquerque: University of New Mexico Press.

Fishler, Stanley A. 1953. *In the Beginning: A Navaho Creation Myth.* University of Utah, Department of Anthropology, Anthropological Paper 13.

Fowler, Catherine S. 1986. "Subsistence." In Warren L. D'Azevedo, ed., *Handbook of North American Indians.* Vol. 11, *Great Basin.* Washington: Smithsonian Institution. 64–97.

Franciscan Fathers. 1910. *An Ethnologic Dictionary of the Navajo Language.* Saint Michaels, Ariz.: The Franciscan Fathers.

Frankfort, Henri, ed. 1946. "Myth and Reality." In *The Intellectual Adventure of Ancient Man: An Essay on Speculative Thought in the Ancient Near East,* ed. Henri Frankfort. Chicago: University of Chicago Press. 3–27.

Frazer, James G. 1958 [1890]. *The Golden Bough.* New York: Macmillan.

Friedman, Richard Elliott. 1987. *Who Wrote the Bible?* New York: Summit Books.

Frisbie, Charlotte J., and David P. McAllester. 1978. *Navajo Blessingway Singer: The Autobiography of Frank Mitchell, 1881–1967.* Tucson: University of Arizona Press.

Fromm, Erich. 1973. *Anatomy of Human Destructiveness.* New York: Holt, Rinehart, and Winston.

Gayton, Anna. H. 1935. "Areal Affiliations of California Folktales." *American Anthropologist* 37:582–599.

Gleick, James. 1987. *Chaos: Making a New Science.* New York: Viking.

Goddard, Pliny Earle. 1911. "Jicarilla Apache Texts." *American Museum of Natural History, Anthropological Papers* 8:1–276.

————. 1919. "Myths and Tales from the White Mountain Apache." *American Museum of Natural History, Anthropological Papers* 24:87–139.

————. 1933. *Navajo Texts.* American Museum of Natural History, Anthropological Papers 34, part 1.

Goodwin, Grenville. 1939. *Myths and Tales of the White Mountain Apache.* American Folklore Society Memoir 33.

————. 1969 [1942]. *The Social Organization of the Western Apache*. Tucson: University of Arizona Press.

Goody, Jack. 1977. *The Domestication of the Savage Mind*. Cambridge: Cambridge University Press.

Gordis, Robert. 1951. *Koheleth: The Man and His World*. New York: The Jewish Theological Seminary of America.

Gough, Kathleen. 1961. "Variation in Preferential Marriage Forms." In *Matrilineal Kinship*, ed. David M. Schneider and Kathleen Gough. Berkeley: University of California Press. 614–630.

Gould, Stephen Jay. 1996. "This View of Life: Up against a Wall." *Natural History* 105, no. 7:16–22, 70–73.

Gribben, John. 1993. *In the Beginning: After COBE and before the Big Bang*. Boston: Little Brown.

Gunn, John M. 1917. *Schat-Chen: History, Traditions, and Narratives of the Qeres Indians of Laguna and Acoma*. Albuquerque, N.Mex.: Albright and Anderson.

Gunnerson, Dolores A. 1956. "The Southern Athabascans: Their Arrival in the Southwest." *El Palacio* 63:346–365.

Gunnerson, James H., and Dolores A. Gunnerson. 1971. "Apachean Culture: A Study in Unity and Diversity." In *Apachean Culture, History and Ethnology*, ed. Keith H. Basso and Morris E. Opler. The University of Arizona, Anthropological Paper 21:7–27.

Gutheil, Emil. 1959. "Sexual Dysfunctions in Men." In *American Handbook of Psychiatry*, ed. Silvano Arieti. New York: Basic Books. 1:708–726.

Hacker, Andrew, ed. 1983. *U/S: A Statistical Portrait of the American People*. New York: Viking Press.

Haile, Berard. 1917. "Some Mortuary Customs of the Navajo." *The Franciscan Missions of the Southwest* 5:29–33.

————. 1938. *Origin Legend of the Navaho Enemy Way*. Yale University Publications in Anthropology 17.

————. 1943a. *Origin Legend of the Navaho Flintway*. University of Chicago Publications in Anthropology.

————. 1943b. "Soul Concepts of the Navajo." *Annali Lateranensi* 7:59–94.

————. 1947a. *Head and Face Masks in Navaho Ceremonialism*. St. Michaels, Ariz.: St. Michaels Press.

————. 1947b. *Navaho Sacrificial Figurines*. Chicago: University of Chicago Press.

————. 1950. *Legend of the Ghostway Ritual in the Male Branch of Shootingway and Suckingway: Its Legend and Practice*. St. Michael's, Ariz.: St. Michaels Press.

————. 1978. *Love-Magic and Butterfly People: The Slim Curley Version of the Ajilee and Mothway Myths*. Flagstaff: Museum of Northern Arizona Press.

————. 1979. *Waterway*. Flagstaff: Museum of Northern Arizona Press.

————. 1981. *The Upward Moving and Emergence Way: The Gishin Biye' Version*. Lincoln: University of Nebraska Press.

————. 1984. *Navajo Coyote Tales: The Curly Tó Aheedlíinii Version*. Lincoln: University of Nebraska Press.

Hallpike, Christopher R. 1979. *The Foundations of Primitive Thought.* New York: Oxford University Press.

Harris, Marvin. 1968. *The Rise of Anthropological Theory: A History of Theories of Culture.* New York: Thomas Y. Crowell.

Headley, Lee A. 1983. "Conclusion." In *Suicide in Asia and the Near East,* ed. Lee Headley. Berkeley: University of California Press. 350–365.

Henderson, Eric. 1982. "Kaibeto Ceremonialists, 1860–1980." In *Navajo Religion and Culture—Selected Views: Papers in Honor of Leland C. Wyman,* ed. David M. Brugge and Charlotte J. Frisbie. Santa Fe: Museum of New Mexico Press. 164–175.

Hewitt, J. N. B. 1900. "Iroquoian Cosmology." *Bureau of American Ethnology Annual Report* 21:127–339.

Hill, W. W. 1935. "The Status of the Hermaphrodite and Transvestite in Navaho Culture." *American Anthropologist* 37:273–279.

———. 1938a. *The Agricultural and Hunting Methods of the Navaho Indians.* Yale University Publications in Anthropology 18.

———. 1938b. "Navajo Use of Jimsonweed." *New Mexico Anthropologist* 3:19–21.

Hoijer, Harry. 1956. "Athapascan Kinship Systems." *American Anthropologist* 58:309–333.

Honigmann, John J. 1946. *Ethnography and Acculturation of the Fort Nelson Slave.* Yale University Publications in Anthropology 33.

———. 1954. *The Kaska Indians: An Ethnographic Reconstruction.* Yale University Publications in Anthropology 51.

Hultkrantz, Åke. 1953. *Conceptions of the Soul among North American Indians.* Statens Etnografiska Museum (Sweden) Monograph Series 1.

———. 1980 [1967]. *The Religions of the American Indians.* Trans. Monica Setterwall. Berkeley: University of California Press.

Irwin, William A. 1946. "The Hebrews." In *The Intellectual Adventure of Ancient Man: An Essay on Speculative Thought in the Ancient Near East,* ed. Henri Frankfort. Chicago: University of Chicago Press. 223–360.

Jochelson, Waldemar. 1905. *The Koryak. Reports of the Jesup North Pacific Expedition.* American Museum of Natural History Memoir 10, part 2.

Jorgensen, Joseph G. 1980. *Western Indians: Comparative Languages and Cultures of 172 Western American Indian Tribes.* San Francisco: W. H. Freeman.

Kaplan, Bert, and Dale Johnson. 1964. "The Social Meaning of Navajo Psychopathology and Psychotherapy." In *Magic, Faith, and Healing: Studies in Primitive Psychiatry Today,* ed. Ari Kiev. London: The Free Press of Glencoe, Collier Macmillan, Ltd. 203–229.

Kaufmann, Yehezkel. 1960. *The Religion of Israel: From Its Beginnings to the Babylonian Exile.* Trans. and abridged by Moshe Greenberg. Chicago: The University of Chicago Press.

Kellert, Stephen H. 1993. *In the Wake of Chaos: Unpredictable Order in Dynamical Systems.* Chicago: University of Chicago Press.

Kirk, G. S. 1970. *Myth: Its Meaning and Functions in Ancient and Other Cultures.* Berkeley: University of California Press.

Klass, Morton. 1995. *Ordered Universes: Approaches to the Anthropology of Religion.* Boulder, Colo.: Westview Press.

Kluckhohn, Clyde. 1962a. "Ethical Relativity: *Sic et Non.*" In *Culture and Behavior: Collected Essays of Clyde Kluckhohn,* ed. Richard Kluckhohn. New York: The Free Press of Glencoe. 265–285.

———. 1962b [1944]. *Navaho Witchcraft.* 2d ed. Boston: Beacon Press.

Kluckhohn, Clyde, and A. Kimball Romney. 1961. "The Rimrock Navajo." In *Variations in Value Orientations,* ed. Florence Kluckhohn and Fred L. Strodbeck. New York: Harper and Row.

Kluckhohn, Clyde, and Dorothea C. Leighton. 1974 [1946]. *The Navaho.* Rev. ed. Cambridge: Harvard University Press.

Kneal, Albert. H. 1950. *Indian Agent.* Caldwell, Idaho: Caxton Press.

Kroeber, Alfred L. 1907. "Ethnology of the Gros Ventre." *American Museum of Natural History, Anthropological Papers* 1:145–281.

———. 1925. *Handbook of the Indians of California.* Bureau of American Ethnology Bulletin 78.

Kunitz, Stephen J., and Jerrold E. Levy. 1991. *Navajo Aging: The Transition from Family to Institutional Support.* Tucson: University of Arizona Press.

———. 1994. *Drinking Careers: A Twenty-Five-Year Study of Three Navajo Populations.* New Haven: Yale University Press.

Ladd, John. 1957. *The Structure of a Moral Code.* Cambridge, Mass.: Harvard University Press.

Landar, Herbert, Jr. 1961. "A Note on the Navaho Word for Coyote." *International Journal of American Linguistics* 27:86–88.

Lang, Andrew. 1898. *The Makings of Religion.* London: Longmans Green.

Lantis, Margaret. 1984. "Aleut." In David Damas, ed., *Handbook of North American Indians.* Vol. 5, *Arctic.* Washington: Smithsonian Institution. 161–184.

Leighton, Dorothea, and Clyde Kluckhohn. 1947. *Children of the People: The Navaho Individual and His Development.* Cambridge, Mass.: Harvard University Press.

Levinson, David, and Martin J. Malone. 1980. *Toward Explaining Human Culture: A Critical Review of the Findings of Worldwide Cross-Cultural Research.* New Haven: HRAF Press.

Levy, Jerrold E. 1964. "The Fate of Navajo Twins." *American Anthropologist* 66:883–887.

———. 1965. "Navajo Suicide." *Human Organization* 24:308–318.

———. 1992. *Orayvi Revisited: Social Stratification in an "Egalitarian" Society.* Santa Fe, N.Mex.: School of American Research Press.

———. 1994. "Hopi Shamanism: A Reappraisal." In *North American Indian Anthropology: Essays on Society and Culture,* ed. Raymond J. DeMallie and Alfonso Ortiz. Norman: University of Oklahoma Press. 307–327.

Levy, Jerrold E., and Stephen J. Kunitz. 1974. *Indian Drinking: Navajo Practices and Anglo-American Theories.* New York: John Wiley and Sons.

———. 1987. "A Suicide Prevention Program for Hopi Youth." *Social Science and Medicine* 25:931–940.

Levy, Jerrold E., Eric B. Henderson, and Tracy J. Andrews. 1989. "The Effects of Regional Variation and Temporal Change on Matrilineal Elements of Navajo Social Organization." *Journal of Anthropological Research* 45:351–377.

Levy, Jerrold E., Stephen J. Kunitz, and Michael Everett. 1969. "Navajo Criminal Homicide." *Southwestern Journal of Anthropology* 25:124–152.

Levy, Jerrold E., Stephen J. Kunitz, and Eric B. Henderson. 1987. "Hopi Deviance in Historical and Epidemiological Perspective." In *Themes in Ethnology and Culture History: Essays in Honor of David F. Aberle*, ed. Joseph Jorgensen and Leland Donald. Berkeley: Folklore Institute. 355–396.

Levy, Jerrold E., Raymond Neutra, and Dennis Parker. 1987. *Hand Trembling, Frenzy Witchcraft, and Moth Madness: A Study of Navajo Seizure Disorders.* Tucson: University of Arizona Press.

Li, Fang-Kuei. 1933. "A List of Chipewyan Stems." *International Journal of American Linguistics* 7:122–151.

Linton, Ralph. 1936. *The Study of Man.* New York: Appleton—Century—Crofts.

Llewellyn, Karl N., and E. Adamson Hoebel. 1941. *The Cheyenne Way: Conflict and Case Law in Primitive Jurisprudence.* Norman: University of Oklahoma Press.

Lovelock, James. 1988. *The Ages of Gaia.* New York: Norton.

———. 1991. *Gaia.* London: Gaia Books.

Lowie, Robert H. 1912. "Chipewyan Tales." *American Museum of Natural History, Anthropological Papers* 10:171–200.

———. 1924. "Shoshonean Tales." *Journal of American Folklore* 37:1–91.

———. 1940. *An Introduction to Cultural Anthropology.* New York: Rinehart.

———. 1956 [1935]. *The Crow Indians.* New York: Rinehart.

———. 1961 [1920]. *Primitive Society.* New York: Harper and Brothers.

Luckert, Karl W. 1975. *The Navajo Hunter Tradition.* Tucson: University of Arizona Press.

———. 1977. *Navajo Mountain and Rainbow Bridge Religion.* Flagstaff: Museum of Northern Arizona.

———. 1978. *A Navajo Bringing Home Ceremony: The Claus Chee Sonny Version of Deerway Ajiłee.* Flagstaff: Museum of Northern Arizona Press.

———. 1979. *Coyoteway: A Navajo Healing Ceremonial.* Tucson: University of Arizona Press.

Malinowski, Bronislaw. 1954 [1948]. "Myth in Primitive Society." In *Magic, Science, and Religion, and Other Essays.* Garden City, N.Y.: Doubleday. 93–148.

Mason, J. Alden. 1946. *Notes on the Indians of the Great Slave Lake Area.* Yale University Publications in Anthropology 34.

Matthews, Washington. 1887. "The Mountain Chant." *Bureau of American Ethnology Annual Report* 5:379–467.

———. 1897. *Navaho Legends.* American Folklore Society Memoir 5.

————. 1902. *The Night Chant*. American Museum of Natural History Memoir 6.

McNeley, James Kale. 1981. *Holy Wind in Navajo Philosophy*. Tucson: University of Arizona Press.

Merchant, Carolyn. 1980. *The Death of Nature*. New York: Harper and Row.

Mitchell, Emerson Blackhorse, and T. D. Allen. 1967. *Miracle Hill, the Story of a Navajo Boy*. Norman: University of Oklahoma Press.

Mitchell, Frank. 1978. *Navajo Blessingway Singer: The Autobiography of Frank Mitchell*. Ed. Charlotte J. Frisbie and David P. McAllester. Tucson: University of Arizona Press.

Monroe, Robert L., John W. M. Whiting, and David J. Halley. 1969. "Institutionalized Male Transvestism and Sex Distinctions." *American Anthropologist* 71:87–91.

Mooney, James. 1888. "Myths of the Cherokees." *Journal of American Folklore* 1:97–108.

Morice, Adrien G. 1907. "The Unity of Speech among the Northern and the Southern Déné." *American Anthropologist* 9:720–737.

Murdock, George Peter. 1955. "North American Social Organization." *Davidson Journal of Anthropology* 1:85–97.

————. 1965. *Culture and Society*. Pittsburgh, Pa.: University of Pittsburgh Press.

————. 1967. *Ethnographic Atlas*. Pittsburgh, Pa.: University of Pittsburgh Press.

Murphy, Jane M. 1964. "Psychotherapeutic Aspects of Shamanism on St. Lawrence Island." In *Magic, Faith, and Healing: Studies in Primitive Psychiatry Today*, ed. Ari Kiev. London: The Free Press of Glencoe, Collier Macmillan Ltd. 53–83.

Newhouse. S. R., and J. Amodeo. 1985. "Native American Healing." In *The New Holistic Health Handbook*, ed. Shepard Bliss. Lexington, Mass.: Stephen Greene Press.

Nisbet, Robert A. 1966. *The Sociological Tradition*. New York: Basic Books.

————. 1980. *The History of the Idea of Progress*. New York: Basic Books.

O'Bryan, Aileen. 1956. *The Diné: Origin Myths of the Navaho Indians*. Bureau of American Ethnology Bulletin 163.

Opler, Morris Edward. 1938. ""Ethnological Notes." In *Chiricahua and Mescalero Apache Texts*, ed. Harry Hoijer. Chicago: The University of Chicago Press. 141–156, 190–213.

————. 1940. *Myths and Legends of the Lipan Apache Indians*. American Folklore Society Memoir 36.

————. 1965 [1941]. *An Apache Life-Way: The Economic, Social, and Religious Institutions of the Chiricahua Indians*. New York: Cooper Square Publishers.

————. 1994a [1942]. *Myths and Tales of the Chiricahua Apache Indians*. Lincoln: University of Nebraska Press.

————. 1994b [1938]. *Myths and Tales of the Jicarilla Apache*. New York: Dover Publications.

Ortiz, Alfonso. 1969. *The Tewa World: Space, Time, Being, and Becoming in a Pueblo Society.* Chicago: University of Chicago Press.

Osgood, Cornelius. 1936. *Contributions to the Ethnography of the Kutchin.* University Publications in Anthropology 14.

———. 1937. *The Ethnography of the Tanaina.* Yale University Publications in Anthropology 16.

Parsons, Elsie Clews. 1916. "The Zuni La'mana." *American Anthropologist* 18:521–28.

———. 1926. *Tewa Tales.* American Folklore Society Memoir 19.

———. 1929a. *Kiowa Tales.* American Folklore Society Memoir 22.

———. 1929b. *The Social Organization of the Tewa of New Mexico.* American Anthropological Association Memoir 36.

———. 1974 [1939]. *Pueblo Indian Religion.* 4 vols. Chicago: University of Chicago Press.

Peck, M. Scott. 1983. *People of the Lie: The Hope for Healing Human Evil.* New York: Simon and Schuster.

Piers, G., and Milton B. Singer. 1953. *Shame and Guilt: A Psychoanalytic Study.* Springfield, Ill.: Charles C. Thomas.

Plaut, W. Gunther. 1981. *The Torah: A Modern Commentary.* New York: Union of American Hebrew Congregations.

Prigogine, Ilya. 1980. *From Being to Becoming.* San Francisco: W. H. Freeman and Company.

Radin, Paul. 1927. *Primitive Man as Philosopher.* New York: D. Appleton and Company.

———. 1937. *Primitive Religion: Its Nature and Origins.* New York: Viking.

———. 1956. *The Trickster: A Study in American Indian Mythology.* New York: Schocken Books.

Ramsey, Jarold. 1973. *Love in an Earthquake.* Seattle: University of Washington Press.

Rasmussen, Knud. 1929. *Intellectual Culture of the Iglulik Eskimos.* Vol. 7 of *Reports of the Fifth Thule Expedition.* Copenhagen: Gyldendal.

———. 1931. *The Netsilik Eskimos.* Vol. 8 of *Reports of the Fifth Thule Expedition.* Copenhagen: Gyldendal.

Redfield, Robert. 1953. *The Primitive World and Its Transformations.* Ithaca, N.Y.: Cornell University Press.

———. 1955. *The Little Community: Viewpoints for the Study of a Human Whole.* Chicago: University of Chicago Press.

Reichard, Gladys A. 1963 [1950]. *Navaho Religion: A Study of Symbolism.* New York: Pantheon.

Ricketts, Mac Linscott. 1965. "The North American Trickster." *History of Religions* 5:269–307.

Roberts, John M., Malcolm J. Arth, and Robert R. Bush. 1959. "Games in Culture." *American Anthropologist* 61:597–605.

Roessell, Ruth, ed. 1971. *Navajo Studies at Navajo Community College.* Many Farms, Ariz.: Navajo Community College Press.

Russell, Frank. 1975 [1898]. "Myths of the Jicarilla Apaches." *Journal of American Folklore* 40:253–271.

Russell, Jeffrey Burton. 1977. *The Devil: Perceptions of Evil from Antiquity to Primitive Christianity.* Ithaca, N.Y.: Cornell University Press.

———. 1986. *Mephistopheles: The Devil in the Modern World.* Ithaca, N.Y.: Cornell University Press.

Saladin d'Anglure, Bernard. 1984. "Inuit of Quebec." In David Damas, ed., *Handbook of North American Indians.* Vol. 5, *Arctic.* Washington: Smithsonian Institution. 476–507.

Sapir, Edward. 1936. "Internal Linguistic Evidence Suggestive of the Northern Origin of the Navaho." *American Anthropologist* 38:225–232.

Saunders, E. Dale. 1961. "Japanese Mythology." In *Mythologies of the Ancient World,* ed. Samuel Noah Kramer. Garden City, N.Y.: Doubleday. 409–442.

Schlegel, Alice. 1983. "CA Comment," remarks in "The North American Berdache," by Charles Callender and Lee M. Kochemis. *Current Anthropology* 24:443–470.

Schmerler, Henrietta. 1931. "Trickster Marries His Daughter," *Journal of American Folklore* 44:196–207.

Schmidt, Wilhelm. 1939. *The Culture Historical Method of Ethnology.* Trans. S. A. Sieber. New York: Fortuny's.

Searle, John R. 1992. *The Rediscovery of the Mind.* Cambridge, Mass.: MIT Press.

Shepardson, Mary. 1978. "Changes in Navajo Mortuary Practices and Beliefs." *American Indian Quarterly* 4:383–395.

Smith, Anne M. 1993. *Shoshone Tales.* Salt Lake City: University of Utah Press.

Spencer, Katherine. 1957. *Mythology and Values: An Analysis of Navaho Chantway Myths.* Philadelphia: American Folklore Society.

Spencer, Robert F. 1959. *The North Alaskan Eskimo.* Bureau of American Ethnology Bulletin 171.

St. Clair, H. H., and Robert. H. Lowie. 1909. "Shoshone and Comanche Texts." *Journal of American Folklore* 22:265–282.

Stephen, Alexander M. 1929. "Hopi Tales." *Journal of American Folklore* 42:1–72.

———. 1930. "Navajo Origin Legend." *Journal of American Folklore* 43:88–104.

Stevenson, Matilda Cox. 1894. "The Sia." *Bureau of American Ethnology Annual Report* 11.

———. 1904. "The Zuni Indians." *Bureau of American Ethnology Annual Report* 23.

Steward, Julian H. 1933. "Ethnography of the Owens Valley Paiute." *University of California Publications in American Archaeology and Ethnology* 33, no. 3:233–250.

———. 1943. "Some Western Shoshone Myths." *Bureau of American Ethnology Bulletin* 31:249–299.

Stirling, Matthew W. 1942. *Origin Myth of Acoma and Other Records.* Bureau of American Ethnology Bulletin 135.

Stocking, George W. 1987. *Victorian Anthropology.* New York: The Free Press.

Swanson, Guy E. 1960. *The Birth of the Gods: The Origin of Primitive Religion*. Ann Arbor: University of Michigan Press.

Swanton, John R. 1922. *Early History of the Creek Indians and Their Neighbors*. Bureau of American Ethnology Bulletin 73.

Teit, James A. 1912. "Mythology of the Thompson Indians." *American Museum of Natural History Memoir* 12:199–416.

———. 1917. "Kaska Tales." *Journal of American Folklore* 30:427–473.

———. 1919. "Tahltan Tales." *Journal of American Folklore* 32:198–250.

Textor, Robert B. 1967. *A Cross-Cultural Summary*. New Haven, Conn.: HRAF Press.

Thompson, Stith. 1966 [1929]. *Tales of the North American Indians*. Bloomington: University of Indiana Press.

———. 1989. *Motif-Index of Folk-Literature*. 6 vols. Rev. ed. Bloomington: Indiana University Press.

Titiev, Mischa. 1944. *Old Oraibi: A Study of the Hopi Indians of Third Mesa*. Peabody Museum of American Archaeology and Ethnology, Harvard University, Papers, vol. 22, no. 1.

———. 1972. *The Hopi Indians of Old Oraibi*. Ann Arbor: University of Michigan Press.

———. n. d. "Census Notes from Old Oraibi." Peabody Museum of Archaeology and Ethnology. Cambridge, Mass: Harvard University.

Tyler, Hamilton A. 1964. *Pueblo Gods and Myths*. Norman: University of Oklahoma Press.

Tylor, E. B. 1958 [1871]. *Primitive Culture*. New York: Harper Torchbooks.

Underhill, Ruth M. 1948. *Ceremonial Patterns in the Greater Southwest*. American Ethnological Society Monograph 13. New York: J. J. Augustin.

———. 1979. *Papago Woman*. Prospect Heights, Ill.: Waveland Press.

Voth, H. R. 1903. *The Oraibi Summer Snake Ceremony*. Field Columbian Museum Publication 83.

———. 1905. *The Traditions of the Hopi*. Field Columbian Museum Publication 6.

Wheelwright, Mary C. 1942. *Navajo Creation Myth*. Navajo Religious Series 1. Santa Fe, N.Mex.: Museum of Navajo Ceremonial Art. 39–125.

———. 1945. *Atsah or Eagle Catching Myth and Yohe or Bead Myth*. Museum of Navajo Ceremonial Art Bulletin 3.

———. 1946. *Nilth Chiji Bakaji (Wind Chant) and Feather Chant*. Santa Fe, N.Mex.: Museum of Navajo Ceremonial Art Bulletin 4.

———. 1949. *Emergence Myth According to the Hanelth-nayhe or Upward Reaching Rite*. Navajo Religion Series 3. Santa Fe, N.Mex.: Museum of Navajo Ceremonial Art.

———. 1951. *Myth of Mountain Chant and Beauty Chant*. Santa Fe, N.Mex.: Museum of Navajo Ceremonial Art Bulletin 5.

Wissler, Clark, and D. C. Duvall. 1918. *Mythology of the Blackfoot Indians*. American Museum of Natural History, Anthropological Paper 2:1–163.

Witherspoon, Gary. 1974. "The Central Concepts in Navajo World View (I)." *Linguistics: An International Review* 161:41–59.

Wood, John W. 1982. "Western Navajo Religious Affiliations." In *Navajo Religion and Culture—Selected Views: Papers in Honor of Leland C. Wyman,* ed. David M. Brugge and Charlotte J. Frisbie. Santa Fe: Museum of New Mexico Press. 176–186.

Wyman, Leland C. 1936a. "Origin Legends of Navaho Divinitory Rites." *Journal of American Folklore* 49:134–142.

————. 1936b. "Navaho Diagnosticians." *American Anthropologist* 38:236–246.

————. 1962. *The Windways of the Navaho.* Colorado Springs: Taylor Museum.

————. 1965. *The Red Antway of the Navaho.* Santa Fe, N.Mex.: Museum of Navajo Ceremonial Art.

————. 1970. *Blessingway.* Tucson: University of Arizona Press.

————. 1975. *The Mountainway of the Navajo.* Tucson: University of Arizona Press.

Wyman, Leland C., and Flora L. Bailey. 1943. *Navaho Upward-Reaching Way: Objective Behavior, Rationale, and Sanction.* University of New Mexico Bulletin 389.

Wyman, Leland C., and Clyde Kluckhohn. 1938. *Navaho Classification of Their Song Ceremonials.* American Anthropological Association Memoir 50.

Wyman, Leland C., and B. Thorne. 1945. "Notes on Navajo Suicide." *American Anthropologist* 47:278–288.

Wyman, Leland C., W. W. Hill, and Iva Òsanai. 1942. *Navaho Eschatology.* University of New Mexico Bulletin 377, Anthropological Series 4, no. 1:1–49.

Yazzie, Ethelou, ed. 1971. *Navajo History: Volume 1.* Many Farms, Ariz.: Navajo Community College Press.

Young, Robert M., and William Morgan. 1980. *The Navajo Language: A Grammar and Colloquial Dictionary.* Albuquerque: University of New Mexico Press.

Young, Stanley Y., and Hartley H. Jackson. 1978 [1951]. *The Clever Coyote.* Lincoln: University of Nebraska Press.

Zolbrod, Paul G. 1984. *Diné Bahane': The Navajo Creation Story.* Albuquerque: University of New Mexico Press.

Index

Compositor:	BookMasters, Inc.
Text:	10/13 Galliard
Display:	Galliard
Printer:	Data Reproductions, Inc.